TARKENTON

TARKENTON

By Jim Klobuchar and Fran Tarkenton

HARPER & ROW, PUBLISHERS

NEW YORK · HAGERSTOWN · SAN FRANCISCO · LONDON

Photographs on pages 247–257 by Bud Skinner.

Designed by Sidney Feinberg

Library of Congress Cataloging in Publication Data

Klobuchar, Jim.
  Tarkenton.
  Includes index.
  1. Tarkenton, Francis A. 2. Quarterback
(Football)—Biography. I. Tarkenton, Francis A.,
joint author.
GV939.T3K56 1976   796.33′2′0924   [B]   75–5791
ISBN 0–06–012412–1

76 77 78 79 80 10 9 8 7 6 5 4 3 2

This is for a man who laughed and loved the world, and finished his course.

Contents

A section of photographs follows page 116.

Foreword

The glamorization of today's pro football hero has made the more gifted or brazen ones richer than kings and more visible than presidents. The game the pros play on Sunday afternoon has created a popular culture unrivaled by any in America since the movies of the 1930s and 1940s. It has become a national devotional, offering serious competition to the churches and a playground for psychologists.

But it has been tough on legendmakers.

The most successful of the professional football players have been so merchandised and envied they seem to have arrived as prepackaged supermen, flung wholly grown from another planet into the middle of a stop-action frame. If Jim Thorpe played in the 1970s, he would not be harassed by the Olympics rules committees. Since it is almost impossible to win in the Olympics today and not be a professional, Jim could keep his medals. His trophy case would thus be enhanced, but his legend as the persecuted athletic prodigy would be deflated.

Thorpe remains safely a legend. A somewhat different fate awaits today's jock hero. A Joe Namath or an O. J. Simpson can generate money and adoration, but no minstrel's ballads. Television exposure and investment agents have destroyed the myths and removed the fables from the arena.

In the case of Francis Tarkenton, this is the minstrel's loss, for Tarkenton's career has the properties of legends, particularly the

American variety. Let's say that the architects of capitalism, the work ethic, the Frank Merriwell series, and the Dale Carnegie program all got together to create a figure who epitomized their doctrinal virtues. He should be born of good but virtually penniless parents. In his childhood he should dream, and believe, and strive. As an eight-year-old he should decide to become not only a great athlete, but a professional athlete. In later years he should choose to become a quarterback in spite of those who expressed doubts that his arm was strong enough to beat a drum. He should smile at the critic-sages and offer the view that if they couldn't be outargued, they could be outlasted. He should adopt this as a working commandment: To win and endure you don't have to be brilliant, but you do have to be dogged.

Tarkenton met all the specifications.

Early in his professional career they defined his doggedness as scrambling. In order to secure himself within the football establishment, he rebelled against it. He did this in the way he played, the way he negotiated, by his conviction that he was good enough and independent enough to play where he pleased. His performance as a maverick against the institutions of his game was so impressive that he attracted much attention and sponsorship, and therefore he was stamped enthusiastically as the true establishment man.

Wherever Tarkenton went he made touchdowns, money, friends, commercials, and new corporations. But one thing he didn't make for a long time was championships. The critic-sages nodded and called him an aberration and a fifty-fifty quarterback. Huffily, they refused to call him an all-pro. And then one day in 1975, when he was already a millionaire, a triumph of the free-enterprise system but still not an all-pro, the sages looked up—and lo, his name led all the rest.

By the definition that counted, the one of the yardstick, Francis Tarkenton was the greatest. He had thrown more touchdown passes, completed more passes, and run for more yardage than any quarterback in professional football history.

The sages immediately decided he was an all-pro and the most valuable player in the National Football League, and they marveled at the strides he had made since 1974.

I first met Francis Tarkenton in the summer of 1961. We chatted pleasantly on the steps of the gymnasium at Bemidji State College in Minnesota. Francis had been in a professional football training camp for 3½ days. Although not an impetuous young man, he seemed anxious to share a discovery. I invited him to confide. He revealed his intention to become a starting quarterback in his first year in pro football. I detected no braggadocio. Francis was simply making a sunny affirmation of the inevitable. He was later appalled to realize how little he knew in 1961. At the time, however, he felt that all the riddles had fallen into place and, after a few days of pro quarterbacking, it was a joy to have all that learning behind him.

He may not have been wise then, but he was accurate. He *was* a starting quarterback in his first year, and he has never stopped. His extraordinary career both as a player and as a creative businessman is a mirror of the pro football cult and a testament to the individual's still-great power to exert his will on his surroundings.

But if pro football has become a cult, it is still a game. And if Francis Tarkenton has become the video-age version of a legend, he is still a man. When we started to collaborate on this book, we looked for a way to describe the clash of vanities, the hilarities, and the solemnities of the game, and to express the feelings and insights of one man who plays it. We decided to share the load. I have traced the steps in Francis Tarkenton's career from the point of view of a newspaperman. In alternate chapters, Francis Tarkenton speaks for himself.

We are friends, but we also have a professional relationship, and therefore we are hardly sweethearts. I think that Francis is a hopeless mossback in player association-management dealings, and that some of the eternal truths he espouses this year on a few other matters may change the next. Francis, in turn, cannot understand my abnormal fascination with what the quarterback and the coach say to each other on the sidelines, and why that might be more interesting than the AT&T annual report he carries in his attaché case.

Whatever our disagreements, Francis Tarkenton is an unassailable authority on his game. His wits lifted him to the summit of his trade. Whether the room is filled with players, coaches, writers, or schoolboys, when Tarkenton talks football—its mechanics, tactics, development, and future—people listen. Here he also talks about himself, and about his frictions with Norm Van Brocklin and Wellington Mara, his admiration for Bud Grant, Chuck Foreman, Freddie Dryer, Dick Butkus, Jim Marshall, and a few hundred others. He identifies the dirtiest football player he has met (not a bad guy personally) and the best. But he is also a party at interest in feuds, struggles, triumphs, humiliations, and a lot of spectacular deeds. And these, we decided, would probably be better seen through my eyes.

The moods of our recital shift, as they do in the locker room and in the six-month life cycle of a football team. But one impression remains constant in my mind: I have found Francis Tarkenton to be a rare athlete, an engaging human being, a tireless authority, and, as his father must know, a good and loyal son.

Jim Klobuchar

April 1976

December 28, 1975

1

Cliff Harris of the Dallas Cowboys stared into the Minnesota backfield. The vibrations he transmitted were intended to convey menace. Among the safetymen in professional football, he had more than the normal allocations of shrewdness, range, and ego. What set Harris apart from most of his peers at that position was the maniacal zeal with which he collided with people. These urges were almost totally impartial. He crashed into enemies and friends (if they happened to be in the target zone) with equal enthusiasm.

His belligerence was both heartfelt and calculated. He understood that there are certain types in football, particularly the thoroughbred wide receivers, who are capable of being terrorized. That he had a bald head and weighed only 195 pounds in no way discouraged Harris in the pursuit of this mission. Although he was one of the most skilled craftsmen of all National Football League defensive backs, he was much more touched by his reputation as the thinking man's sadist.

Walking to the line on the Vikings' first offensive series, Francis Tarkenton glanced at Cliff Harris. It was a subtle movement in no way recognizable to the crowd, which was zestfully burrowing in for 2½ hours of December football in suburban Minneapolis' Met Stadium. Out of the grandstands wafted the usual light mist created by more than 46,000 frosted breaths. The communal exhalings had more intensity today. This was playoff football, the Vikings against

1

Dallas, December 28, 1975. Whatever the emotional status of their football team, the Viking crowds were always keyed up psychologically for December football. They came in bizarre antifreeze dress that gave the occasion the tone of a polar Mardi Gras. They also had commitment, because playoff football meant their team once more was within two games of the Super Bowl. And today, as they almost always were when icicles formed on the goalpost crossbars, the Vikings were favored.

Yet it was a relatively congenial day by Minnesota's nostril-numbing standards for winter, and Cliff Harris was grateful for that. Tarkenton saw him standing there poised, mustache and all. He would be a man to contend with. Tarkenton's brain spun a few cogs. What Harris valued above most of the treasures of life was to knock somebody's jock off. The owner of the most endangered member that day, Tarkenton determined, was Jimmy Lash. Lash was one of the Vikings' regular outside receivers, a young man who was tall and capable but largely anonymous in the eyes of the nation's television audiences. The main-eventer on the outside for Minnesota was John Gilliam. Yet in the past two years Lash was almost as productive as Gilliam and possibly more reliable, although never the same deep touchdown threat as his faster and more dramatic partner.

Tarkenton had important schemes involving Jimmy Lash, Cliff Harris, and John Gilliam.

All right, Cliff, he was going to say, come with all of your *machismo*. Lash would run some slants and curls and Zs that waved the red flag at Harris, challenging Cliff to make a commitment. Gilliam, in the meantime, would run foot races with young Mark Washington on the Dallas corner. If Harris committed prematurely to Lash, believing the ball was going into an intermediate zone, the swirl of all the bodies downfield would leave Gilliam one-on-one against Washington. For quarterbacks and flankers it was the big banana split in the sky. It never happened quite that simply in the era of the zone and oddball defenses, but it was a situation that a quarterback with fifteen years' experience could connive for and create. It demanded patience, art, and a memory bank with miles of invisibly filed printouts that Francis Tarkenton brought to the ball park every Sunday afternoon.

So this was another Sunday afternoon at the ball park. It was burdened by the orthodox pressures of a divisional playoff game. Tarkenton felt no grimness, no sense of being measured for excellence or immortality. It was his seventh playoff game, his how many hundredth day at the ball park?

The arena had no more mysteries for him. The phantoms were gone, the genii and the visions. The juices always flowed faster when it was a day of occasion, and in his own private critiques he was gratified to feel that he usually played better on these days. Yet even to this variable he had made his adjustment.

If you played badly, it didn't mean you choked. And if you lost, it didn't mean you played badly. Or if you won, you had a lock on the next reservation in Valhalla. The slogans of the grandstand absorbed a lot of earthy derision in the locker rooms of the pros. But they fascinated Tarkenton because the whole canvas of football was his milieu. He was paid better than two hundred thousand dollars a year to play the game. But to him the psychology of the fan was just as provocative—if not quite as rewarding—as the evolution of the blitz.

At the age of thirty-five, with most of his personal ogres buried, with most of his personal goals achieved, he was simply comfortable to be back in the arena each week on Sunday afternoon. The record book now said bluntly that Francis A. Tarkenton was the No. 1 passer in pro football history. It didn't say that he had the most powerful arm or the biggest harem or the loudest mouth. It certified that somewhere in the snowstorm at Buffalo the week before, he had thrown his 290th touchdown pass to tie John Unitas' record, and then a few minutes later threw his 291st. The record book might not explain that Chuck Foreman had dragged half of the Buffalo defense into the end zone to pull Tarkenton even with Unitas. But it was equally silent on the kind of defenses Unitas was throwing against fifteen years ago. And if statistics are reality, or at least an unbiased measure of it, Tarkenton in his fifteenth year of pro football stood on a special kind of mountaintop that no other quarterback had reached.

Although he didn't plaster it on a billboard, it mattered. Nobody who had exercised any control over his early career—from Wally Butts, his coach at the University of Georgia, to Norm Van Brocklin, his first coach in the pros—believed him capable of enduring in pro football, much less outdistancing all his fifty-five years of predecessors. It mattered because in his deepest heart was the sure knowledge that the public now recognized what the game's old lions—in front of their stuffed jockstraps in their trophy rooms and from the broadcasting booths—had declined to recognize for so long: He belonged with the masters. It wasn't a revelation to the football public from the critics or the ghosts of Walter Camp and Vince Lombardi. It was the evidence of fifteen years on their television screens. They had once colored him fluky. Wind up the little quarterback and see him run. Blitz the linebackers and watch him scramble.

But line him up with a team of quality and let him quarterback.

Tarkenton not only preferred it that way, he also insisted on it. He always believed that the choice of the team he quarterbacked was much too important to be left to general managers and the operation of the Rozelle rule. And so he returned to the Vikings in 1972, the result of what was called a trade but was really closer to a personal ultimatum. A quarterback could stage-manage a choice like that if he had the brains, the testicles, and an independent income.

The fact that the cup of recognition was now filling for him did not lift Tarkenton into trances of self-glorification. He had proved. He had made much money. And he had achieved. They were goals for which no professional athlete need blush. But among all the commandments by which the athlete lives (or is made to live), he recognized one of unshakable truth: The really unforgettable moments are the ones he shares with the men he plays beside.

He had a private credo he lived and played by, stapled to a wall of his business office in Atlanta:

I have come to really believe that the people who make it in the world aren't the most talented ones or the smartest or the luckiest, or necessarily the bravest. The ones who make it are the dogged ones. Just plain tenacity. Those are the ones who take the jolts and get up and look at the sky. And no matter what's there they'll say, "well, I've got to do it; so let's go." The athletes have an expression for it—suck it up. Other people do the same thing, in their own fashion. And whether they realize it or not, that's the real serenity of living. Coping in some civil, meaningful and positive way with the problems that come.

Today the problem was the Dallas Cowboys. He was ready, controlled, at ease. All the auguries were right. It could be a day he would remember above almost all others because it had been a season in which so much success had coalesced around him: a ten-game winning streak for his football team, the personal satisfactions, the enlargement of his life through the deepening joy of watching his children grow. All of this suggested it might, and probably would, be the year for the surmounting deed of his competitive life, the winning of the Super Bowl.

The thought exhilarated him, although he had made no such announcements when the telephone rang at 8 A.M. that Sunday morning in the Holiday Inn, where the Vikings were sequestered for home games. Mick Tingelhoff, the center, was not the kind of guy to whom you said, "Let's hear it for a good, good morning!" Buddies and old heads, they lost count of the guffaws they had milked from the other jocks with stories about their special kind of relationship: one spending the better part of his professional life with his hands on the other's crotch.

Tarkenton never ate breakfast. Others wolfed steak; he drank black coffee. It wasn't nerves; it was his modest digestive powers. There was a chapel meeting thereafter, attendance strictly voluntary among members of the Fellowship of Christian Athletes. Jeff Siemon, Nate Wright, Chuck Foreman, Fred Cox, Terry Brown, Roy Winston, Paul Krause, and Tarkenton sat around exchanging thoughts low-key, considering a passage from the Bible, reciting a brief personal testament. Tarkenton's father was a preacher in the Pentecostal Church. In the newspaper stories about his son, the Rev. Dallas Tarkenton was usually transformed into a Methodist minister, which is not quite the same. But it was close enough and also considered more respectable in some places in the South.

From the earliest moments of his professional career, Tarkenton's religiosity had attracted the sports authors as magnetically as his statistics. And it was probably correct that he was measured for heaven on the sports pages far earlier than he was for the Hall of Fame. He tried not to make a display of his beliefs. From the beginning, his Christian witness was probably more casual and chummy than that of the born-again Fundamentalists who made up most of his father's congregations. After a while it became something of a weight, the swarms of requests—even demands—for his speaking services at father-and-son meetings and the full spectrum of benefit programs.

Only a saint could or would have wanted to deliver on all of them.

Since Tarkenton admitted his mortality early in the game, he found himself withdrawing from that kind of public witness. Some saw this as sophistry. Tarkenton preferred to call it privacy. But his alleged sainthood was retreaded when he was traded from the Vikings to the New York Giants in 1967. The impresarios found it impossible to resist the metaphor of matching the apostle who quarterbacked the Giants against the Jets' Joe Namath, who had managed so far to avoid canonization.

Friends of both would explain wearily that neither completely deserved the casting, but what chance does accuracy have against poetry?

Tarkenton's perception of what constitutes A Good Christian had undergone change over the years. It might partially explain his rise from the streets and alleys of Richmond, Virginia, and Washington, D.C., to the level of a net-worth millionaire by the time he was thirty-two. He tended now to define goodness more humanistically than he did in the days of the hallelujah commitment of his youth. What was godlike now, he decided, were qualities like loyalty and truth and understanding among human beings. Some people said he ran too hard in too many directions and was a conglomerate frantically capitalizing himself; they said he was a smoothie as a politician, plausible and adaptable. But you didn't have to be a pauper or a 'round-the-clock psalm singer to be a Christian. Tarkenton cared about people in the abstract, all right, but far more inquisitively when he was face to face and could establish something in human terms, not on a jock-fan basis, which sometimes he hated.

But in all his modification of values he never let himself forget the message—and more importantly, the simple inspiration—of the little preacher he sometimes called Squat: his father, Dallas Tarkenton. And so in his reflections three hours before a playoff football game Tarkenton remembered his daddy, and Frances, his mother. They were part of the thanksgiving of this day, in this year of years for their quarterback son.

His mother was an authentic fan. The last week of November she flew up from Georgia to attend the game in which her son broke Unitas' career record for most completed passes. Francis asked his wife, Elaine, to outfit her in suitable polar equipment for the game. Dressed in snowmobile boots, a half-dozen sweaters, an overcoat, and a Viking stocking cap, Mrs. Dallas Tarkenton witnessed her first game on the icecap, and was enchanted. The reverend wasn't there. He arrived a day later at the Tarkentons' seasonal home on Lake Minnetonka fifteen miles west of Minneapolis. His ignorance of football was deep and impregnable. It resisted television, the press, his wife's enthusiasm for the game, and table conversation with a houseful of his middle son's beefy friends. It wasn't that Dallas Tarkenton objected to football or was indifferent to it, he just never had the time to understand it. He had been born in the slums of Norfolk, Virginia. His policeman father died when he was five, and his mother when he was seventeen. From his adolescent days he had had the urge to preach. He was going to be a Pentecostal preacherman, and that, together with the rearing of his three sons—Dallas, Jr., Francis, and Wendell—would be enough to occupy a man who in 1950 was willing to serve the Lord and support a family of five on fifty dollars a week.

He was a little man in constant motion as a herald of salvation. He was one of those unapologetic strict constructionists who didn't believe in using aspirin and didn't allow the shining of shoes in his house because these were quackeries or frivolities. So were motion pictures, none of which Francis Tarkenton saw until he was a fresh-

man at the University of Georgia when he was already a campus
figure. On reflection, movies were worse than frivolities. They were
the flashcards of the devil.

While he was rough on the devil and implacable on shoeshine,
the parson Tarkenton was essentially a man with a friendly heart and
a bounding style in his pursuit of redemption for the souls around
him. He was the kind of man, his son remembers, who really saw no
wickedness in other human beings, only confusion now and then.
Dallas Tarkenton would rise at 6 A.M., read his Bible, and pray. Then
he would stroll the neighborhood, shaking hands and socializing.
The minstrels would have called him a man who liked to smell the
roses, which he did. He also enjoyed his music but avoided controversy because he connected conflict with destruction, and perhaps
this is why football sometimes befuddled him, although he never
discouraged his sons from playing it.

A few days after his arrival in Minneapolis, Dallas Tarkenton did
watch his son in a practice session. Standing on the sidelines at
Metropolitan Stadium in midweek of late November, the little
preacher had a difficult time releasing his eyes from his quarterback
son. They had filled out the reverend with a Viking sweatshirt, a big
purple jacket, and oversized boots. Somebody from the defensive line
squawked a warning that Grant might fine him for wearing his
shirtsleeves longer than prescribed. On the practice field even Bud
Grant, the expressionless Sheriff Iron Eyes of football coaching, was
hazable. This time the coach smiled a ton. It would have been a scene
for CBS. The parson stood in the cold for two hours, and it was a
reasonable surmise that he did not have the foggiest clue to what he
was watching. Did it matter? This was his boy's world, and these
were Francis' friends. The parson had the normal gratifications in his
son's long-standing celebrity, but it was more important to see him
in his true environment: bantering, working, enjoying, getting ready
for a game millions would see. There was no intimation that the
young man was consumed by tension over the significance of it.
Francis never was.

A few days later, the family had dinner at the Radisson Flame
Room downtown. Francis would treasure that night because his

mother and father seemed so graced by the relaxed pleasure of this interlude. It was a vintage hour for his daddy especially, a night out with his son and daughter-in-law, and his twelve-year-old grand-daughter, Angela. Francis' longtime teammate and closest friend, Grady Alderman, and his wife, Nancy, sat across the table. The Radisson had a big violin ensemble called the Golden Strings, which spun rich Viennese mosaics and Hungarian gaiety. The parson beamed. He talked about his other grandchildren back at the Lake Minnetonka home, Matthew, six, and Melissa, five. And he confided to Alderman that it was a delight knowing there were still places where a family could be entertained without apologizing to heaven. He talked about his little church in Savannah, where he would return in a couple of days with his wife. He admitted not knowing much about the mathematics of the playoff system, but he expected the Vikings to be on television on December 28, and he would be man-ning the galleries in front of the living room set. Smiling, Francis lightly squeezed Elaine's hand. It seemed to him that all the work and praying his father had done for others, his cheerful sacrifices as a husband and father and parson, had reaped for him the surmount-ing contentment of a night like this.

For that and all the other gifts the year had provided, Tarkenton gave unspoken thanks at the brief pregame chapel meeting. There was time enough for his game face. The motel room was not the place. Laurel and Hardy were on the tube. It was the only act in show business, the quarterback observed with baffled respect, that would outlast George Blanda. The telephone rang: Cowboy Nelson, the trainer's assistant, was making his usual Sunday morning summons.

Cowboy always taped Tarkenton. Cowboy fended off insults with a fine blend of martyrdom and contempt and, therefore, was per-fectly suited to minister to Tarkenton. Francis rarely solemnized the pregame hours of a football game. He turned himself on an hour before. They might have gone through walls at Alabama and in South Bend and Texas, but Grant discouraged such behavior as unbecoming and probably dangerous.

Tarkenton stuck the telephone under his pillow and let Cowboy strangle a little.

At the team meeting in the motel, Grant spoke for a few minutes. He was a tall man with dissecting blue eyes and a bristle haircut unchanged since the 1950s. His language, typical of all of his personal habits, was thrifty, disciplined, and functional. As a consistent winner in pro football, he ranked with Don Shula of Miami and Tom Landry, his rival today. In ten years at Minnesota Grant had become sanity's fixed beacon at Metropolitan Stadium, nerveless and impregnable, an emotional Sahara. When he spoke to the players it was usually to remind them in broad outline of their purposes, to focus them. The assistants handled the tactical briefings. For games of special importance he tried to impart some sense of the occasion without delivering an oration, which was as foreign to him as a sideline cartwheel or an upraised fist.

He could not remember another game that he personally had looked at with such anticipation, he told his players. From the first day of training camp they had expected to win their division championship. It was a judgment that reflected both the quality of their team and, the players conceded, the beneficence of the schedule. The organization would never admit it, but the only easier recorded schedule in recent years was Richard Nixon's in the 1972 election.

That aside, Minnesota had played well and consistently in the 1975 season. It harvested swarms of team and individual records in winning twelve of fourteen games. Now, in the playoff, it confronted a team that always stimulated Grant because Landry, and therefore the Cowboys, approached the game in the same tenor and with the same respect for untheatrical professionalism.

"It's here today," Grant said. "It's a new season. Three games long. I think you've looked forward to it as much as the coaching staff has."

Tarkenton, the quarterbacking sophisticate and mahogany-office tycoon, hung on Grant's every syllable in a way that might have startled the television fan whose own image of Grant was not so flattering. Some of Tarkenton's teammates themselves were not overpowered by Grant's terse wisdom before the games, regarding it as pro forma vapor like any other coach's. But Tarkenton didn't see it in those colors. Grant impressed him in a hundred different ways.

He did it with his perceptions, his control, his understanding of the athlete's nature. Grant recognized strengths that could be appealed to, vulnerabilities that could be healed or outflanked, hungers that could be appeased, and, above all, doubts that could be cleared with straightforward talk.

Standing next to Grant on the sidelines, even in the midst of a critical football game, was invariably a learning experience for Tarkenton. The multitude could be in tumult. The hostilities on the field might offer all the prospects of a riot. And Grant could say aside, "Their quarterback has thrown five straight balls seventeen to twenty yards." It was a remark that might have no special profundity except to reveal that his mind was working deductively while everybody else in the joint was ready to come on with broadaxes and hand grenades. Tarkenton recalled a couple of years before when the Vikings played in Los Angeles in a game widely advertised as a collision of defensive goliaths. The Rams got off to a 17–0 lead. Grant gazed out on the proceedings in characteristic posture, resembling a displaced face from Mount Rushmore. He then spoke to his quarterback: "I don't think we are going to beat these people by running." Tarkenton nearly collapsed in giggles.

Restored, he charged onto the field to start throwing against the Ram's quarterback, Roman Gabriel. It was one of the great javelin contests of the decade. The Vikings won it, 45–41. They considered giving the game ball to their trainer, Fred Zamberletti, for keeping the wide receivers conscious between sixty-yard downfield sprints.

Grant's brief pregame speech at the Holiday Inn demanded no mass decimation of the Cowboys in memory of Hiawatha or Leif Ericson. Grant believed that a manageable kind of emotionalism was a cardinal part of winning football. But he, like Landry, expected each of his players to generate his own passion in accordance with his own disposition and glands. With this Tarkenton agreed. But if the quarterback had one reservation about the Minnesota football team, it was in the scarcity of let-'er-rip swashbucklers, the kind who could infect football teams with the fever of their mission. The team had a few emotional players by Tarkenton's definition. Wally Hilgenberg, the snarly, curly-haired linebacker, was one. Alan Page, the great defensive tackle, sometimes played in a frenzy, particularly when he saw himself as the victim of an unforgivable screwing by an official. Carl Eller once rescued a helplessly taut football team by smashing a blackboard at half time so wrathfully that Tarkenton had to duck into his locker to escape the shrapnel.

Tarkenton considered himself an emotional player in spite of his reputation as a cool dude and august head. It was a thought, however, that scarcely concerned him an hour before kickoff. He drove into the Met Stadium parking lot with Fred Cox and Mick Tingelhoff, through the acres of quilt-suited tailgaters. Some of the tailgaters were still sober. Tingelhoff had borrowed a housekeeping van in which they planned to spend a postgame hour unwinding with their wives, watching the second half of the Oakland-Cincinnati game and waiting for the traffic to thin.

The subterranean corridor leading to the Vikings' dressing room was drafty and chilly, like the tunnel of an iron ore mine, Tarkenton imagined. It never changed—the condition and the temperature never seemed to vary much from the Fourth of July to the end of December. Outside it was a jewel of a Minnesota day in December. The temperature was twenty-six degrees, and a ten-mile-an-hour wind was blowing out of the southwest. Somebody had plowed off a tiny rink fifteen yards from the end zone for a half-time figure-skating exhibition. In Los Angeles they paraded bikini girls at half time, and in New Orleans they refought the battles of 1812. In Minnesota they held dogsled contests and snowmobile races.

At the doorway to the Viking dressing room Unitas said hello. Johnny U., with his blazer, overcoat and lumpy smile. "Good day, considering," he said.

"I'll take it, John," Tarkenton said convivially. "How yah been?" He had an impish temptation to say, "How yah doin', Avis?"

Unitas was now a licensed oracle, an expert analyst on the CBS Sunday afternoon telecasts. By no coincidence whatever he had been assigned to the Viking games when Tarkenton verged on breaking his career record of 290 touchdown passes. But to the sorrow of the network choreographers, Tarkenton broke the record when Sonny Jurgensen was doing the masterminding. The nation was thus deprived of a carefully plotted poignancy wherein the old king would lay anointing hands on his successor—or wrap them around his throat, if the old king felt aggrieved.

Unitas' evaluation of Tarkenton's quarterbacking had aroused some indignation from the Viking audiences two and three weeks before. Unitas didn't intend any slurs. They happened to be two different quarterbacking creatures. Unitas flourished when it was the emblem of honor and an assertion of the American way to stand in the pocket and get disemboweled if it came to that. In addition, Unitas couldn't beat an egg as a runner. Tarkenton was spontaneous and adjustable. He was cunning and, in his fashion, great. Unitas was methodical, precise, brave, and, in his fashion, great. His usual public assessment of Tarkenton was something on the order of "a really outstanding quarterback; the best thing he does is scramble." Tarkenton heard that often enough to have a stomachful. And when Unitas disclosed a few weeks before in midgame that "Francis didn't throw with much precision on that play," Tarkenton simmered in the aftermath, primarily because Green Bay's Alden Roche had just rapped him in the crotch before he threw, disturbing the precision.

But nobody in football had much anger for Unitas; Tarkenton had none that clung for any length of time. Unitas was earnest and likable, a clubby guy. He might not electrify television on Sunday afternoon, but who did? In their occasional encounters, Francis and John always hit it off with the conventional hazing. And because Tarkenton construed himself not only as a celebrity jock but also as an interpreter of the whole phenomenon of pro football, from the huddle to the grandstand, he could not resist probing the life cycle of the Tarkenton-Unitas relationship.

John Unitas was the first great contemporary quarterback Francis followed when he was crafting his own game in high school at Athens and at the University of Georgia. He observed him on television, and envied the strength of his arm and the late-game heroics that became the wellspring of the Unitas cult.

In the second exhibition game of his pro career, Tarkenton stood on the sidelines in juvenile rapture at a personal glimpse of the real, the live John Unitas. Yet three months later, Tarkenton and his roisterers, mavericks, and innocent rookies defeated Unitas and his battle-ribboned veterans 28–20. And Unitas, asked to comment on his performance, blurted: "Why me? I wasn't even the best quarterback on the field." They became peers and rivals, but the *cognoscenti* rarely spoke of Tarkenton in the same frame of values as Unitas. Johnny U. had staked out the territory. He was the classicist, the man who belonged to history as the architect of that most momentous victory in the annals of mankind, the Colts' sudden-death defeat of the Giants in 1957. When Unitas retired, the heretic scamperer suddenly began overrunning all his statistics. Now, in 1975, the man who had been the model and icon of Tarkenton's schooldays, to be venerated but not touched, had become his chronicler in the television booth.

There was almost a tribal law at work there, but Tarkenton saw no special vindication in it, nor did he extract much personal triumph from it. Unitas was a decent enough guy, whatever the tangents of history.

"Congratulations on the record, Fran," Unitas said. "Good luck today."

Tarkenton nodded, and cuffed him on the shoulder. Neither one of them had any identity problems.

Tarkenton ducked through the locker room doorway, and inside said hello to Bob Berry and Bobby Lee, the reserve quarterbacks and his locker room neighbors. Also anybody else within range. Some ballplayers arrived at work with a prefabricated grimness, a kind of opaque absorption that was their armor for the pain and pressure. For some it involved an actual change in character. Tarkenton accepted that. Each by his own devices. But Francis was a social animal, and his temperament didn't change much despite the largeness of the event. He rapped a little with Jimmy Eason. Jimmy was the veteran equipment man who was simultaneously the hard-butt quartermaster, confessor, and mother hen of the expensive wards in his custody.

Tarkenton trussed himself in some of his gear and reconnoitered through the thin smoke camouflaging the outlying commodes, the only habitation allowed for smokers by Bud Grant. Grant firmly believed that both hell and the waiver lists are overpopulated with smokers. Tarkenton walked to the training room to heft a six-pound shot-put ball for a couple of minutes, in the fashion of a baseball hitter swinging the weighted bat. The therapy had been part of his routine since his arm nearly went dead a couple of years ago. But now it was restored. If John Gilliam got out there fifty-five yards today, Tarkenton would find him. As a matter of fact, the quarterback was planning on it.

He finished dressing and sat in front of his locker, leafing through a copy of *Pro,* the NFL program. He often found it very instructive. A few weeks ago he read where a highly successful NFL quarterback was now the operating head of a behavior-management service that promised dramatically to increase the profits of American industry by reducing absenteeism and heightening productivity. He could quote the pitchman's speech almost verbatim: "Gentlemen," the quarterback was telling personnel managers representing companies with more than a billion dollars in assets, "I don't think I have to tell you there is a close correlation between a man's productivity and his happiness. The unhappiest worker is one who is bored. We think we have a system, a program, that will heighten the efficiency of the employees in your company. It can do this by humanizing the conditions of their work, by recognizing, rewarding them when they do good work. This can raise productivity by cutting absenteeism, turnover, and low performance. All of this means more revenue for your company."

The reason Tarkenton could quote it almost syllable for syllable was that the speech and the company were his.

But today the quarterback was not a corporation. He was very much pads and sinew and hard ambition. The program lay at the bottom of his locker now, and he was staring at the clock. Time to go. Jim Marshall was waiting for him at the doorway. What was the ultimate phenomenon in pro football? It might be Jim Marshall. Tarkenton could not think of an equal. How many consecutive games? Over two hundred now. It was a record that did not depend on token appearances here and there to glue it together, or walk-ons in the fashion of the field goalers. For fifteen years Marshall was a starter at defensive end, where year in and year out 270-pound offensive tackles were shooting at him and cracking back on him. Years ago they laughed at him when he ran the wrong way with a fumble. But he outlasted all of them with his miraculous body and his singing heart. Fevers, pneumonia, busted ribs—they came with the equipment. Marshall went into the pit with all of it. His inquisitive spirit conjured other identities for himself, and he fulfilled some of them. One day he was a treasure-hunter, or a mountain climber, the next a make-believe entrepreneur. But on Sunday he was a ballplayer.

Fifteen years ago Tarkenton and Marshall had been teammates on the first Viking opening day, when Van Brocklin sent his unpedigreed roustabouts against the Chicago Bears, lampooning George Halas' blooded maulers as "the biggest marshmallows in football." When it was over, and the Vikings won, 37–13, Halas agreed with him. Everybody else was gone now, even Grady Alderman. But Tarkenton and Marshall were still wearing the purple heads and white horns. They congratulated themselves for this honor with a private ritual before leading their teams out for each game, half in parody and half seriously. Like the World War I combat pilots in the scrambling room before takeoff, they touched their rights fists before the man opened the door.

They did it now, the mustached black lineman from the ghettos of his childhood and the worldly southern white, a poor preacher's kid who became a millionaire by declining to follow the precept that the meek shall inherit the earth. They had played chess together, suffered, won and lost together, and roasted each other. They were ship's cronies adjusted to each other's strengths and limitations. They were never really intimate friends. Away from football they walked in different rhythms. But each understood what goaded and sustained the other, and this they respected.

The field was slow. Gilliam informed Tarkenton of that after running three or four downfield patterns in the pregame warmup. It was an informal briefing, part of a pro football game's intelligence operation that begins the moment the players leave the tunnels and continues until the final play. Much of it was funneled to the quarterback, the kind of information a military commander receives from his scouts: effects of the weather, condition of the terrain. Is a weak point ready for exploitation?

The slowness of the field bothered the quarterback because he *was* a quarterback and he lived on the forward pass, and forward passes had to be caught. All right, so it was just as gloppy for No. 12, the Cowboy quarterback, Roger Staubach, and for Staubach's deep receivers, Drew Pearson and Golden Richards. But the quarterback had to file the information. His receivers would have trouble making precise cuts. It was critical information, but Tarkenton really didn't know what he was going to do with it. If he was throwing on rhythm or the rush was staring down his throat, somebody better make the right cut at the right time.

Tarkenton stepped back for a moment, hands tucked inside his belt. They told horror stories around the league about December football in Minnesota, but most of them were fairy tales. Tarkenton remembered only one or two games of painful cold, and even then the cold was academic, by decree of Bud Grant. Grant refused to recognize cold weather. He banned butane heaters on the sidelines, no matter what the temperature or wind chill. The player who is preoccupied with being warm starts thinking about those heaters when he's supposed to be blocking and tackling, Grant maintained. If there are no butane heaters, nobody thinks about them. Tarkenton, with a little time to ruminate about that, smiled. Grant's logic was undefeatable.

Tarkenton's eyes swept the homely little stadium. There were less than thirty minutes before kickoff, but the arena was 85 per cent empty, although it would be virtually filled to its forty-eight-thousand-seat capacity by game time. The players were accustomed to this pregame solitude at Metropolitan Stadium. The absentee customers were congregated on the vast asphalt acres of the parking lot, tending their hibachis, their grills, and their cauldrons. They wore snowsuits that had the general form-fit contours of a barrage balloon. To an outlander they were incomprehensibly happy, stoking their fires, sipping their booze, munching their bratwurst, and predicting the margin of the newest Viking triumph.

Tarkenton was not all that festive about the game. But he did expect the Vikings to beat the Cowboys. Dallas had football players, but it missed the commanding presence of a Bob Lilly on the defensive line and the power and recklessness of a Calvin Hill in the backfield. In running situations and especially on first down, the Cowboys' defensive front would align itself in the so-called flex, dropping two of the heavyweights a yard off the line. These placements were intended to snag the enemy ground game by giving the co-ordinated Dallas defense better angles of pursuit once the direction of the play was established. Two years ago the Vikings scrambled it early by introducing a couple of influence or misdirection plays. Their intent was to dupe the middle linebacker, Lee Roy Jordan. Lee Roy was savvy and spry, a dynamic fellow Dallas liked to unleash to roam the field. But in the 1974 playoff Lee Roy was railroaded, and the Vikings won the game. With it they won the National Football Conference title. It is *de rigueur* for all professionals, winners and losers, to deny that tactics or trickery in any form influence the result of a game. All hands dutifully made their denials after the 1974 playoff. But the misdirection plays did terrible mischief to the Dallas defense early in the game, and the Cowboys never regrouped.

No misdirection plays would beat the Cowboys today, Tarkenton understood. Landry long ago found ways to neutralize or at least minimize those. Minnesota had some new material in for the flex today, altered blocking, a little different emphasis on some of Chuck Foreman's plays. Tarkenton was certain he could throw against the Cowboy zone, in spite of the menace of Cliff Harris, who was wise and shovey back there. Mel Renfro, although a convalescent, also had to be respected on the Dallas right corner, and Charlie Waters was okay at strong safety. Mark Washington on the left corner was less experienced. Would Tarkenton snipe at the cornerback, fling the heady speedster, John Gilliam, against him? Of course he would.

Quarterbacks never admit that anymore. They consider it lowbrow and unethical to finger the enemy. It also makes your offense sound simplistic. But Tarkenton had not played pro football for fifteen years to ignore the fascinating possibilities of a meeting between Gilliam and young Washington. He planned such a meeting on the Vikings' first possession of the ball.

The introductions were delayed by the verdict of the coin flip. It came up Dallas, and Freddie Cox, kicking off for the Vikings, flopped the basic Freddie Cox kickoff. It was short and treacherous. Dallas, almost mishandling it, had to start from the nineteen. The Cowboys intended to surprise nobody. Landry's over-all concept of offense was essentially no different from Grant's or anybody else's in pro football. You didn't plan beforehand to throw forty times, or to run on three out of four plays. Events determined that. The controlling conditions in the opening minutes were the high stakes of the game and your field position. The Cowboys were starting from a long way out, in a foreign arena. So they ran.

Roger Staubach directed, via Landry's messenger service from the sideline. Like Tarkenton, Staubach had to stand off the sour prophets early on in his career. He ran too much. He could disorganize his own offense. But he could also compete, passionately and without much thought of personal safety. A Heisman trophy coverboy when he played for the Navy, he was forgotten during his service days by almost all save the Dallas scouting system. Landry believed in him, saw in him genuinely heroic qualities, strength under fire, willingness to sacrifice, the ability to deliver the climactic play. With him, Dallas had won a Super Bowl. If Dallas was going to win today, Landry understood, Roger Staubach would have to be the instrument of it, throwing the football. From your own nineteen, though, you better run.

It didn't surprise Grant to see Dallas move out on the ground early, but the Cowboys weren't going to beat him running. They held the ball for six minutes and came up with nothing. Mitch Hoopes punted into the end zone, and Tarkenton trotted on with the Viking offense.

How about something a little rakish early, to let Dallas know the Vikings were not chary about taking risks? Tarkenton threw to Stu Voigt, the muscular tight end. Not too rakish, Grant might have suggested. It wasn't. The completed pass cost Tarkenton a yard. Show the run, he thought. Foreman for one. Throw some more, get them loose. He hit Gilliam for fifteen. And now he would maneuver Jimmy Lash against Cliff Harris, the violence-loving safetyman, in the hope of springing John Gilliam one-on-one against Mark Washington. Gilliam cut once and broke free. Tarkenton threw deep, a touchdown special.

It missed by four inches.

A few minutes later Tarkenton gunned with another pass that oozed through Gilliam's hands at the same range, fifty yards.

The Vikings' own ground game was moving with no noticeable destructiveness. Tarkenton was annoyed and puzzled by that, because the Dallas defense, while sound and statistically impressive, did not seem that good to him.

So in the absence of a quick-strike touchdown to Gilliam, it was becoming a struggle. What else is new? Tarkenton asked himself. He felt strong and confident despite the blanks on the scoreboard. Like any other veteran player, he had a total respect for Murphy's law when applied to the football field: "Anything that can go wrong, will." He lived with that kind of wariness. But he was a man of elemental optimism from Day 1 as a professional football player. He believed with the force of the evangelized that the man who made things happen was the one who won.

At the quarter no one had made anything happen yet. Tarkenton would be startled if this turned into one of his team's memorable hours, but they were going to win. He felt too good and assured to consider any alternative. In December of 1975, all the planets were in order for Francis Tarkenton.

The self-acknowledged hillbilly of the team, rookie Neil Clabo from Tennessee, punted from midfield for the Vikings. Neil was mustached and twangy, and took a large pride in being able to drop the ball near the goal line in situations like this. The Cowboys' Harris was waiting just outside the end zone. As the ball descended, the Vikings' rookie defensive back, Autry Beamon, stared squarely into Harris' tonsils as the Cowboy safety tried to field the ball. Autry, in fact, nearly had him garroted. He gave him no room at all. It was very intimidating and quite illegal, although somehow ignored by the officials. It was also unsettling to Harris, who never touched the ball in its downward flight. It bounced around at the four-yard line and would have been given to Dallas there except, in the judgment of the officials, it touched Harris as it was flopping around. Or maybe it was Pat Donovan, one of the Dallas blockers. The touchee was never clearly identified. Whatever the ball did beforehand, it wound up in the embrace of the Vikings' Fred McNeill, and was awarded to Minnesota. Three plays later, Foreman smashed into the end zone, and the Vikings led, 7–0.

Nothing that happened in the remaining twelve minutes of the half ignited either the blimp-suited thousands in the arena or the millions in front of their television screens. It was stolid football, not always cautious football, but uneventful football. It did not offend the Met Stadium audience, which was unaccustomed to the rhapsody of easy winning. Grant's formulas militated against it. Get a lead, make the others pass, force a mistake, lead comfortably, and then *don't do anything stupid.* The Viking offense in 1975, ironically, was one of the most versatile in recent football history. But playoff games are not necessarily the times to showcase versatile football.

Tarkenton frowned. The Vikings weren't moving on the ground as well as they had programmed. The passing was mixed. Their problems had something to do with Harris. He could have played the heavy in a Gay Nineties melodrama, with his mustache and all the consternation he was causing. He tackled, loused up passing patterns, and in general raised hell. Offensively, Tarkenton calculated on the sidelines, Dallas was running better than a team with Robert Newhouse, Preston Pearson, and Doug Dennison in the backfield should run against a prospective Super Bowl defense. He wasn't downgrading anybody, least of all the Viking defense. The Vikings led, 7–0, but a deflected punt was responsible for that, not the Minnesota offense.

They jogged into the locker room, awaiting the arrival of the muses in their coaching caps. The professional teams didn't squander half time with hot-breathed elocution. Jerry Burns, the Vikings' offensive coach, led the contingent down from the press box observatory. The offense assembled at one end of the locker room, the defense at the other. Burns always salted his technical talk with punchy four-letter connectives. Plays 37 and 57 ought to go. He wanted Foreman running off tackle, to take advantage of the pinching-down tactics of the Dallas defensive ends, Too Tall Jones and Harvey Martin. They had pretty well killed the Viking inside running game. Also, Fran, Burns was saying, the bootleg and sprint-out actions are open for the passing game.

Burns didn't have an immediate antidote for Harris, nerve gas and grappling hooks being illegal.

Bud Grant brought the squad together. To win, he said, the team would have to play better, execute better. But he wasn't going to sound alarmist. Hardly. He reminded them they were leading, 7–0, and they knew they were capable of playing better. Trailing, Dallas would have to come to them.

At about the time the Vikings clattered back through the tunnel, the half-time conversation ebbed in the Dallas Tarkenton living room in Savannah, Georgia. The preacher draped his leg over the arm of an easy chair and listened to Wendell and Dallas, Jr. He conceded they had cleared up all the first-half mysteries to his satisfaction. His wife, doing something busy in the kitchen, prepared to join them.

On the field in Minneapolis, his third son decided to discard the long bomb in deference to Cliff Harris. It was back to the beanbag offense on the third quarter's first play. Tarkenton lobbed the ball to Eddie Marinaro to explore. Marinaro hustled it forty yards. *Now.* They were at the Cowboy thirty-five, and Tarkenton's filaments told him that Dallas was prepared to be disorganized. He remembered Burnsie's briefing. He would hammer them off-tackle with Foreman, where Yary and White and Chainsaw Voigt lived, on the Viking right side. Tarkenton could see the opening widen and Foreman churning. He might go the distance. But Too Tall Jones slipped off Chainsaw's block with an acrobatic movement when he had only an eyelash of time left.

At the Viking bench, John Michels, the offensive line coach, gasped. It was an incredible play.

Two lousy yards, and they had a touchdown in their pocket. All right, same guy, same place. It was open again. Foreman was barreling. He had it broken. Tarkenton lifted his arms and he wanted to cheer. But Jones came off Chainsaw's block again.

Michels was stunned. The Viking execution had been perfect.

Five bleeping yards. So third and three. Would the Cowboys blitz? Probably. Tarkenton squinted out to Gilliam on the flank. Here they come. Dallas was blitzing. Somebody fouled the blocking assignment, but Gilliam was cutting for the sideline. Too Tall lunged, too late. Tarkenton got rid of it. Gilliam caught the ball for a first down, bobbled it, caught it. He was doing some of both, going out of bounds.

Incomplete. The Cowboys were ready to go over the cliff, but nobody obliged them with a shove.

Freddie Cox came in and methodically missed a field goal from forty-five yards out.

Zero points.

"The hell with running on the first down," Tarkenton told the gray eminence on the sidelines. The quarterback wasn't rebellious or mad at anybody except the Viking offense, Francis A. Tarkenton included. Dallas allowed him adequate stewing time. The Cowboys labored seventy-two yards. From the Viking four on third down, Landry opted for Dennison smashing the line. The Cowboy staff beside him nearly fainted. Dallas *never* ran on third and four in that situation. Not only did the Dallas staff know it, but Jeff Siemon and the Viking defense knew it. Dan Reeves, one of the Cowboy assistants, was so unsettled he wanted to call a time-out. But Dennison was a quick accelerator, an obsessed, straight-ahead runner in critical situations. This was the moment, Landry decided, for some deviousness.

They came off the ball, and Siemon flew out from his middle linebacker position, looking for the pass. Who could blame him? Certainly not Reeves. Dennison rammed straight up the middle into the end zone.

Almost at that same moment, a little sixty-three-year-old preacher in Savannah, Georgia, groaned softly and closed his eyes. His head fell backward in the chair, and he breathed deeply.

In a moment he was gone, dead of a heart attack.

His sons tried to revive him by breathing into his mouth. One of them went into another room, where their mother must be told why they were calling the doctor, must be comforted, offered some hope, although they knew there could be none.

In Minneapolis, the fourth quarter opened with a Toni Fritsch field goal that sent Dallas into a 10–7 lead.

Nobody had to hold up bulletin board maxims for Tarkenton, or Yary, or Tingelhoff. About sucking it up. They had been there a hundred times. If you've got the insides, and if there is any excuse for calling yourself a championship football team, you do not die there.

A procedure penalty sandbagged them. Clabo punted. The defense stopped Dallas. With eleven minutes to go, the Vikings were seventy yards away. It doesn't matter how, Tarkenton told himself. This time we get in. Drive on them. Throw the ball fifty yards, kick them in the balls. Nobody is going to ask how you did it.

Yary was downfield on first down. It was a tribute to his hustle but a stain on his discretion. He wasn't supposed to be downfield. So it was first and twenty. The heroics can wait. Be patient.

Foreman for seven. Tarkenton was a hard man to amaze. But Foreman amazed him a half-dozen times a game, with his spontaneity, his guts, his hands, whatever he needed to advance the ball. Throw now. Sixteen yards to Foreman. Foreman for seven more. Now to Marinaro. How about McClanahan? When are they going to give me *all* the tools? Tarkenton would puzzle. Nobody on the team ran quite like McClanahan. Heedless, driven, and productive. So in came McClanahan.

Tarkenton ran him on a reverse. The quarterback had been holding the play face down in his little pile of hole cards. You save the reverses for the other guy's twenty to forty. In his own territory he has to react to any movement to protect the goal line, which makes the deception of the end-around or backfield reverse all the more potent. McClanahan went for thirteen.

Now they had it going. For the ballplayer, when he feels it in his marrow and groin, a touchdown drive becomes an ecstatic, Freudian ride on the wind. The men in his huddle are more than teammates.

They are kin, united by the zealotry of the moment and the shared sacrifice. It sometimes heightens the euphoria, nourished as it is by violence and pain, to have swatches of blood on the uniform—an opposing player's, your own, it doesn't matter. The Vikings' Ed White explained it: "No matter what your mentality is, and how you sublimate the game and make it an intellectual as well as physical experience, you play it—or at least you used to—in mud, on half grass, half scrabble, on frozen dirt. There's no way you can get around the objective of the game when you're slugging it out on the line of scrimmage. It's force against force. You're hammering each other. And as long as you're doing it that way, you may as well do it on God's good earth, or frozen earth, whatever he gives you on Sunday afternoon. The artificial rug just doesn't seem like the right environment for all the mauling you have to do. You come out of it with the uniform looking pretty, and you wonder why you have to shower. I'm no bloodthirsty beast. But when you cut your knuckles lining up in the stance and you've got red streaks on your jersey, it makes the game seem a helluva lot more believable."

White, Tarkenton remembered, had some red flecks and jagged stains on his forearms. Did that seem melodramatic? Certainly. Nobody seriously maintained these were real wars. For three hours people grunted and gouged, tried to run faster, throw better, and score more than the fortune hunters like themselves who were arrayed on the other side of the line. Yet when it was over they didn't burrow in for the night but went out to some chichi supper club and partied for a couple of hours.

But the physical sacrifices it demanded, the hurt it imposed, the fellowship it forged were genuine enough. And that is why the ballplayers sometimes accepted the metaphor of the battlefield, and why the fans insisted on it.

Tarkenton would have wagered his four-hundred-thousand-dollar manor back in Atlanta that they were going in. He had felt it a thousand times. Vince Lombardi maintained that Paul Hornung could smell the goal line. The biographers of Patton said he could sense the presence of an ancient battleground. Tarkenton felt a tingling in his insides when a long drive was going to make it to the end zone. It was like rising cadenzas in the orchestra hall. The whole team felt it. The big people on the line couldn't wait for him to call the play, roll the cadence on the line. They wanted him to go for it on the ground. We can beat them running. Us against them. We've got it together. The Cowboys felt it. Old Lee Roy Jordan was jacking around in front of Mick Tingelhoff, and Lee Roy would bust his tubes chasing Foreman, but Lee Roy must feel it, too.

They were on the sixteen, first down. Half the game they had run on first down, half of it they had passed. Jordan knew they were going to run, all right. Tarkenton would never screw this up with four downs to work on. Foreman dipped to the outside. Somebody had a leg at the scrimmage line, but he was powerful and possessed. Harris finally got him at the five. Foreman again? Who else? He was all legs and moves, and he faked himself into slipping, as he often did. But he recovered at the five and bored to the one. The Cowboys anchored for the Vikings' double-flyover, Jerry Burns' jabberwocky for the Sam Bam Cunningham play, the helmet-first dive over the line of scrimmage. The upback flew in first, the ball carrier next. The play had the delicate nuances of an earthquake. They stacked in on Foreman, but it was McClanahan, blasting the left side. Stopped once, he blasted again through Lee Roy Jordan into the end zone.

Tarkenton trotted off briskly.

The professional's trot. Seventy yards and six minutes in eleven plays. It was 14–10, and the gin-laced snowmobile pilgrims in the gloomy tiers of Met Stadium screeched and stomped and clutched their Thermoses in the air.

The Cowboys were dying. A veteran ballplayer can sense that as acutely as he can sense the irresistible momentum of a touchdown drive. They were not only dying, Tarkenton told himself on the sidelines, they looked terrible doing it. It was no judgment of the Cowboys' effort or their performance. For much of the game Dallas looked like the stronger team. Its play was smoother, and its statistics were more impressive. Yet heading into the final minutes, the Cowboys seemed unco-ordinated and lost. Centering deep to Staubach in the shotgun formation, John Fitzgerald rolled the ball on the freezing turf and dirt a couple of times. Staubach groused the second time.

Marshall and Page heightened his distemper by racking him for an eight-yard loss. With 3½ minutes to go, Mitch Hoopes punted for Dallas. It was short and almost abject. To compound the unsightliness, the Cowboys had an illegal man downfield. You could almost hear the air going out of Dallas.

The Vikings had possession. Their tactical situation was almost unbeatable. It was third and two on the Dallas forty-seven when Lee Roy stopped the clock. With just over two minutes left, and two yards to go, the Vikings could put it away right here. But Tarkenton needed more than a short-yardage play. The Cowboys were going to stack enough people on the line to hold the levees at Galveston. He wanted a rollout option to keep the Dallas secondary loose.

Tingelhoff snapped it, and Tarkenton rolled right. The strong safety, Waters, *had* to respect a possible pass there. It was in capital letters in the defensive playbooks. But Waters didn't. "They're not going to throw that thing on third and two at midfield," he counseled himself. Waters flew up to the line. Tarkenton tried to step inside, but there wasn't room. He couldn't throw because there wasn't time. He held the ball and got nailed. And Clabo punted one more time.

The pros sanctify the big play, which sometimes takes a very prosaic form. In all the shock waves ten minutes later, nobody remembered how Charlie Waters defied the manuals and buried the quarterback on the play Dallas needed if for nothing more than the usual doomed thrashings at the finish.

With Dallas in possession, Fitzgerald bowled the ball back to Staubach, who responded by barking and fuming. The Cowboys were disordered. On fourth and sixteen from the twenty-five, Drew Pearson told Staubach, "Me, throw it to me on the sideline. I can beat Wright with an out ball." Staubach lofted it amid a flutter of "Ave Marias," and Pearson leaped to spear it at the fifty as he was going out of bounds. Nate Wright nudged him while he was descending. Even without Wright's assistance, Pearson was likely to land out of bounds. The official, Jerry Bergman, could have seen it that way, but didn't. The catch was allowed. It was a marginal play, and not many officials want to decide a playoff football game with a penalty call in the final minute. Bergman was under an even larger gun. He had been wounded by all the recriminations following the Mercury Morris fumble play in the Miami-Buffalo game a few weeks ago.

The hairy-chested tycoons would decide this on their own. Flags are okay early in the game. In the last minute of this one, Dallas and Minnesota were going to police themselves.

Tarkenton's view of the midfield pass was obscured. There was some bitching around him, but he couldn't join because he didn't really see the play. Staubach had thirty-seven seconds left from midfield. Tarkenton didn't visualize Tarkenton calling the play in this circumstance. He rarely looked at the other quarterback that clinically. All he wanted Staubach to do was get wiped out by the Viking rush. From the shotgun Staubach threw to Preston Pearson, who dropped the ball. Now thirty-two seconds left. Staubach set up again. The Viking rush was urgent but a half-second off and a half-yard late. Drew Pearson was flying shoulder to shoulder down the sideline with Nate Wright. It was a prevent defense, all right. But still, it wasn't preventing the Cowboys from loosing the jackrabbit flanker one-on-one against Wright. Krause was coming over, but Golden Richards was on the other side, and Krause had to worry about that. The ball was nosing down through the wind. Under-thrown. Pearson had to slow down. Aware, Wright tried to adjust to the changed rhythm. They made contact, and Wright fell. Striding over him, Pearson hooked the football on his hip with one hand. It was a kind of catch only heaven could understand, or ordain. But Pearson had the ball and was stepping into the end zone in astonish-ment, almost in guilt, because even the professional flankers with all their big talk about catching anything in sight don't catch a football like that.

Pearson looked at the official slackly. Was it all right? Any flags? There was something yellow on the field. Pearson could have sworn it was a flag, but it was nothing more accusatory than a tennis ball flung from the stands.

Wright got up and charged the official with Krause. On the sidelines Tarkenton screamed and swore. He ran onto the field with a half-dozen others. The crowd was comatized in silence. The sounds were from the players, not the spectators. "You dirty son-of-a-bitch," Tarkenton yelled crossfield to the official. "It was interference! Call it!"

The culminating year. The season of seasons for the conglomerate quarterback, and the year of the Super Bowl championship for his football team. They were going to beat the Steelers somehow, and all the old derisions and neglects would be wiped away. And now a hotdog, cocksure official, which is the way Tarkenton characterized Bergman, pulled the plug on Tomorrowland. The screen went black.

And it all came tumbling down.

Tingelhoff got Tarkenton back to the sidelines. The Vikings couldn't stop yammering. These were the good, disciplined, mechanical men. Calculating professionals. And in this ugliest, wrenching moment of their football lifetimes they were acting like deranged dockyard toughs.

Grant restrained his players, but he couldn't blame them.

Page was chewing out one of the officials. "Take it," he said, "and stick it up your ass."

They docked Minnesota fifteen yards for that on the kickoff. Fritsch hammered the ball deep, and McClanahan brought it out to the fifteen. Tarkenton ran on with the offense, looking for Bergman.

He cursed the official from cap to shoelaces, accused him of losing his guts and blowing the ball game. Bergman flung his replies, then told the quarterback to play football or he was going to run him off. Tarkenton called a pass play, and Too Tall Jones ripped him on the one-yard line for a loss of fourteen. Tarkenton got up and renewed his assault on Bergman. Christ, he couldn't believe it. Six months down to this. The day of days for the quarterback and his football team. Bergman told him to stop or he was out. "Go ahead," Tarkenton railed. "You already took it away from us." Bergman wasn't going to run him in a championship game. But he might as well. As they were arguing, the official nearby, Armen Terzian, grabbed at his head, struck by a bottle thrown from the stands. Other bottles were falling. Foreman raced to the railing. A week before, other dues-paying morons in Buffalo threw rock-hard snowballs and ice chunks at the Vikings and caught Foreman in the eye. He had double vision for three days. "Knock it off," Foreman pleaded. "You already hurt one guy."

Tarkenton closed his eyes. It was degenerating. It was a living horror. The day that began with sunbeams and gold dust, with the intimations of Jubilee ahead, was winding down with a cruelty and vindictiveness that made the whole progression of events seem like a mindless mockery. They were losing the football game in a way they couldn't possibly lose it. The season was in ashes. And now an official knelt bleeding from a missile flung from the stands by some drunken fan.

The pain was still too raw for Tarkenton to yield any remorse. He knew later he would experience that. But at the moment he could not summon compassion for Terzian, the fallen official. The officials had lost their nerve and changed the verdict of the scoreboard, he felt inflexibly. In the back of his head he understood the evil and cowardice of the bottle-throwing. He even remembered talking to a newspaperman three hours after the game in Buffalo. Minnesota liked to congratulate itself on the civility of its athletic crowds. Alongside the bleacher jungles of Boston, Baltimore, and Philadelphia, theirs had a drawing-room restraint. But Tarkenton maintained there were just as many brainless spectators at Metropolitan Stadium as there were in Buffalo or at Shea.

It did not occur to him at the moment that the anarchy could also spread to the field.

A game. Tarkenton himself insisted football was a game too solemnized by the American public, its true purposes and values perverted. Yet in the final moments of this game, animalism, shock, and frenzy took possession of the stadium—and the field.

There were still ten seconds remaining when Page and Eller started walking off the field. Their act was a violation of the most rudimentary codes of the solidarity of the team. But it was over, and the two saw no need to observe some sepulchral formality.

At the gun the quilted multitudes in the stands headed wordlessly for the corridors. The Cowboys danced and howled, and the Vikings moved stricken, like armored zombies, toward their tunnels.

Grant left them alone in the locker room. What was he going to tell them? That they had had a great season, but you can't win them all? That they had had the game won but were jobbed by an official? Nothing the coach could say to them was going to lift the big round rock in their stomachs.

Tarkenton lingered in the locker room long after the others left. He had been obliging in the postgame inquisition, responsive to all of the questioners, the incisive ones as well as the dullards. He was composed and articulate. The four-letter words belonged to the combat. This was the epilogue. It deserved some contemplation. His judgment hadn't changed. The Vikings were beaten, he said, by the failure of an official to make an interference call that was obvious to anyone with eyes.

But his responses were quiet and measured, even when a young eastern journalist asked him, "Does a game like this bring back the old ghost, that you still aren't able to win the big one?"

An explosion might have followed in another locker room, or even from Tarkenton himself in an earlier year. But in Tarkenton's eyes the Big One syndrome was now so old and so discredited that it required no militant rebuttal. Tarkenton turned slowly, smiling. He was not amused, rather resigned, to a familiar penance.

"I don't play football for the adulation of the fans or to survive their boos," he said. "I don't play it to achieve somebody's conception of greatness. I play it because I enjoy it. The opinion others have of you may be interesting and important, but the one that is the most important is the honest feeling you have about yourself. Have you done your best, have you conducted yourself as well as you can as a competitor, allowing for your human mistakes?"

He talked about the Dallas defense, which he said was sound and powerful, about the dedication of the Vikings' fourth-quarter touchdown drive. He talked slowly, until he was talked out. He rose, but he could not leave. Even on the days of the worst disappointment, he could shake it off and head for the parking lot with lift in his stride. But today the barrenness of the locker room seemed to imprison him. He couldn't bring himself to walk out, although by now all but Stu Voigt were gone. He paced slowly among the discarded towels and strips of tape, the trunks Eason and his helpers were filling with the soiled garments of a beaten football team. The locker room is sometimes the athlete's playpen. Sometimes it is his sanctuary, and sometimes his limbo.

He was oblivious of a far deeper grief ahead.

Tarkenton walked over to Stu and dropped a hand on the curly-haired outdoorsman's big shoulder.

"A nightmare, Fran," Voigt said, "the way the game ended."

Tarkenton walked back to the washroom, pretending to himself he had to clean some dirt off his hands. He stared into the bowl, making an examination of himself. He had never wasted much time in depression, over defeat or bad news generally. At the moment he couldn't remember having experienced such a foul sequence of blows. The defeat, the hysterically bad ending, the bottle-throwing, the ranting. Hideous. But he wasn't especially depressed now. Puzzled. "Why and how?" nudged his brain. He understood now why he wasn't leaving the locker room. He didn't really want to accept the finality of it. It was as if postponing his departure kept open the possibility of some made-in-heaven recount or, even more miraculously, an official's admission of error.

"Come to," he said. "Get out of here."

His daughter, Angela, was waiting in the corridor. An eleven-year-old girl with a mature woman's wisdom about the vulnerability of heroes.

They talked calmly, about this and that. He didn't want her to sense his futility, and she preferred not to let on that she did. Angela led him to the van where Elaine and his son Matthew were waiting, with Grady and Nancy Alderman, Mick and Phyllis Tingelhoff.

They had done this before. But for the first time Tarkenton could not find the handle to join the conversation, with Elaine and the kids, let alone with his friends. He was uneasy and unhinged, palming a soft-drink glass as he stared at the television screen. It was half time in Oakland. The talk from Grady and Mick came to him in distant gutturals, halfhearted and indistinct. They tried to bring him into the conversation. He was appreciative, but the talk didn't interest him. He didn't want to be in the van, but he didn't want to be anyplace else, either. It was a kind of half stupor that was new to him and bothersome. A voice on television was saying something about wanting "to express our sympathies." He heard the name Tarkenton, and he looked at the screen again. Why the sympathies to Tarkenton? Jack Buck was talking. He said Mr. Tarkenton was sixty-three years old.

Mr. Tarkenton was dead.

He died watching the Minnesota-Dallas game with two of his sons.

Tarkenton put his hand to his face. Please turn the television set off, he wanted to say.

Elaine's hand gripped his. The others' eyes were moist. Other hands touched him. Lips.

Tarkenton rose. He wanted to go home. He put Matthew's coat on and took the boy by the hand to walk him to the car. Nancy Alderman was weeping. Grady and Mick offered to drive them home, but Tarkenton said he could handle it. In the car Elaine said she could drive. He shook his head and turned the key.

They were on the freeway going west, toward Minnetonka. When did I see him last? Tarkenton asked himself. His father was at the Minneapolis–St. Paul airport, big grin and all because he was glad to have spent an eventful week with his quarterback son, but he was going back to work for the Lord. Daddy was like the good soldier that way. Pastoring was what his life was all about. The little church in Savannah had pleaded with him to help out. It didn't have much money, and it had only seventy-five members. So Dallas Tarkenton came out of his semiretirement and went back to pastoring.

Tarkenton had another picture of his father. He saw him by the big coffee urn in the Viking dressing room during practice week before the Washington game. He was listening attentively while Grant made a little testimonial of his own: "I never take anything addictive when I'm working," Grant said. He spoke mischievously, but it was the truth. The parson said he liked that, really liked it. He was wearing those oversized boots and the long-sleeved purple jacket. He looked ready for a rummage sale, but they all liked him, and that pleased his son.

He died watching his son play football. A game. The parson

never understood the game but his son loved it, and that made it all right. His other sons, Dallas and Wendell, had tried to reach their brother at the stadium, but they missed him. NBC was unaware that Tarkenton did not know about his father.

"He's gone," Tarkenton said. He could think of nothing else to say. He wanted to speed home to talk to his mother, but the day needed no more tragedy. The blows had come with a terrible, concussive cadence. The grossness of the last minute, the end of the season and the Super Bowl mirage, the loutish bottle barrage, the official bleeding, and now the death of his father.

Even that seemed psychically laden. Dallas wins. Dallas dies.

And five hours before, the world whirled brightly and beautifully, all synchronized. What better than to be Francis Tarkenton and playing a big football game with millions watching on December 28, a game that had no more surprises for him, no mysteries?

He asked Angela to hold his right hand.

Matthew slid his own hand into it.

Tarkenton drove the rest of the way silently. Five-year-old Melissa was home with the baby-sitter. "Granddaddy's dead," she said. Her mother hugged her, and her father went to the phone. In a few minutes he had talked to all of them in Savannah. He would fly there tomorrow.

Grady, Mick, Bill Brown, and Mike Lynn, the general manager, visited later in the evening. He needed them, almost as much as his family, because he wanted to talk about the parson and what a lovely, unselfish man he was. And he wanted to explain some of the things he had said that afternoon. He didn't apologize for his competitiveness, but he was ashamed of some of his hard rhetoric. His father's forgiveness? He would have that. The parson would have said it's just a game. But sometimes it's more than just a game, even when you deny it. It's your blood and dreams, Freud, Midas, God, and the big down. Tarkenton had chided apoplectic fans for transforming a football game into something larger than reality. But in the final minute at Metropolitan Stadium that afternoon, the accidents of luck, an official's decision, time, and even nature's wind had perverted the orderliness of the six months of his team's careful planning, and the aspirations of years. It all blew up capriciously, a blind disintegration.

Daddy didn't know about football, so he might not understand how it could become that desperately important to a civilized person. But he did know humanity, and therefore he would not have seen it as anything evil.

The parson, as much as any man he had met, Tarkenton now recognized, grasped the most enduring realities. He had sought to be a good person and to encourage others to so strive. He had expended all the energies God gave him, and he had never really slowed in his pursuit of goodness for those willing to listen. But he had still had time to smell the roses and to enrich daily the imperishable reality of his life, his family.

Tarkenton drew his wife and children to him, and said his father was the wisest man he knew.

The Quarterback

2

When I came back to Georgia after my first year in professional football and my exposure to people like The Dutchman, Ray Nitschke, and Alex Karras, people said, "My, that must have been a shock going into that world from the University of Georgia." I'm just not so sure it was all that shocking. My life at Georgia had just as much suspense. It had almost as many hazards. It certainly had the full quota of characters.

I wasn't generally heralded as the football messiah at Georgia because I played high school ball in the same town, Athens. The townspeople had theories about that. Athens kids weren't supposed to get a fair shake at Georgia because they were fully exposed week in and week out to the Georgia staff, and everybody was conscious of their limitations. It was the kind of theory that had something in common with many theories: It was really pretty hard to prove, and it was probably filled with gas.

I don't know how I could have been better programmed for a high school career. By the time my family left Washington, D.C., and came to Athens where Daddy was going to preach, I had decided without equivocation that I was going to be a professional athlete. I fantasized with bubble-gum picture games in the attic, and I fantasized in the sandlots. I played all the time. I was bigger than the other kids my age, and I tended to dominate the ball games. I don't blush to say I had big feet. Somebody started calling me "Foots." Why not?

36

At the age of thirteen I was 5 feet 10, weighed 145 pounds, and wore a size 10½ shoe. Today I'm 6 feet and wear an 11 shoe. The way my feet developed early, some guy said I was wasting my time trying to be an athlete and should grow up to be a detective.

But Athens was great for kid ball, and I played everything. In high school football we had a coach named Weyman Sellers, who was notorious. He wrote the book on how to be a tough football coach, and is known in southern football almost as well as Bear Bryant. If you lost a ball game Friday night, Weyman Sellers was the kind who would bring you back on the field Saturday morning and scrimmage you for four hours. At practices we would run a mile, take our exercises, run ten fifty-yard wind sprints, and *then* start playing football. It was incredible. When I was introduced to the Dutchman's two-a-day drills at the Vikings' camp in Bemidji everybody seemed appalled. They could never figure out why I was so calm about it. Actually I was grateful. If Sellers ran the Vikings he would have scheduled a third one at night. But he taught me the fundamentals of playing quarterback, the techniques that stood up for the rest of my career. He was relentless about teaching the quarterback to make the right moves taking the ball, handling it, handing off. Most of what I still use I got from the Athens High School Trojans and Weyman Sellers.

It's still probably the best thing I do as a quarterback, handle the ball, which is an acknowledgment I know John Unitas will be pleased to hear. But in my junior year at Athens something traumatic happened. I got a bad shoulder separation and just couldn't throw the ball for more than fifteen to twenty yards. But we had a great team and killed everybody. I quarterbacked, ran, and tried to sound inspirational. We got into the state championship against Valdosta, which was the Massillon, Ohio, of Georgia football. I ran a kickoff back ninety-nine yards and threw one pass the whole game. It was incomplete. We won, 41–20, and please don't draw any conclusions.

Because we moved up in classification and we lost some fine players, we didn't do much my senior season, but the colleges seemed interested in me. I couldn't think of a better place to become a football hero than the University of Georgia, which already had two quarterbacks who aspired to that status, Charley Britt and Tommy Lewis. Although younger and respectful, I decided it was just a matter of time until I would take over. One of the people who didn't necessarily agree with this logic was the head coach, Wally Butts. Coach Butts was the first in a long line of brilliant football minds who didn't think that Francis Tarkenton had much future as a professional football player. At the time, though, he thought I had a reasonable chance of lettering at Georgia eventually. Our timetables just happened to disagree.

Coach Butts was really far ahead of his time in his approach to football tactics. He was a pugnacious little guy who could talk like a carny worker on the practice field and lead us in prayer the next day. We always had a devotional before the game, of course. It was part of the southern tradition, and the coach was a churchgoer who came from a Baptist college, Mercer. He also conducted a prayer session afterward, unless we lost.

Another thing we did before the game once in a while was to go over the opposition's game plan—if it happened to fall into our hands. We were in the midst of this quiet, contemplative period on a Saturday, listening to soft background music of University of Georgia fight songs and alma mater anthems and trying to feel very fierce about facing Vanderbilt in a couple of hours. Coach Butts called me in and explained that some bellhop at the hotel where Vanderbilt was staying had "stumbled into" the Vanderbilt game plan. By the rankest coincidence we now had it. It told all about how Vanderbilt was going to use the monsterman on defense, and what stuff they were going to use against our passing game. All of that and more. I figured they must know what they're doing, I mean our board of strategy, so I just filed away the information. I don't think we called our agents "plumbers" in those days. And I'm sure the bellhop just didn't flat-out steal that game plan. I have no idea how he came into possession of it, and I'm also mortally sure that most teams in the Southeastern Conference had some version of this intelligence system. We did beat the daylights out of Vanderbilt that year.

The guy who really got me ready psychologically and technically for college football was a man named Quinton Lumpkin, the freshman coach at the University of Georgia. He had been a great center at Georgia. He was the kind who lived in the dormitory with the players, a principled, hard-fibered, decent guy who was a man among men. Nobody ever challenged Quinton Lumpkin. He was tough, all right, but a gentle guy at the core, a man you could confide in if things got rough. We played three freshman games and won them all, and two weeks before the varsity's opening game, we beat the varsity.

As a sophomore, I naturally began as the third-string quarterback behind Charley Britt and Tommy Lewis. Charley later played defensive back in the pros and was a teammate of mine for a while with the Vikings in the middle sixties. Until Terry Bradshaw, I never saw a quarterback with Britt's physical qualifications. He was six-two, had a powerful arm, and ran like a deer. Tommy Lewis was a tremendous passer, too. And then there was Tarkenton, with the kind of arm you can define any way you want. In the face of this, I still thought I would be the starting Georgia quarterback in a couple of weeks. I really didn't look on that as bravado. I actually thought I had enough to give the team.

We opened at Texas, and I watched most of the game from the bench. I don't think we made a first down the first three quarters. I was standing next to Wally Butts, convinced the Georgia coaching staff had decided to red-shirt me, hold me out of competition my sophomore season. To hell with that noise. I started telling Coach Butts, "I can do it, I can get you a touchdown in this game, I can get this thing going." I still hadn't regained the full strength in my right arm in the two years since my shoulder separation, but I could throw adequately.

In the last quarter, Texas punted the ball down to our five. Before Butts could haul me back, I was running out to the huddle. Somehow the University of Georgia football team went ninety-five yards with Francis Tarkenton at quarterback on his first series. To compound the absurdity of it, he passed for the touchdown. He also passed for the two-point conversion, and Georgia led, 8–7.

Texas had a bunch of strong runners, though, people like Walt Fondren. So they went the length of the field to score, and we had four minutes left. I was poised on the sidelines, the adrenalin oozing. And what does Coach Butts tell me? He says Charley Britt is going in there to win the game.

I have never really been able to persuade many people right out of the blocks—I mean, for the first five or ten years they have watched me play—that I belonged in the front row in football. My high school team obliterated everybody in sight in my junior year, and as a senior I played very well, yet I never made the first team all-state team. In basketball I made it as a freshman. But not in football. The number of nonbelievers in Francis Tarkenton in football has been very impressive, and you might even say scary. This might make it easier to understand why Coach Butts went immediately to Charley Britt after I took the team ninety-five yards in the fourth quarter. Butts was looking to play the big, strong quarterback. Charley tried his damnedest, but we lost.

You can imagine the reaction in Athens. I was an instant martyr. They thought Butts was crazy, and they thought the old proverb about Athens boys getting screwed at the University of Georgia surely had been confirmed. The next week they practically passed a town ordinance demanding that Tarkenton should start the second game.

Coach Butts was no greenhorn as a politician. He read the polls shrewdly. He decided an excellent choice for his starting quarterback the next game would be the sophomore from Athens. I quarterbacked the first three plays of the game. Butts then substituted Charley Britt, who played the rest of the game, which we lost.

In the next two or three weeks I got in once in a while, but on one particular Saturday I was something less than the next Sammy Baugh. In practice the following Monday, Butts gave me the full barrage—language I just didn't think a coach was capable of using on a football player. Some really awful stuff. I was the child of a Fundamentalist church, you should remember, and even "hell" and "damn" were foreign to me then. Here was my head coach calling me names I had only seen on the washroom walls. I knew Butts' reputation as a slaughterhouse orator when he was chewing out a player, but this was the first time it had happened to me, and it wasn't going to happen again. I was finished with Georgia, and I walked off the field.

I met with Butts that night and I told him I wasn't coming back because I didn't have to accept his kind of abuse. He tried to talk me out of it. I said my mind was set. One of my teammates, Pat Guy, felt as strongly as I did about dehumanizing coaching tirades. Another was Phil Ash, who lived in Stone Mountain, a town a few miles east of Atlanta. The three of us took off together. I think Phil was pretty much along for the ride, but we spent the night in his home, planning to enroll at Florida State and leave the Bulldogs and Wallace Butts far behind.

The next day, we had a visit from Quinton Lumpkin, the only coach in the world we would have listened to under the circumstances. He just walked in quietly and sort of sat around, talking a little about hunting and fishing. We told him about our intentions. He said he understood all that, and how things happen the way they did on the practice field, but Georgia really needed us, and our teammates needed us, and none of the strong words spoken by Coach Butts were in any way personal. He would guarantee that.

I think Quinton Lumpkin meant every word he said because it never occurred to me then, and never will, that this man might be capable of saying something he didn't believe. Naturally, we went back to Athens. From then on I quarterbacked a lot, and Charley Britt played defense primarily, and a first-rate defense at that. We started winning. In my junior year Britt would start at quarterback and then shift to defense. I'd come in on offense in the first quarter and quarterback the rest of the game. I'm not sure how Wally Butts arrived at this formula, but it worked.

We were selected to finish tenth in the Southeastern Conference that year, 1959, and when you examined the rosters of the other teams it was not hard to understand why. Louisiana State had people like Billy Cannon, Johnny Robinson, and Warren Rabb; Mississippi had Charlie Flowers and Jake Gibbs. Jackie Burkett and Zeke Smith and a half-dozen other outstanding players were at Auburn. But we opened the season by beating Alabama, and when we went into the ninth week, it was Georgia and Auburn for the championship and the Orange Bowl. The finish was the kind you wouldn't have believed if you saw it in the old Monogram movies. It was tied, 7–7, and Bobby Walden went back to punt: the one, the only Bobby Walden who starred for the Cairo, Georgia, Syrupmakers, my teammate later with the Vikings, and now annually picking up Super Bowl checks with the Steelers. Bobby lined up to kick, and Charley Britt, who was then in at quarterback, was the blocking back. I think Charley dropped back a little deep, because Bobby delivered a terrific effort and kicked the ball right into Charley's rear end. In front of sixty thousand people. I never saw a guy look more shocked in all my life. I don't mean Charley. I mean Bobby.

Auburn revived before either one of them and recovered the ball on our one. When they scored it was 13–7. The game wound down to a minute and a half left. We recovered a fumble on their forty-five and I threw three straight passes, incomplete. On fourth and ten I hit one. We reached the Auburn seven, but they snarled up a screen pass, and with thirty seconds left we're on the thirteen-yard line, fourth down.

It was a huge game—for the championship, the honor of Georgia, Coach Butts, and all of the good, great Baptists. The whole South was tuned in. I called a time-out but did not go to the sidelines to visit Coach Butts. We just didn't have any plays programed for fourth and thirteen with thirty seconds to go and the whole reborn Confederacy hanging on the outcome. I drew up a play in the huddle. I actually did, just like the John R. Tunis books I grew up with.

We didn't have split ends in those days. The two pass-catching ends were always lined up tight, and there were the conventional three running backs in the backfield. Essentially the play was a quarterback rollout to the right in which everything would flow right, the blocking and the receivers except for the left end, a fellow named Bill Herron. I told him to stay in and block, and count, "One thousand one, one thousand two, one thousand three, one thousand four." When he finished the count I wanted him to sprint into the left corner of the end zone.

We got the play going and I rolled right. I was dying to see what was happening with our left end. I wanted to look back, but I made myself carry out the deception. The whole stadium was looking at the rightward flow of the play, and all I could do was pray that the Auburn secondary was just as attentive. When I finished my own "one thousand four," I stopped and pivoted for a look at where Bill Herron was supposed to be. And Lord have mercy, there he was, wide open.

I ripped it crossfield, scared to death he was either going to drop it or the ball was going into the stands. Neither happened. We had the touchdown. Durwood Pennington kicked the extra point, and Georgia was in the Orange Bowl. I almost *never* call plays like that in the NFL, and I don't usually admit it when I do. Unprofessional. The computer has a play for every contingency. Except not quite, and the computers don't have to explain it all to the fans after the ball game.

We beat Dan Devine's Missouri team, 14–0, in the Orange Bowl that year. And the next season, my senior year at Georgia, was presentable. So I decided the world was now ready to bestow its rewards on Francis Tarkenton. Elaine and I were married at the end of the season. We had met three years before at a fraternity party when we were both freshmen. My date was her roommate, but it didn't take me long to rearrange the pairings, making myself quickly unpopular with my date and Elaine's in the process. Elaine was the kind of girl who made you stop surveying. She was—and is—a beautiful dark-haired woman with stunning blue eyes and a brightness of personality and mind. She was a majorette, but the band played for varsity games and she had no knowledge whatever of the freshman quarterback. I thought I might help familiarize her. I asked her to church services the next morning, and we were a twosome thereafter. She enjoyed my playing football in college, but she was never overwhelmed by it. So she needled me more than somewhat when we went directly from our wedding night to the practice camp for the annual Blue-Gray game after the 1960 season. She said the romanticists would be horrified.

We became close friends of the Norman Sneads at the Blue-Gray game. Both of us were waiting on word from the NFL draft. Snead's Wake Forest team was 1–9 for the 1960 season, but he was a big guy with a cannon arm and it was generally assumed he would go on the first round. I don't know what was generally assumed about Francis Tarkenton. *I* was assuming he would be picked on the first round. The team I wanted to draft me, of course, was the Washington Redskins. They were having organizational problems, but Washington was the city of my boyhood excitements and where I had built up my own Hall of Fame invincibles—the Sammy Baughs in football and the Bones McKinneys in basketball. When Daddy had to take the family out of the city and move South, I had made this very solemn personal pledge to the nation's capital that I would return. I don't think Douglas MacArthur could have made such a vow more significantly.

Like any other pending draft choice, I had been getting letters and telephone calls. One of the calls came from a man named Billy Bye. I later found him to be a very companionable fellow. He was a former star of the University of Minnesota, a high school coach, and for a couple of years a member of the Viking organization. Bye introduced himself and said he represented the Vikings. I never heard of the Vikings. They sounded like an eight-man team playing in northern Georgia. But Bye said they were a new franchise in pro football.

I still didn't connect the Vikings as an expansion team in the National Football League. I thought they might be in one of the minor leagues, like the Bethlehem Steelers. But Bye said they would be playing in the National Football League in 1961, and would I be interested in playing for them if I were drafted? I said, well, sure, I'd be glad to consider the Vikings. But privately I'd rather not, because Washington was where I wanted to go, not with the Vikings or the new American Football League, but back to the Potomac. I was even prepared to row a football over the river if that's what it took.

The Washington Redskins drafted Norman Snead on the first round. I was deflated. Just smothered. I then waited for the news report or the telephone call that would identify the NFL team that had drafted Tarkenton on the first round.

Nothing showed.

I thought the wires must be down. I had been fully impregnated by the quarterback syndrome of the time. All the first-rate college quarterbacks, the ones with any prestige and promise as professionals, were automatic first-round choices. I was not a first-round choice. I wasn't picked in the second round either. Finally, I received a telephone call from Bert Rose, the Vikings' general manager. He informed me I had the distinction of being drafted on the third round by the Minnesota Vikings, and that I could expect a visit shortly from their traveling agent, Joe Thomas.

I think my end of the conversation was courteous, but brief. Thomas did materialize in a day or so, followed by Ed McKeever, representing Boston—now New England—of the AFL. Both of them were likable and talked straight. Thomas offered a figure he thought was generous but within the Vikings' means, a package of about $15,000. McKeever was prepared to pay me $17,500 in salary and $5,000 in bonus to sign with Boston. I had to tell him the National Football League was my idea of the zenith in athletics, and I would therefore sign with the Vikings.

I think the exact figure the Vikings offered was $12,500 in salary and $3,500 in bonus, which the accountants tell me is about what I now make in one game. But at the time my untoppable goal was to make $20,000 in one season. If I could do that, I told myself, I would have achieved everything in pro football within my capabilities and visions.

I asked Joe Thomas who the Viking coach was. He said the coach hadn't been selected yet. But when he was, it was sure to be a choice that would enrich my career as a pro football player. Joe said the new coach would be a man I would spend many hours of warm society with.

A Team of Orphans and Outcasts

3

As an outpost of human sensitivity, the Minnesota Viking training camp in the early years of Norm Van Brocklin fell somewhere between Devil's Island and Buchenwald.

For this reason history has dealt shabbily with Van Brocklin's football teams of the early 1960s, virtually ignoring them in the attention focused on such fastidious idols as Vince Lombardi's Green Bay Packers. The Vikings won only a fraction of the games Lombardi won, but they compensated with wrath, gusto, and lunacy. They may have been raucous, but at least they were unaccountable. They paid no heed to Lombardi, the curfew laws, and the established codes of football propriety.

In their original trappings the Vikings were not so much a team as a loosely maintained wildlife preserve.

Their first-year roster was the post office wall of the National Football League. The Vikings were the only team in pro football whose press book compilers seriously considered including fingerprints. Some of the heroic renegades and aging desperadoes of football found lodgings with the 1961 Vikings. Many of them were men who had once played honorably but had sinned by getting old, rebellious, or fat. None of these qualities underwent any substantial change when they got to Minnesota. Consider the sadly underreported achievement of Don Joyce, for example, in the Vikings' first summer in Bemidji, Minnesota.

Bemidji is a northern Minnesota community largely isolated from the main currents of communication. Until a few years ago it was uncorrupted by progress. Because it presents a lovely aspect in the firs and the glacial lakes, however, it was deemed by the Vikings' pioneer general manager, Bert Rose, to be an ideal site for a training camp.

One of the Minneapolis sports editors objected. He claimed Bemidji was too far removed from the centers of publicity to permit the Vikings adequate coverage.

"Coverage," Van Brocklin snarled, scanning his roll call of discredited antiques and derelicts. "With these guys we don't need coverage, we need concealment."

Don Joyce was a widely respected antique. In his best days as a defensive end and tackle with the Baltimore Colts, he was one of the most dreaded linemen in pro football, a man of deep antagonisms and bone-shattering strength. The glamour attached to Gino Marchetti, Artie Donovan, and others, but Joyce was the one who made harsh men quiver. Among his versatile tastes as a Louisiana-bred gourmet was his enthusiasm for beer. This was a boon to the brewing industry in Baltimore but a source of dismay for the official weight watcher in the Colt training room, and in the summer of 1961 Joyce found himself exiled to Bemidji. His distress was soothed by his discovery of a 3.2 tavern entitled "The Dutchess." It was an odorous relic constantly in danger of collapse into the hillside willows that served as the coeducational bathroom. Architecturally "The Dutchess" had the appearance of a stockade. Older natives claimed it once was all that stood between Minnesota and reconquest by the Chippewa Indians. The condition of its sills and floorboards suggested the Chippewa may have rejected title and ownership of "The Dutchess" as too high a price to pay for the repossession of Minnesota.

When the Vikings arrived in Bemidji, the chairs of honor as the team's grand lamas at "The Dutchess" were accorded by popular will to Don Joyce and Bill Bishop. Bill Bishop had played for ten years for George Halas in Chicago. Bishop regarded this as unnatural servitude and the most inhuman punishment imaginable. Like

Joyce, he played football with a natural animosity and a disregard for everybody's safety, his own and the enemy quarterback's particularly. Neither Joyce nor Bishop, understandably, reached the competitive heights for Minnesota they had achieved in greener times. But they did experience one much-treasured moment of revival when together they threatened to throw Van Brocklin off the team's flight to Minneapolis after the last game of the season. Van Brocklin responded with the impartiality bred in all great leaders. Before the start of the next season he fired them both.

For Don Joyce in the Vikings' first summer, the start of the season months away seemed so remote that he was imperiled by the loss of his competitive edge. Accordingly, he challenged a few luckless teammates to a beer-drinking contest. It began in the hour immediately following a Viking exhibition game in Fargo-Moorhead and continued at "The Dutchess" the next day. One by one the victims of Joyce's remorseless offensive disappeared into the willows or passed out under the tables. Even witnesses fainted. The bartenders, being men of firmer substance, are the authorities for the final statistics of Don Joyce's devastation of the NFL record book for beer consumption in a twenty-four-hour span. They insist he emptied seventy-five bottles. They also attest that at the finish Joyce was largely sober. Certainly he was controlled enough to rouse his prostrate buddies and to stop at Hernando's Hideway for a civilized nightcap of pizza, which he dispatched just before curfew in the team dormitory.

Not all of the combatants in Bemidji were as loyal to Van Brocklin's curfew as Joyce. To correct the legends, it should be noted that Van Brocklin had every intention of running a slack ship his first year. As an amateur historian, he had read that this policy was pursued with passable success by managers of the first boatload of convict-settlers to reach the American colonies. In addition, he was only a few months retired as an active player. He never found authoritarian coaches very believable, which may shock the Atlanta Falcons of the early 1970s. He pledged to allow maximum liberties, within the framework of two-a-day scrimmage sessions and an 11 P.M. curfew.

The Dutchman outlined this policy in a soulful conversation with Hugh McElhenny, by far the most distinguished of the expansion-draft veterans whom The Dutchman immortalized as "The Thirty-six Stiffs."

"King," Van Brocklin said in his Bemidji office, "you're the leader. Everybody looks up to you. You and I have both enjoyed our good times and our beers with the boys, but we want to have some discipline along with the fun here. I want you to be the man who encourages that by example."

The King stood significantly and nodded, recognizing the simple truth The Dutchman had spoken. They clasped hands, respectful old rivals now united in common cause.

The next morning one of Van Brocklin's adjutants handed him the dormitory report. "Our first curfew violation," the aide sighed. "After a perfect record of two days we have a violation."

The Dutchman scowled. "Who," he demanded, "is the god-damned crook?"

"He gave his name," the aide reported, "as Hugh McElhenny."

Coincidentally the Vikings had an intrasquad scrimmage booked that morning. Feeling unsettled by effects of the local grog, McElhenny tried to maintain a low profile during the calisthenics, camouflaging himself in some tall grass at the forty-yard line. He was not immediately recognized, his face having attained a rich chartreuse cast. Van Brocklin spotted him nonetheless. "McElhenny," he barked to his lieutenants, "carries the ball on every play."

This was not quite correct. McElhenny merely carried the ball on twelve straight plays, the total number attempted before he collapsed on the fifteen-yard line from the effects of a hard tackle and a hangover.

The Dutchman smoldered over such acts of ingratitude. He considered them an abuse of his lofty attempts at humanitarianism.

That night the staff turnkey reported another one of the warriors missing past the dormitory deadline. Van Brocklin waited at the doorway, sitting in granite silence for an hour to welcome the delinquent, who was a veteran receiver of some national repute.

Two hours after curfew Van Brocklin rose, kicked the small

mountain of cigarette butts at his feet, and churned into the night in search of the absentee. The Dutchman found him in a nearby parking lot, entwined with a young woman in the back seat of a car. Coupled, the polite expression goes. Under these conditions, the Dutchman recognized no such standards of politeness. Opening the back door, he reached into the car and with one hand yanked the receiver from the arms and other accouterments of his adored, declaring with more bitterness than charity: "You've got better moves here than what we pay you for."

The reaction of the lady has never been recorded.

Friends later chided The Dutchman for his abruptness and lack of romanticism. "You could at least," one suggested, "let them have a good-night kiss."

A similar charge of unsentimentalism was lodged against The Dutchman a week later when two of the squad redoubtables, Bill Bishop and Charley Sumner, along with a 250-pound rookie fullback, Raymond Hayes, were busted by Van Brocklin's truant officer for coming in late from a Saturday night social at "The Dutchess."

At 8 A.M. Sunday morning, Van Brocklin barged into the sleeping room occupied by Jimmy Eason, the equipment manager. Eason had served valiantly in the Italian campaign of World War II. But he never experienced raw terror until Van Brocklin kicked out the metal pipes of his cot as an announcement that day had dawned in Bemidji by decree of The Dutchman. It was a revolting discovery since this was a Sunday morning and Eason himself had barely made it to the dormitory ahead of the roosters.

From the debris of his cot, Eason regarded Van Brocklin with a mixture of clinical interest and foreboding. The Dutchman's eyes were streaked, his cheeks were puffed, and he was chewing gum savagely. In the short time he had known Van Brocklin, Eason understood the symptoms well enough to realize that somebody was going to be lynched.

"Get down to the locker room," Van Brocklin said. "There'll be three guys there. All of them get full pads. Have them on the field by nine."

The three were Bishop, Sumner, and Hayes, and together they

trudged the quarter mile from the dressing room to the practice field. They walked with the fatalistic slouch of Batista loyalists approaching Castro's firing squad.

Van Brocklin waited for them on the goal line, simmering in the August sun that sent heat waves rising languorously off the grass. He had decided to take no prisoners. It would have to be unconditional surrender.

"What you're going to do," he said, "is roll end over end down the field to the other goal line."

They so rolled.

Their destination achieved, they lay panting in the end zone.

"Roll back to the other goal line," The Dutchman said.

They complied, on a much more erratic course, but they completed the mission.

For a half hour they rolled from one end of the field to the other, taking time between laps only for enough air to sustain them for a hundred more yards.

They then leapfrogged a hundred yards at a time. And after fifteen minutes of that they somersaulted a hundred yards at a time.

The temperature was nearing ninety degrees. After an hour of these groaning gymnastics, Bishop, Sumner, and Hayes made their way on hands and knees toward the only available sanctuary, the shadows of the goalposts.

The sight touched Van Brocklin, evoking merciful impulses that he forced himself to suppress.

"On your feet," he said.

They rose in fragments, their eyes lacquered. By now, awed teammates were staring out on the grim tableau from dormitory windows and other vantage points behind trees. Two of them, attempting a closeup, launched a rowboat on Lake Bemidji just off the practice field. They nearly drowned when Van Brocklin whirled at the sound of a rusty oarlock. The boat capsized, as though terrified itself.

Back in the end zone, the rollers finally got sick. They were also very contrite.

"Coach," one of them said, "you can take two grand in pay outa my pocket, but don't make me roll down that field one more time."

"Roll down that field," Van Brocklin said, "one more time."

At 11 A.M. he ended the morning's calisthenics and departed the field, leaving the prostrate players to meditate upon their wrongdoings. They lay there for two hours. They may have been meditating, but some of their buddies would have sworn they weren't meditating at all; they were unconscious.

Sumner, Bishop, and Hayes were the last reported curfew violators in camp.

Into this jungle of crime and punishment and biblical justice walked the bouncy young innocent from the University of Georgia.

Van Brocklin called him Peach or P.K., for Preacher's Kid. From the very first days Tarkenton was The Dutchman's Exhibit A of the eager youngbloods—although in Van Brocklin's earliest judgment not necessarily a gifted one—who stood ready to topple the complacent or jaded veteran.

Like the patriarch of a caveman colony, The Dutchman developed predictable patterns in his choice of field leaders. He would first make a public show of esteem for some old soldier, a Hugh McElhenny or a George Shaw, the quarterback. It was usually an esteem that was genuine. But if and when the old soldier faltered or failed, The Dutchman could not confine himself to replacing him. He had to cashier him. As part of the process he would enlist one of the youngbloods, a Tarkenton or a Tommy Mason. Van Brocklin would befriend him, counsel him, tease him with practice field diminutives, and generally let the world and the disgraced old soldier know about the line of succession. But when Van Brocklin tired of Tarkenton, he bestowed the same affections on Ron VanderKelen and Bob Berry. For The Dutchman it was part of the renewal process. For Tarkenton in 1961 it was the introduction to his craft, the beginning of the emotional roller coaster that marked his first years in professional football and the discovery that ignominy and bliss were interchangeable qualities of life on The Dutchman's football teams.

The conventions of his trade required Tarkenton to serve a respectable apprenticeship as a second- or third-string quarterback. In this role he would sponge up knowledge, learning from the triumphs and pratfalls of his elders. Tarkenton acknowledged the reasonableness of the role, but he never intended to accept it. In a couple of weeks he had appraised his competition. George Shaw was an experienced quarterback, technically able as a player, a man of intelligence and decency. But injuries and blighted hopes had beaten him down. He had lost the edge of assertiveness Tarkenton believed all successful quarterbacks should have.

Later, Tarkenton would define that quality as arrogance. The exact terminology varied according to whatever was in vogue at the time. The clichés of football are trendy. For a while everybody talked about pride. When Lombardi was winning, it became love. Well, arrogance could wait. Whatever was needed to cope with Van Brocklin and the burdens of quarterbacking a team of derelicts and untrained young veterans, George Shaw lacked it in 1961. By early season, Tarkenton projected, he would be starting for the Minnesota Vikings. Van Brocklin doubted this, but he was also aware that Tarkenton as a rookie quarterback presented an unusual resource. As a learner he was facile and decisive. He had self-confidence and technical adroitness well beyond that of the average kid quarterback. Personally he was sociable and well adjusted, a mixer and a hustler.

"If you could throw," Van Brocklin would tell Tarkenton, needling, "you'd be a real menace."

Despite the hairiness of his new football society, Tarkenton never underwent any jolting loss of innocence. He had already encountered the tough language and boozing as a collegian. Why should it bother him, a preacher's kid? He didn't happen to drink or smoke or wench around. That some of his teammates did gave him no offense nor, he granted, did it instantly consign them to hellfire. The gruff veterans with their codes of loyalties and willingness to extend their friendship to a twenty-one-year-old novice aroused his admiration and, in one case, his wonderment.

"I'll never forget the first time I saw Hugh McElhenny," he told friends later. "They called him The King. The King of the Halfbacks. The rookies had been in camp for about a week, and the veterans were due in a few days. McElhenny drove in a day early. He showed up in the afternoon unannounced, standing in the shade under one of the pine trees, watching our workout. What a sight. He came in driving a big black Cadillac towing a trailer painted black. He was dressed in black jeans with some kind of matching T-shirt and tennis shoes that matched his outfit. He had this weathered complexion with little pockmarks and a few small scars in his face that gave it extra character. His hair was jet black, and he just stood there looking like the incarnation of the pro football star: glamour, strength, aura, whatever you wanted. All my life I had read about Hugh McElhenny. Van Brocklin saw him and went over to where he was standing. They shook hands and gabbed for a little while, and then The Dutchman brought him over to us and introduced him. 'I want you to meet The King of the Halfbacks,' he said. 'This is Hugh McElhenny. He's going to be one of your teammates.' McElhenny waved to us like we were all going to be in the Hall of Fame inside of a couple of months. What a moment."

Of all the football exiles forced into the doubtful shelter of Minnesota in 1961, Hugh McElhenny least deserved such destiny. In his nine years with the San Francisco 49ers he had been one of the unrivaled prodigies of professional football. His abrasions with Coach Red Hickey in San Francisco made McElhenny deportable. But he retained in his tenth year the panache and grace that made him an object of deference wherever professional players gathered. The fans may lionize football players, but only a few of them achieve the open-mouthed homage of their peers. Jimmy Brown was one of them, Dick Butkus another. And McElhenny. He was among the last of a species, the open-field runners who lived on guile, their instincts, on nuances of the matador's art. These they flung at the dreadnoughts of football, huge and violent men whose pursuit of them often took on an extra dimension of malice because it hurts to look foolish in view of sixty thousand people. But if the McElhennys imposed this embarrassment on them, it was totally impersonal.

A typical McElhenny run belonged more in the concert hall than it did on a battlefield. Which is why his performances in an enemy stadium rarely met the hostilities and silences that partisanship would otherwise dictate. His controlled gymnastics, his escapes, the spectacle of one man against the herd, dependent on his intuition and his reflexes—all of these appealed to a higher ethic in the football fan. The response they evoked was not the thunder of a glandular crowd. It was rolling applause and a head-shaking of true believers seeing their faith vindicated. And it was not until one of his great runs was finished that he would yield himself to a piece of excusable showmanship, throwing back his head and lifting his knees as he trotted into the end zone. A finale? Certainly. From the stands you could almost hear "Bravo!"

Shortly before he played his final game of the Vikings' first season, the Chicago football writers awarded him a plaque. "Wouldn't football be a beautiful game," it read, "if everybody played it like Hugh McElhenny?"

And fifteen minutes later McElhenny fielded an Eddie Brown punt, slickered the first wave with a feint to the sidelines, coaxed some daylight, and then ran eighty-one yards into the Bears' end zone.

Tarkenton marveled at him as the apotheosis of the great professional football player. McElhenny was a good trouper and a leader of the team, but he played without pretense. He didn't project any special kind of heroism. When he was hurt, he would rather sit it out. He didn't play well when injured, which his admirers might say was simply pure thoroughbred and which a detractor might say was simply Hugh McElhenny. He had no ego problem with that, or with his philosophy as a runner. He did not perceive every play as an examination of his manhood. Neither his money nor his place in history depended on his hurling himself into a homicidal defensive tackle. It offended both his sensibilities as a creative runner and his shins and ribs. Other men could run recklessly. McElhenny ran with a sense of time and place. He had all the crafts—a slack leg for the linebacker, a disappearing shoulder for the defensive end. He would pivot, change speeds, and run laterally when necessary, but he never lost sight of the goal line or the great open-field runner's first principle: When everything else fails, gut out a couple of yards. He did that well, too.

McElhenny was the showpiece of the first football team of Francis Tarkenton's pro career. But Tarkenton himself stirred some wonderment. His first few exhibitions told him he belonged with the pros. His arm was adequate to good. He could take their shots physically. Van Brocklin's offense was sophisticated. But attacking it with constant curiosity, Tarkenton discovered with satisfaction after a couple of weeks that he was compatible with it. He struck his teammates as being unusually secure, a forthright kid who was agreeably chesty, preparing himself for a professional career the right way. He respected the game's demands and was wise enough to see his imperfections. He had a sense of mission acute enough to want success in pro football more than anything in life at that point, yet he did not allow himself to be consumed by the goal. It did not alter his personality nor change his child's excitement in football as a game in the sun in the park.

The Chicago Bears tried to change both. After Tarkenton played acceptably in his first few exhibitions, Van Brocklin gave him half of the ball game against the Bears in Cedar Rapids, Iowa. The Bears at the time played in the full, rich tradition of Chicago Bear defenses. They were belligerent, obnoxious in behavior, and erratic in style. They were also, at the time, very good. The three linebackers, Bill George, Joe Fortunato, and Larry Morris, were the toughest such combination in football. In Cedar Rapids the Bears assaulted the bumbling expansion team with a succession of blitzes and just plain battery. Tarkenton could handle the roughhousing, but he did not have the wisdom to find and exploit the weaknesses. Each play drained a little more confidence and control from his shrinking reserves. The Bears were also pounding dents in his body. And so each play became a mortification. Van Brocklin tried to help him, suggesting plays, shouting obscenities at his old antagonists on the Bears. It ended 30–7 in a cloudburst, and Tarkenton could not remember aching more or suffering more internally after a football game.

"It'll get better," The Dutchman said helpfully. And then, painting on the old battle face, he added: "It has to."

Nobody brooded long on the Vikings of that era. Depression was always overtaken by some new hysteria or burlesque. An hour after the Bears game Tarkenton was sitting in the front seat of the team bus. Like the others he was awaiting the arrival of one of the team owners, car dealer Bill Boyer. Boyer was a congenial sort. But he was unaware at that early date of the acerbic nature of a football player forced to wait in discomfort and defeat for a tardy football owner.

Boyer stepped into the bus.

"Hooray for Bill," a guttural baritone began from the rear of the bus.

"Hooray at last," responded a mounting chorus.

"Hooray for Bill, he's a horse's ass."

Boyer was not sure whether to bow, depart, or fire the chorale. He compromised by sitting down.

"I can't," Tarkenton whispered to Tommy Mason, "believe it."

A similar attitude was expressed by the Bears themselves two weeks later when essentially the same Viking football team, with the same kid quarterback playing the last 3½ quarters, won the first regular-season football team it ever played by a score of 37–13. What made the Bears especially despondent about the whole thing was the identity of the Vikings' opponents: the Chicago Bears.

The enormity of that Sunday in Metropolitan Stadium has never fully penetrated the national consciousness. It was comparable to the Soviet Army's being overwhelmed by the Estonian beach patrol. Relatives of George Halas, hearing the news in Chicago, telephoned a radio station to upbraid it for inflicting another Orson Welles hoax on the listening public. It astounded the entire football establishment except for the minority voice of Norm Van Brocklin, who honestly expected his scruffy collage of malcontents and apprentices to contend for the championship and possibly go undefeated.

As part of this conviction Van Brocklin had invited Tarkenton and his wife to dine with the Van Brocklins at their lakeside home. It was just after a 21–17 loss to the Rams in the Vikings' final exhibition. But in the Dutchman's judgment Tarkenton had clearly beaten George Shaw for the regular quarterbacking job, and he so confided to Tarkenton in the mellowness of the hour. He conducted a tour of his trophy room, disclosing all the emoluments that lay ahead for a quarterback who threw accurately, played bravely, and listened to the coach.

Despite substantial evidence to the contrary, The Dutchman was not a full-time, hard-barked character. He did have sensitivities. In midweek, he began to squirm about his decision to start Tarkenton. Shaw, after all, was the veteran. He had not played well in the exhibitions, but that was hardly unique. Some courtesies were due. Also, starting Tarkenton against Bill George, the Bears' middle line-backer, compared in fairness with matching a romper room valedictorian against a devious professor. On a drive to the Vikings' practice site at Midway Stadium, Van Brocklin confided his dilemma to a reporter (me).

"The kid deserves it," he said, "but I'm trying to build some squad loyalty, and there's such a thing as veterans' rights. I thought the kid played a helluva game against the Rams. He's got the head for this game. He's going to make it. He's going to be my quarterback eventually. Why not now?"

The Dutchman's monologue subsided, and the automobile's drone offered suitable sound effects for a mind in ferment.

"So how do you think I should go?" The Dutchman asked, casting a hook into unpromising waters.

"I don't think it matters," I said.

The Dutchman seemed saddened. "Doesn't matter? This is a football game. We're playing the Bears!"

"What I meant," I said, "is I don't think it matters what a neutral party thinks about it. I think you have made up your mind."

"If you would be so good," The Dutchman said with elaborate etiquette, "would you kindly tell me who I have decided to start at quarterback?"

"Yes. You are going to be chivalrous, and you are going to start George Shaw."

"That's right," The Dutchman said. "I'm going to be a friend to man and start George Shaw at quarterback. The thing that worries me is, am I doing him a favor?"

Posterity may never be clear on that point. Shaw did start and was confronted with early opportunities. The game was five minutes old when the Bears gave evidence of being geared to play their worst game in history. The symptoms of this were two fumbles, an intercepted pass, and a snap from center that sailed ten yards over the punter's head and nearly reached the scoreboard. Shaw showed no disposition to exploit this bounty. After a couple of series, Van Brocklin substituted Tarkenton. Within five minutes he had thrown his first touchdown pass, a fourteen-yarder to Bob Schnelker. He threw two more in the third quarter, to McElhenny and Jerry Reichow, and a fourth later to Dr. Dave Middleton. Tarkenton scored a fifth touchdown himself. In his first regular-season game as a professional, playing with and against some of the glowering old knights who populated his bubble-gum games, Francis Tarkenton threw 17 completions in 23 attempts, 4 touchdown passes, and accumulated 250 yards through the air.

Long before the game ended, George Halas made a vow to his private saints. He would not speak to the miserable, floundering incompetents who had brought disgrace on his organization's coat of arms. He would reveal his contempt with suffocating silence. And when the game was over, Halas held his resolve. Not one word of reproach. He would let the Bears soak and muck around in their own humiliation while he, George Halas, the founder of an empire, the Charlemagne of pro football, would carry off this hour of shame wordless as stone, bitter but dignified.

When the Bears boarded the team bus to return to the airport, Halas waited until all of the wretches had time to accept the full horror of their deeds. The time finally arrived when he as coach must make some terse, meaningful summation of the day's events. He should briefly but accurately convey what was in his mind and heart, without spilling into empty oratory.

Halas stood, turned, and rendered his evaluation:

"You *pussies!*" the coach said.

Whereupon he sat down. It was the shortest postgame speech that ever went unrecorded.

Van Brocklin was the kind of competitor who considered every yard gained by the enemy a personal assault on his honor and a renunciation of duty by his own team. The victory over the Bears convinced him the Vikings could probably win fourteen in a row with luck and a decent break from the officials.

Their march to the championship, unfortunately, was interrupted by seven straight defeats, beginning with a 21–7 loss to Dallas.

The following week the young quarterback who threw four touchdown passes in his first game as a professional made nine appearances against the Baltimore Colts—each time to hold the ball for a field goal or extra point. It was all very bewildering for Francis Tarkenton, because there just wasn't enough room in his old bubblegum games for immortality and obscurity to appear on the same card.

George Shaw eventually fell into permanent disfavor, however, and Tarkenton was launched on an eighteen-touchdown season as rookie passer. But his team, while often inflamed by the Dutchman's exhortations, was a pauper miscast among football's lusty aristocrats. As a result, Tarkenton frequently found himself without friends at the most embarrassing times, such as third and fifteen when he was exploring twenty yards behind the line of scrimmage. He had not entered pro football as a self-ordained scrambler. But it was not exactly an impulsive decision. As a collegian he had watched telecasts of the pro games and observed the quarterbacks, when surrounded, ritualistically bow their heads to their executioners and disappear beneath a thousand pounds of linemen. "I'd sit there," Tarkenton said, "and I'd say, 'God, do something. Don't just accept defeat.' They would just stand there in the pocket. If it held up, they threw. If it broke down, they got blasted for seven yards, or ten. If they weren't rushed, their teams won. If they were, they lost.

"I just didn't feel I wanted to play it that way," Tarkenton said. "I wasn't setting myself up as a trailblazer. You do what you can to win. In my early years with the Vikings the only way I saw open to keep a drive alive, or to salvage a play where the blocking broke down, was to turn it into a helter-skelter situation where instincts and adlibbing gave you a chance. If you couldn't get time with blocking, you tried to do it running. Despite a lot of things that were said about our early teams, I never really thought I played behind bad offensive lines. They were the best we had, and I never stewed about being hurt by poor blocking. Lord knows the linemen might have said the same about my scrambling. But there were some plays and some games where I just thought I had to do it myself. I would get into situations where I would take gambles and risks to win. If I came up with the Green Bay Packers, I would have been a different quarterback. But I started with an expansion team, and I used what was available to me—my quickness, reaction time, sandlot intuition, I don't really care what you call it. Sometimes it worked, sometimes not. The Dutchman never really discouraged me. I'm sure he knew what I was trying to do, and why. We had some colossal boomerangs, of course. I set a still-standing record by fumbling into a forty-five-yard loss against the Rams. I once actually heard Deacon Jones of the Rams groan as I was looping behind the line, 'Jesus Christ, here he comes again.' "

Admirers of the modern-day Tarkenton may not grasp the magnitude of some of the odysseys of his youth. He was the Magellan of pro football. Visiting scouts assigned to chart the Viking offense would be on their third box of tranquilizers by the second quarter. There was no known system for diagramming a Tarkenton scramble. The defensive ends would pinch on him, and Tarkenton would pivot and flee, bound for one sideline or other but occasionally his own end zone. By the time he had retreated thirty yards, his location had been fixed by most of the defensive team but not always by Van Brocklin. Crossfield the herd would come, pounding and snorting while Tarkenton, large-eyed but usually under control, would calculate the exact moment when he had to change course to avert decapitation.

On the Viking sideline Van Brocklin would curse quietly. "Jesus," he would say, "all we needed was five yards. And he decides to be creative."

Even in his most stressful moments, though, Tarkenton was looking for a receiver. Unlike some of his imitators, he ran wildly in order to pass.

"But he *did* run wildly, didn't he?" Gino Marchetti used to ask, seeking some confirmation to explain the violent trembling in his calves and the rebellion from his lungs after an encounter with Tarkenton. It was Marchetti, later an admirer of Tarkenton's, who issued a public ultimatum. Scrambling quarterbacks, he said, were an annoyance to the linemen's fraternity. They should either reform or lose their heads.

Marchetti never personally molested Tarkenton, aside from tackling him a few hundred times, but Gino's teammate, linebacker Bill Pellington, did.

In Tarkenton's judgment, Pellington was the dirtiest football player he ever played against. His specialties were late hits, out-of-bounds tackles, judo chops, and other discourtesies too numerous to mention. Pellington, his teammates maintained, had a mood so foul he would order his training room milk in a dirty glass. Removed from this environment, it should be noted, he was the most affable of men.

Education and knobs on the head were delivered to the rookie quarterback by odd tutors. The Lions had a defensive lineman named Bill Glass, an active and devoted member of the Fellowship of Christian Athletes and a man Tarkenton made a point of visiting on the Saturday before the Vikings played their first game in Detroit.

"I was completely impressed," Tarkenton said. "Here was a widely respected football player, a key man on a team with a lot of gruff characters, telling of the spiritual challenge before us and how it was possible to be a fully aggressive athlete and a soldier in the Army of Christ at the same time.

"We played the Lions a surprisingly close game the next day. I scrambled one time near midfield and got walloped on the head after I ran ten yards out of bounds. Ten yards! I turned around to confront this torpedo. It was Bill Glass. Nobody else. He clapped me on the shoulder and said, 'Praise the Lord.' "

From the very beginning, the Vikings fielded a big-league offense. Van Brocklin's head, McElhenny's finesse, Tarkenton's youthful defiance, and the seasoned receivers, Jerry Reichow and Dave Middleton, assured that. The Vikings' defense was pugnacious but fundamentally awful. This quality disclosed itself most painfully when the Green Bay Packers appeared at Metropolitan Stadium that year, destined for the first of Vince Lombardi's championships. The Vikings' roster of defensive backs was constantly changing, the names and faces seldom known to the fans and not always to the coaches.

At one stage the defense was being mangled so badly that Van Brocklin considered releasing the names only to the next of kin.

One of the defensive backs was Rick Mostardi, a youngster from Kent State who was fast but fragile, bright but eminently beatable. In 1961, playing against the Packers, he established a rarely threatened NFL record by being beaten by forty yards on a routine pass to Boyd Dowler.

"It was one of those play-action passes," Mostardi told his interrogators afterward. "Starr sends a back into the line pretending to hand off. Unless the defensive back is careful, this may make him forget all about covering Dowler and go for the fake.

"I'm covering Dowler. Starr sends Taylor into the line. I'm damned if I don't take the fake and come up on Taylor. Then Starr sends Hornung into the line, and I'm damned if I don't get faked by Hornung, too. I'm trying to sort them out, but neither one has got the ball.

"By deductive reasoning I figured there is only one place the ball can be at that exact moment. Right. It is floating high overhead. Dowler was standing there so long by himself he got impatient and started tapping his foot waiting for the ball to come down."

Despite the expansion team's inevitable disorderliness, the Vikings played their first season—and virtually every season under Van Brocklin—with zeal and a certain hunted desperation. They also often played with intent to do bodily harm, although The Dutchman never so instructed them apart from stenciling Van Brocklin's law on the mind and soul of all his employees: "Go get yourself a jock."

They did it often enough in their first season to win three games. And they didn't do it all on Van Brocklin's blast-their-eyes leadership or on the élan of Tarkenton and the Viking offense.

"There was a lot of snickering in those years about the quality of the Viking castoffs," Tarkenton remembers. "But I'll always respect those guys. They had no reason to be loyal to the Minnesota Vikings as such, and no responsibility, I don't suppose, to build any kind of togetherness. But they did. Guys like Hugh McElhenny, Bill Bishop, Don Joyce, Dave Middleton, Jerry Reichow, and old Mel Triplett, the fullback, who may have been the strongest blocking back I ever played with. They integrated the kids with the vets. They organized parties, established traditions that are still with the team. They have played only a year or two, and they knew it wouldn't be much more. But this was their breeding as football players, and the young ones benefited.

"We had a puffy-cheeked guy named Ed Culpepper playing defensive tackle. He was squat and wide, and his greatest achievement was draining a whole big brandy snifter full of goober peanuts with one gulp in a bar one day. Just chugged the whole thing. They called him The Penguin. He didn't make much money but he played his guts out, and he'll always have my respect."

In tone with the temperament of their coach and the eccentric collection in the huddle, the Vikings rarely won or lost uneventfully. In the third game of the season, the retread ragamuffins verged on an authentic miracle, leading the Baltimore Colts of John Unitas, Lenny Moore, Gino Marchetti, and Jim Parker by two points with one play to go. The Vikings were beaten with zero time remaining on the scoreboard when Steve Myhra kicked a fifty-two-yard field goal after being benched earlier in the game because he could not kick the ball more than forty yards on kickoffs.

And in the final game in Chicago, the team produced another statistical breakthrough: Everybody showed up for the opening kickoff but the head coach.

Dispatched on a negotiating mission the day before the game in the wake of the league player draft, Van Brocklin was marooned overnight in Pennsylvania by storms. For hours the next morning he stood beside his hotel room window demanding a change in the weather. He was the jockstrap version of King Lear. It finally subsided in late morning, but The Dutchman's charter fought a losing battle with the prevailing westerlies and did not touch ground in Chicago before the Vikings had built a 21–7 lead.

Behind wailing police sirens, Van Brocklin set an impassioned course for Wrigley Field. He arrived in time to see his warriors blow their two-touchdown lead. The Dutchman's presence just failed to ignite the faltering Vikings. They lost, 52–35, despite Tarkenton's four touchdown passes.

A baggage handler's strike delayed the homeward cortege by four hours, time that Van Brocklin and most of the athletes found ideally suited for a traditional season-ending auld lang syne. From the airport terminal the festival moved unevenly to the airliner. Champagne was served.

"What are the owners celebrating?" Culpepper asked. "The fact," Bishop explained, "that we got out of the season without creating a riot."

This oversight was almost rectified. Angered by the presence on the plane of a team hanger-on, Van Brocklin accused Eason of cadging a free seat for a crony. It was a bum rap. Eason objected. Whereupon The Dutchman launched Eason's food tray into the aisle. Van Brocklin now found himself surrounded—by Bishop (who was holding a magnum of champagne) and by Joyce (who never touched the stuff but could surround you just by being in the vicinity).

Bishop thrust his impressive jaw into Van Brocklin's and accused The Dutchman of mishandling him during the season. It was impossible, The Dutchman argued, to mishandle Bishop.

From there the conversation lost some of its character but compensated with expanding volume and novel threats, such as Bishop's sudden decision to throw Van Brocklin out of the cabin into the Wisconsin snowdrifts thirty-one thousand feet below. Bishop was interrupted by a passing champagne split and forgot the project.

It was an idle thought, Bill explained later, a boyish prank never intended to be executed.

A bigmouth mutiny, Van Brocklin said.

Bishop was on the payroll of a Chicago truck company the following autumn.

The bubble-gum cards, Tarkenton told Tommy Mason, never said anything about champagne flights from Chicago.

The Dutchman

4

The Tarkenton–Van Brocklin relationship in Minnesota is some-times likened to the one between Aaron Burr and Alexander Hamilton. Like most such comparisons, it has a fine cut of credibility. It also has flaws.

Van Brocklin and Tarkenton never actually shot at each other.

They coexisted in reasonable harmony, in truth, for most of their six years together. The fact that they have not spoken to each other in the ten years since suggests a certain cool-off in their mutual affections. Both have exerted a fair degree of ingenuity in avoiding each other during that period, maneuvers required by their joint citizenship in Atlanta since 1968.

Their actual collisions were rare and, until both exited from opposite ends of the stage almost simultaneously in Minnesota—like some Grecian playactors—they never experienced any continuing alienation. Just a few weeks from their parting they spent hours conspiring a new era in Minnesota Viking football in which both would last forever, or at least until their contracts were up.

From the beginning Van Brocklin saw Tarkenton as bright and adaptable, a young man whose cheeky spirit did not conflict with his coachability. There was an unshowy discipline about Tarkenton that governed his conduct and shaped his goals, and Van Brocklin decided Tarkenton quickly could and probably would be a winner. He was a rookie whose broad optimism and purposes did not leave much room for the average rookie's doubting depressions. Van Brocklin treated Tarkenton with more courtesy than he gave the other first-year players. He did so partly because a quarterback required such treatment, in the judgment of the quarterback-coach, and partly because Tarkenton's weekly performance did not warrant much haranguing. In later years Van Brocklin regarded Tarkenton as a willful self-seeker in his actions as a quarterback and in his general deportment, and ultimately he appeared to believe his offensive captain was in league with other veterans like Bill Brown, Grady Alderman, and Mick Tingelhoff to bring him down.

Van Brocklin's intensities and early chumminess quickly made an ally and disciple of Tarkenton. By the end of the first year, however, Van Brocklin's mercurial shifts in mood puzzled the young quarterback. The Dutchman's abuse of his teammates offended him. Their relationships bobbed unevenly for a time and then flew off into mutual suspicions and sporadic eruptions. Tarkenton became convinced that Van Brocklin was unable to share or yield the public's attention for very long. The team, in other words, had to be the Van Brocklin Vikings, or later the Van Brocklin Falcons. If a rival emerged, he had to be downgraded or checkmated. This, in any case, was the quarterback's reading of Van Brocklin's erratic handling of his personnel and his postures with the press.

Despite this subsurface rivalry and distrust between the two, Van Brocklin and Tarkenton avoided—until 1966—any violent rupture that would have crippled the team. Their day-to-day associations were usually calm and sometimes even warm and mirthful. That was especially true in 1964, when the Vikings rampaged through the second half of the season, a team of noisy musketeers, very much the image of their earthy, unquenchable coach.

At the time Van Brocklin was perfectly capable of saying of his quarterback after a victory over the 49ers: "Naturally I'm proud of him. I'm his coach. He's a 100 per cent guy, on and off the field." But at a team meeting a few days later, The Dutchman might be perfectly capable of saying, "Tarkenton, you're not strong enough to throw a pass like that, but you sure are dumb enough."

Nobody ever expected The Dutchman to be intimidated by such

coaching requirements as consistency or a willingness to listen to reason. Whenever pro football people have gathered the past two decades, there is an almost irresistible impulse to stretch Van Brocklin on an imaginary couch and psychoanalyze him. In the locker room's ballads, The Dutchman occupies distinct ground.

As a man capable of roiling his ballplayers' juices, Van Brocklin stands almost unique. The hatreds he generated were real, even though they were punctuated now and then by some shaggy guffaw over a Van Brocklin locker room sarcasm. But while his ballplayers hated or feared him much of the time, they followed him just as intensely. He was hardly a reconstituted Dracula. He was, and is, a man of worth and intelligence. With some he is companionable and generous. For the better part of five seasons he gave the Minnesota Vikings the kind of coaching performance that in terms of games won and lost, starting with nothing more than thirty-six empty pairs of shoes, might not have been equaled by any other coach in football.

But as a coach and a man he was capable of soaring intolerances and tyrannical indictments. Nobody raged like The Dutchman raged. He did it beautifully and with great originality. He could imagine himself surrounded by villains, blackguards, and cutpurses. Sometimes they were officials, sometimes rival coaches. Some were muddleheaded, exhibitionist owners. Others were pointy-headed administrators (George Wallace's term) or goddamned pencil-pushers (Van Brocklin's). Most of them were his own ballplayers. Because of the successes he had achieved as a player, partly with his thundering willfulness, The Dutchman could not bring himself to accept mere mediocrity or incompetence as an excuse for losing. There had to be other reasons. Thus he would accuse his struggling nonentities at Minnesota of sloth and stupidity. He also accused them of ingratitude and selfishness. Sometimes he added cowardice. Now and then, incredibly, he accused them of complacency. He would not make himself believe that his team simply was not good enough, or did not have enough quality football players. And this, like so many of his properties, was both strength and weakness. His refusal to admit the obvious led him into rhetorical follies and finally cost him his credibility. But for a time the turmoil, the now-or-never atmosphere his inner intensities created, drove the football team to levels that might have been beyond it physically.

As a ballplayer he could afford these tempests, because his head was always good in the huddle and his right arm was strong. But as a coach the very qualities that caused his polyglot club to follow him and adopt his competitive boisterousness eventually turned the players against him. There is a high perishability factor in emotionalism as a leadership tool. Fear and embarrassment as motivating forces for football players have a short life. Defused by excess, the rages lie in ashes, to become the charcoal for clubhouse caricature. Instead of being turned on, thrust to competitive heights by fear and charisma, the ballplayer will begin to laugh, or sneer, or adopt whatever attitude he finds suitable to taunt an old disarmed dragon.

And so in the end a man of Van Brocklin's furies will almost inevitably lose control of his players, as Van Brocklin did in Minnesota after he quit in midseason in 1965, and as he did in Atlanta after accusing his players of telling their troubles to the whores of Peachtree Street (who presumably were more attentive and certainly a lot more gentle than The Dutchman).

His wrath during a losing football game was cosmic in its breadth and power. The Vikings in the early 1960s had a field goal kicker named Mike Mercer, a good-natured, nervous football gypsy who had enrolled at more colleges than a CIA plant. He was a kicker of power and well-spaced outbursts of accuracy. But he was also a fundamentally gentle young man who would shrivel before Van Brocklin's blasts. Mercer went to resourceful lengths to avoid them. After flubbing a field goal, he adopted the basic survival tactic of evasion. Instead of jogging directly back to the Viking bench, a course that would put him in the path of Van Brocklin's sixteen-inch guns, Mercer would take the longest way around available. It took Van Brocklin only a couple of games to tumble to this manuever.

In a game against the Lions in 1961, Mike blew a field goal head-on from the twenty-two-yard line. The posts then were located on the goal line, which made missing a field goal at that range an almost impossible feat. Mike accomplished it with remarkable ease because the ball took on the aerodynamics of a corkscrew in flight.

It fell with an unlovely splat five yards in front of the goalposts.

The culprit may have been the oncharging Roger Brown, or Alex Karras, muttering unkind vulgarities in the ear of the Viking center. But Van Brocklin, a man impatient with complicated situations, immediately erased all options but one. Mercer had loused it up, and Van Brocklin seriously considered beheading him in reprisal. Nobler impulses discouraged this, and Van Brocklin decided to wait until Mike reached the Viking bench. Mercer, on the other hand, clearly did not *want* to reach the Viking bench. He undertook one of his marathon exits, bearing toward a point somewhere between the team doctor and the security cops, which would give him a good thirty yards' clearance. But as he reached the apogee of this long orbit, Van Brocklin froze him with the raw finality of his judgment:

"Mercer," he screamed, "you couldn't kick a whore off a piss-pot."

It was the kind of assessment of a man's work not calculated to spur his confidence. Mercer was gone a few weeks later, carrying only his kicking tee and his tender memories.

Yet The Dutchman truly aroused his early Viking teams, transmitting his damn-the-torpedoes code and personality to them. And because they were underdogs, and rather mongrelized at that, the Vikings very early acquired the fraternity of the besieged. It was an attitude Van Brocklin both instigated and nourished with his tirades against officials and conspiring rival coaches, who he was convinced plotted constantly to starve him in the trade markets. His team responded with a camaraderie that combined the revenge motif with the fire of impetuous novices, of whom Tarkenton was the leader and orchestrator. But there were games in which the Viking offense seemed to have been conceived on a doodle pad rather than on the blackboard. The unrehearsed, open-field lateral became an integral part of the attack. Nobody was immune as the target of a lateral. Even 270-pound tackles learned swivel-head tactics, especially when Tarkenton was in the vicinity. Van Brocklin was sometimes as baffled by all of this as the pursuing linemen. No one was as baffled as the official who tried to track a lateral that went from Tarkenton to Reichow to Brown to Mason to Reichow to Alderman and finally to Tingelhoff, who had started it all by innocently centering the ball to Tarkenton.

The official came croaking up to a colleague when it was over. "I damned near called a double dribble," he said.

While his people almost always played robustly, Van Brocklin's shifting moods kept them in an emotional revolving door. He reviled his team for an hour once for displaying assorted timidity and ineptness against Green Bay and then handed a stumpy defensive back named Billy Butler a $500 bonus for rising above all the futility. On the practice field he used ethnic slurs casually, as though his membership in football's old-guard brotherhood gave him that right. Sometimes he didn't realize how deeply they cut. And at other times, almost certainly, he did. He called Italian-American officials "spaghetti eaters," and his off-field vocabulary was splotched with such endearments as "kikes," "jigs," "hunkies," "wops," "phony Notre Damers," "phony newspapermen," and "phony Big Tenners." Some of these labels were jocularly hung, but a lot of the time he was serious. Van Brocklin's level of social sensitivity was about average for the coaches of the 1960s. Where he differed from the others was in his spectacular style of delivery.

In Chicago in 1962 the officials ruled that a Minnesota fullback named Doug Mayberry had failed to reach the end zone on a third-down lunge. Van Brocklin was convinced the officials were insane or blind. He also considered the possibility that they may have been relatives of Halas. The Vikings had to settle for a field goal and lost the game in the last twenty seconds when Tarkenton called a handoff to Mayberry on the Viking twenty-five with his team leading by a point. Mayberry fumbled, Chicago recovered, and Roger LeClerc kicked a field goal for the Bears. When it was over, Van Brocklin streaked after the officials, intercepting them as they were about to disappear beneath the ivy. He howled and cursed. He accused them of every infamy catalogued in both Testaments, and he demanded that they all dissolve on the spot in recognition of their sins. When they refused, he made his way back to the Viking locker room and then embarked on one of the all-time character dissections in NFL history.

A shaken reporter returned to the press box nearly an hour later. "I wouldn't have thought it possible," he said. "Van Brocklin talked for forty-five minutes nonstop, and there isn't one word of it I can use in a family newspaper."

The Dutchman historically reserved some of his most bizarre eloquence for the officials. In one exhibition with San Francisco he christened a bespectacled official "Cyclops" and badgered him savagely the whole game. Sometime late in the fourth quarter the official dropped a flag and signaled fifteen yards against the Vikings. Van Brocklin demanded to know why. "No. 72," the official said, "was holding." No. 72 was Frank Youso, a large and intelligent tackle whom Van Brocklin once accused of authoring the original nonaggression pact. Van Brocklin glared at the official disdainfully. "That's Youso," Van Brocklin shouted. "You got to be blind. Youso couldn't block a hat with a steam iron."

They scored a little slam for Van Brocklin. In one swipe he made lasting enemies out of both the official and Youso.

In the visibility he achieved (and insisted on) and in the dominance his nature and reputation imposed on his football team, Van Brocklin had the same day-to-day presence as the weather. His people were constantly aware of him and had to react to him. They sometimes dreaded him, of course. But often when the storm cleared he was benign and frolicsome. He was at his best in a social hour at the dormitories in training camp when his furies were calmed and he would slip into the room of a Paul Dickson or a Rip Hawkins and talk football. Reminiscing, he would order a couple of six-packs of beer for the congregation and let the hard shell peel away. His devotion to the game was real. When he was able to conjure the good times, and do it with people he regarded as peers or at least confederates, he was at his most human and believable. And although he was probably its chief agent of destruction in the long run, he did think about squad morale, and he tried to reinforce it. Several times each fall he would skim off a couple of hundred-dollar bills, hand them to his captains, and tell them to raise a few with the boys at McNamara's Bar.

But the next morning at practice, if some of them responded with less than hair-trigger alertness, he would roar: "All right, goddamn it, if you're going to blow your brains out in a bar, you're going to pay the price."

He was a legitimate tough guy, but he later became the cartoon of a tough guy because as coach and person he was a man of runaway absolutes. There were no middle roads. If the newspaperman wasn't with him *all* the time, he was against him. If a tackle jumped offside, he needed remedial classes in how to count to three. The enemy was always not only beatable, he was also overrated and very probably a pussy. The Dutchman always tried to give his players an extra dose of defiance or bravado by deflating their opponents with briefings that left them gaping at the novelty of his disparagements. Willie Davis of the Packers, he would say, can't play the run, and once you take away his little outside move, you own him. Henry Jordan of the Packers could be muscled. This guy was a fat ass and that guy played like a fruit. He once dumfounded a team meeting by saying of John Unitas: "He's not a great passer, but he knows how to run an offense."

"Only Van Brocklin," said one of The Dutchman's defensive backs, who had spent a career being undressed by Unitas' zooming touchdown strikes, "could say Unitas wasn't a great passer—and really believe it."

Vince Lombardi suspected The Dutchman of teaching dirty football, but Van Brocklin's players unanimously deny it. He did sometimes recommend open assault. The Vikings in the 1960s had a defensive back named Earsell Mackbee, who attracted Van Brocklin's interest as a rookie in training camp by getting into a bloody fist fight with Ed Sharockman, a Pittsburgh brawler whom rookie rivals usually tried to avoid. Then in midseason of 1965 an injury to one of the Viking veterans presented Mackbee with a starting opportunity against Baltimore and the Colts' wily little veteran receiver, Jimmy Orr.

"The Dutchman came up to me before the game," Earsell remembers. "And he said, 'I know exactly what Jimmy Orr is going to do. He's going to try to psych you out right off the gong. So the first thing I want you to do when he comes off the line of scrimmage, no matter what the play is, you walk up there and hit him in the mouth.'

"In that particular game," Earsell recalls, "they had an article in the program about me, and apparently Orr had read it. So when we line up for the first play he says very politely, 'Nice article about you in the program.' And I say, 'Well, thanks.' And he says, 'How are the wife and kids?' And I tell him, 'Fine.' Now, you tell me how I'm going to hit this sociable fella in the mouth after a conversation like that. The game started and he began putting moves on me. The one that really hurt was right near the end of the first half, when Gary Cuozzo threw one fifty or sixty yards and Orr scored on me. Baltimore won the game.

"That was the game where Van Brocklin quit for the first time and came back the next day. He didn't say anything about me not following directions with Orr, but he wouldn't let me forget it, either. We didn't play the Colts again until the following year, in Baltimore. Orr didn't start. He came in some time in the second quarter, and I decided now is the time.

"So I went up and gave him a forearm, which is legal. He kicked at me, and I took after him. We started rolling on the ground. Big Jim Parker of the Colts came over and took off his helmet to fight, and both benches cleared. Before you knew it, the scene looked like the French Revolution.

"Orr and I both got thrown out. He said something as we were leaving, and I don't remember it, but I know sure as hell it wasn't about the wife and kids."

In Van Brocklin's competitive code, no price was too exorbitant for winning—up to and including the sacrifice of a man's body in the bedroom. Hounded by a losing streak one year, he summoned his backfield assistant, Tom (Motormouth) McCormick and demanded a miracle cure immediately.

"Only thing I can figure out," McCormick said, "is our backs and receivers are too tense. Something's got to be done to loosen them up."

The idea of an all-night drinking party was broached and quickly rejected.

"These guys can't hold onto the ball when they're clearheaded," Van Brocklin pointed out. "If you let them out there with hangovers, they'll endanger human life. What else can you think of to get a man loose?" His voice carried powerful chords of suggestion. It was also somewhat desperate, since the team hadn't won in three weeks.

McCormick summoned his troubled little platoon at the close of Friday afternoon practice. "Men," he said, "I think you've been bearing down too hard lately. Now, we have this 11 P.M. curfew, which is good because it maintains a disciplined tone and also keeps some of our men out of jail. There hasn't been a rule written yet that didn't have to be relaxed once in a while. So tonight I want you men to enjoy yourselves. Sometimes it unlimbers a man to share his troubles with a good woman. The married men here will know what I mean. I'm saying that tonight they should forget about television and bull sessions and let these good women have a chance to relax them. Those of you who are single, well, the coaches believe there are good single women, too. Now, we just don't believe that is too great a sacrifice to make on behalf of this organization."

It was a virtual order, the first of its kind in the recorded history of pro football. For one game it put The Dutchman in the same league with Knute Rockne as an inspirational force, although obviously the saints would never have tolerated such harrowing measures at Notre Dame.

The Vikings won that Sunday by three touchdowns.

The following Friday afternoon McCormick found himself surrounded by backs and receivers, all of them declaring their readiness to make additional sacrifices on behalf of the team. Their number had significantly increased. It also included tackles, guards, linebackers, defensive backs, kicking specialists, and two assistant coaches.

"On this team," McCormick said sternly, "we act in moderation. Knock it off. The curfew is reinstated. We ain't running no escort service."

The satin-sheets approach to the problem of survival as a coach in pro football was usually alien to Van Brocklin's nature. His normal disposition was to outslug his enemies. The number of cases in which The Dutchman actually landed on an opponent will probably disappoint the mythologists. Sometimes it was the other way around. He was belted in the men's room of a club in Atlanta years later by a running back named Harmon Wages, who could take Van Brocklin's criticism of his blocking but couldn't stand it when the coach challenged his taste in sports jackets.

The problem with Van Brocklin's pugilism was not his technique nor his bravery but his aim. In the Vikings' first year in Bemidji he found himself harassed at the bar during a football telecast in a crowded roadhouse; The Dutchman restrained himself magnificently, letting the loudmouth talk for a full thirty seconds before swinging at him. It was a stylish overhand right, the kind the great middleweight Tony Zale used to throw. But it was off-target and landed squarely in the midsection of Bernie Ridder, one of the Viking owners.

"Lord, Dutch," Ridder gasped, "that's a helluva way to campaign for a long-term contract."

Three years later in Birmingham, Alabama, The Dutchman was confronted for an interview by Gary Cartwright, a Dallas newspaperman and author. It was shortly before midnight outside one of Birmingham's colonnaded country clubs. Neither party could claim total abstinence. The interview was brief. It was closed by Van Brocklin with a slight breach of etiquette. Cartwright decided he was hugely offended. He pawed at Van Brocklin with what appeared to be a right hand but might simply have been bad breath. The Dutchman, unwounded but incensed, retaliated with a roundhouse right. Unable to launch any evasive tactics, Cartwright stood and admired the great arc of Van Brocklin's swing. It overshot him by a full two feet and came to a sudden stop flush on a marble pillar.

Van Brocklin left to noisy applause by Cartwright. Witnesses were not certain whether he was applauding the purity of Van Brocklin's style or the intervention of the pillar.

The Dutchman was uncertain how much of this episode would be reported by the sensationalist press. For that reason he called a news conference at seven-thirty in his hotel room the next morning. It was the only such briefing I have ever attended in which the subject presided in a pair of Jockey shorts. Van Brocklin's story was that he was the victim of an unprovoked attack by a pillar. More specifically, Cartwright's brute behavior had forced him to counterattack. The Dutchman's conduct throughout had been that of a man goaded and taunted to the point where he had to throw off all bonds of prudence.

It was a remarkable monologue. When it was over I proposed we should unanimously nominate Van Brocklin for the Nobel Peace Prize.

The workaday journalist lived in suspense covering Van Brocklin's rampages—he was never certain whether he was going to be the reporter or the victim. I dealt with the man daily for six months from 1961 to 1965. Together we have logged hours in front of wailing jukeboxes trying to discover some elusive Rosetta Stone that would solve all the mysteries of his unforecastable football teams. We shared confidences, beer, and frank views of the other's professional behavior. I marveled at Van Brocklin's rapidly changing view of the universe. One day he would call Francis Tarkenton the finest young football player he had ever seen, as responsible as any one man for the Vikings' competitiveness in the early seasons. Two days later he would scorn Tarkenton's skin-deep contributions and accuse him of lack of loyalty to the coach who discovered him.

His most admirable quality as a competitor, I thought, was his total belief in himself—that and his willingness to risk the whole bundle on the rightness of his decisions and the force of his leadership. The picture of this kind of self-reliance in a man who had achieved so much as a player had an enormous impact on his young football teams in the early 1960s. It actually made them contenders before they were prepared mechanically or chronologically.

On the other hand, his most damaging qualities as a coach were his amateurish hunch-playing in the selection of personnel and his destructive personal attacks on his players. And as a human being capable of great sociability and perception, his most grievous wounds appeared to be self-inflicted. He built early loyalties, but he himself had difficulty extending trust. It cost him friendships, and in the end the allegiance of many of his players and coaching assistants. He exalted traditional virtues such as independence, candor, and doggedness, but he had trouble crediting others with those same virtues, or he frequently misread them when he saw them.

Van Brocklin's suspicions had a true Olympian breadth. One night in the lobby of Detroit's Sheraton Cadillac, he saw me in conversation with General Manager Bert Rose, who was troubled because he was slowly being muscled out of the organization by an unusual combination of talents. Rose had hired Van Brocklin, whose roughhouse charm and unchallenged position as the football man in the organization made him unanimously popular among the Viking owners until his very last days. But Rose soon found himself submerged by the power of Van Brocklin's personality. A few personal problems added to Rose's vulnerability. He and The Dutchman began feuding, and H. P. Skoglund, one of the Vikings' owners, decided it was a case for the widely unpublicized crafts of "The Swedish Underground," a one-man espionage agency operated by a happily furtive character named Ray Johnson. He was a Skoglund employee who had once been an FBI agent. Johnson's assignment was to track the general manager of the Minnesota Vikings on the chance that he might perform some indiscretion, behind the wheel or otherwise, that would make him even more vulnerable.

The moral, of course, is never to raise your boy to be a general manager.

In any case, The Dutchman demanded to know what I was doing talking to Bert Rose.

"Dutch," I said, "Mr. Rose's qualifications as a conversation partner are (a) he is a human being, (b) he is the general manager, and (c) he talks better near midnight than you do."

Van Brocklin decided this was a very unsatisfactory answer and possibly insulting. He invited me up to his room to settle it man to man.

"You're crazy," I said. "You are a cinch to knock me out inside of two rounds, but you could go up for manslaughter. Also, some newspaperman is certain to get wind of it, and it will be bad for your image."

Van Brocklin said I was copping out. So I agreed to accompany him to his room and to give battle, if that was the proper expression.

"Go to hell," Van Brocklin said, leaving, "I wouldn't give you the satisfaction."

The Dutchman had spent his adult life around newspapermen, but he never could grasp the phenomenon of deadlines. For some reason never explained, he believed the hour of 5 A.M. was especially fraught with danger for Norm Van Brocklin after he had been outrageous or foolish. I came to expect telephone calls at 5 A.M.

I got a telephone call at 5 A.M. after the aborted Battle of the Sheraton Cadillac. It was The Dutchman's version of an apology.

"I don't want to see you starve, you son-of-a-bitch," he said. "How about breakfast in my room?"

"It's five o'clock, boardhead," I said.

"I'll call room service for eggs and bacon," Van Brocklin replied. "I got a six-pack to break the ice socially."

Room service never produced the eggs and bacon.

The Quarterback

5

It's been years since Norm Van Brocklin and I have talked, which is ridiculous when you come to think of it—two grown men who have made their livelihoods in pro football, living in the same city, two people whose fortunes were tied together so intimately for so many years.

So be it. Attitudes harden. In some places olive branches just don't thrive. Apocryphal stories acquire the force of fact. In a way we drove each other out of Minnesota nine years ago, which may or may not have been a blessing for one or both of us. It did prove that Minnesota is easily capable of surviving calamities, at least the sports-page version of calamities.

I certainly have no compulsion to analyze Norm Van Brocklin at this distance. We have had our separate careers since our six-year relationship in Minnesota. Yet he was an important figure in a critical period of my lifetime, and if the reader asks the quarterback to be candid as well as thoughtful, I would like to talk about Van Brocklin and Tarkenton.

I started out wanting to turn him into a father image. I really wanted to look up to the guy, and for a good deal of time I did. He had command. He didn't constantly throw his playing achievements at you, although you certainly were aware of them. He had tremendous prestige, having quit in his prime as the most valuable player in football. He didn't think I was as strong physically as a good pro quarterback should be, although I believe he felt I had other qualities. He conveyed that recognition to me in the ways he usually conveyed things—by adopting me on the practice field, by needling me, by downgrading my competition. He had a good analytical mind, of course. He taught me much, about pass patterns I had never seen before, about recognizing defenses and how the different defenses evolved, which was valuable.

Also on the positive side, he made me tough quicker than I would have been under somebody else. I say this because before my first season was far along, I found out that coping with The Dutchman was more demanding than coping with the Bears and Lions.

Whatever the reasons, I acquired a hard skin early. And The Dutchman was part of that process. I think a quarterback has got to be a fighter. There are so many people taking shots at you, on the field, in the grandstand, in the newspapers, that you have to block all of that out and fight your way through. Van Brocklin's attitude was "To hell with them." I think the disturbing part about Dutch was that "them" included a sizable list of people he came in contact with. After a while, of course, it included me.

If I have any small virtues, they include an insistence that life is basically good, people are fundamentally good, a person receives from life about what he invests in it, and negative attitudes are a sort of cumulative poison. They slowly kill you as a responsive person, and sometimes those around you. For that reason when I look at the breakdown in the relationship between Van Brocklin and me, I want to do it in the context of his over-all impact on the Vikings. He did many things well as a coach, especially for the first four years. I think he was at his best when we played Green Bay. Maybe the competition with Vince Lombardi, and the idea of matching his underdogs against the champions, motivated him. His preparation for those games was always excellent. We played some tremendous football, tactically as well as physically, against the Packers. But I think a hard but valid comment on his coaching career, or at least much of it, was that he might have achieved much more if he had been able to give to people around him the respect he demanded for himself.

He abused you. He abused you in team meetings, and there were

days when he seemed to want to abuse everybody he could. It just
eroded his credibility with his ballplayers. Oh, some of his sarcasm
was funny, all right. Sometimes intentionally, sometimes not. But it
was never very funny when it was directed at you, and after a while
nobody thought it was funny at all because the price of it could be
somebody's humiliation. I just don't know what there was in Dutch's
nature that made it hard for him to criticize constructively. He could
be cruel and personal. You would hate him for what he did to your
buddy in front of the guys. I think nobody who played for Dutch ever
forgave him for what he did to Red Phillips, the fine veteran receiver
who came to the Vikings from the Rams in 1965. Red had a rare skin
infection on his hand. Once a week he had to undergo treatment for
it. Still, he played. He was one of the most decent, willing men I have
ever played with, and the guys just loved him. And one Tuesday after
a tough game when we were looking at film, we got to a play where
Red failed to hold onto a pass in the end zone. Van Brocklin said
something like "Phillips, I never thought I'd see you sticking around
to pick up another year's check."

There were guys in that room who wanted to walk right up to
Van Brocklin and grind him into the wall. I have never seen hatred
in a football clubhouse as intense as I saw it that day. It was a
degrading scene.

I just don't know what kind of drives burn inside the man. He
was dealing with men who were aware of his accomplishments and
his knowledge of the game. They understood his qualifications to
coach. He didn't have to try to brutalize them. You can lead a man
and instruct him without having to dominate his life. I know Dutch
didn't see himself that way. In his mind he was stripping away all
the alibis that he has seen ballplayers use, confronting them with
what he considered to be the cold truth of their performance. But it
wasn't the cold truth at all. Sometimes a man fails because the man
he's playing against is better. Or the man is better on that day. Or
on that play. If a player fails, it does not mean he is a quitter, or he
has lost his manhood, or that his mother and daddy didn't have
character. You can motivate a man simply by teaching. But so many
coaches believe it is the most critical requisite of their job to prove

to their players that they are brass-balls tough. It works its way all through the ranks to the kid-team coaches, who are among the worst. Their idea is you ram a size 13 shoe into the player's rear end and you are going to get him to play better and harder. They keep doing it and doing it, and it just doesn't work.

Lombardi was a tough guy, and he yelled, but he also taught, and he systematized, and he won because he achieved a constant level of performance from his players. The ballplayers never loafed under Van Brocklin. I have not played with many pro teams of any description where players have loafed. But the Vikings' level of performance technically could go from peaks to valleys because the team was in constant turmoil. The coach was totally unpredictable. He could be the most charming guy in the world, and the next day he could be the most obnoxious. He would call me up at any hour of the night or day, in season or in the off-season. He could be sweet as a lamb or raise holy hell. You never knew which way he was coming from so you were never in a stable situation.

All of us came to hate going to Tuesday meetings after a game. It didn't matter whether we won or lost. We just hated going to the meetings to be subjected to all that crap. I tried to analyze my reactions to it. I'd say, "Fran, maybe it's you. Maybe this really is the pro football world and it's just taking you a little longer to adapt to the warts and boils of it." But after a while I realized that no, I was not a choirboy hearing the facts of life for the first time. Everybody around me, or practically everybody, had the same reactions. And your only defense against it was to stand up to the guy.

He came to me once on a flight home and accused me of being a selfish player. I'd been hearing that one lately from him. I'd had enough of it. I told him if he did not like the way I played to get rid of me and I could think of a helluva lot better things to do with the rest of my life than spend it playing for Norm Van Brocklin. I don't think that gave him any new respect for me. It just got him out of there for a while, which was all I had a right to expect.

There was the time we were playing Atlanta, and a big guy we had traded to the Falcons, Errol Linden, was playing against Moose Eller. It was the game where Dutch benched me to start Bob Berry, then a rookie, against an expansion team—which happened to be Atlanta, where I lived. I think what Van Brocklin was saying was the Vikings don't need Tarkenton, all they need is Dutch. Moose came off one time and Van Brocklin yelled, "Linden is kicking your ass all over the field." Moose wanted to kill Dutch. Moose started walking toward Van Brocklin, and if an assistant hadn't intercepted him, I think he might have.

Dutch knew what you had to do to win. He could equip you tactically. And for a while he got all the passion he could out of his players because they not only wanted very desperately to establish themselves but they actually feared the coach and his intimidation. That may work for a while. Eventually it turns into resentment and disbelief. I don't know specifically how and when that affected the scoreboard, but I know that it did.

One of the things that embittered ballplayers most was his attitude toward injuries. Because he was suspicious, he convinced himself some guys were faking it, pretending they were hurt more than they were. He kept trying to impress us with this Spartan code, of playing hurt. Well, pro football players *do* play when hurt. My buddies have. I have. Anybody who has been through this for more than a couple of years understands that pain is one of the specifications of the job. There just happen to be variables here.

Players have different pain thresholds. That's not mythology. That's fact. Another fact is that players in certain positions might play with the identical injury that would disqualify a player at another position. You might get by with a broken hand playing tackle. But you are not likely to if you play flanker. It's also true that some players simply have more will, more spiritual toughness. Playing *means* more to them. We have a classic case on the Vikings in Jim Marshall. He played with fevers or a bronchial condition that would put a normal person, including some football players, on the critical list in a hospital. But that's Marshall. The fact that another man couldn't do it doesn't mean he's goldbricking or picking up an easy paycheck. But Dutch just had a hard time recognizing that.

I'll never forget what happened to Hugh McElhenny the last game he played for the Vikings. He had a leg injury. There's no question about that, and no question that it hurt him something fierce to run, because when the season was over he needed surgery. Mac was the last guy to claim any lofty bravery. There were times when he just didn't believe he was helping the team by going out there way below his physical capability, and I had to agree with that. But this incident in Baltimore was something else. McElhenny clearly shouldn't have been allowed back into the game. But there he was, ordered into the game on kickoff after kickoff, the deep man running the ball out. It was just grief to see him try.

For a time Dutch intimidated me with all the rest. I really got beaten down. Then I said "Nuts on this" and decided to fight him. We got into some big shouting matches on the sidelines. I just can't imagine what kind of stories the fans in the front rows took home to the kids. With Van Brocklin, you had to shove back. It was the only thing he respected. One of the favorite postgame questions you get from a reporter looking for good inside information is "What went on in the conversation between you and the coach just before that big play?" I almost always give that an intramural smile, not because it isn't a legitimate question but because I remember some of my conversations with Van Brocklin. The television guys call them "sideline consultations." With us they were one of two things, either a monologue by Van Brocklin or a war about something that happened on the previous play.

On almost all football teams I know today, the coach and quarterback will have a meaningful exchange. Even when the quarterback is young, the coach wants to know his thinking. It's crucial, absolutely mandatory, that the quarterback should believe in the play that's being called. I don't care if the coach decides the play, or the quarterback does, or the team physician does. The quarterback should have confidence that this play can get the yardage, or get the touchdown, or *do something*. If he doesn't, the team is almost certain to pick that up. There's a chemistry about those things.

It was beyond belief that Van Brocklin, who took that very position himself as a quarterback, should renounce it as a coach. It was as though nobody else's judgment mattered. His was the supreme knowledge. It was "Here's your list and here are the plays you're going to run and how we're going to do it." I was not asked for an opinion. In time-outs, he would call the play. He didn't use a messenger system during the game, but it was almost as bad, because he set the thing up and had a whole series of plays he wanted called, almost by exact sequence.

Van Brocklin did have a creative mind as an offensive coach. He doesn't need my endorsement for that, and I'd be crazy to deny it. But he was no offensive genius. He had good ideas, but often they weren't well integrated. You had very good plays to use in certain situations. The over-all continuity wasn't always the best. I don't make this as any serious criticism. With Van Brocklin's teams, we almost always scored—one way or another. We did it with stuff that he planned, with stuff that wasn't planned. We did it on tactics sometimes, but whatever else we lacked, we had plenty of firepower.

In their finest years together, Bill Brown and Tommy Mason formed the best backfield in football. As for the quarterback, I never blushed about wanting to get points up there. We didn't have the greatest ends, but we had people like Paul Flatley, who had some psychic power in being able to locate the quarterback. It was better than 9.4 speed. We had young linemen like Grady Alderman, Mick Tingelhoff, and Larry Bowie who could play with the best. We had tremendous unity in our offense, a belief in ourselves, a comradeship.

We scored a ton. We never gave up on a play. We really were a bunch of Gas Housers. In a game in Los Angeles on the last play of the half, we came up with a wild crossfield lateral to a kid fullback named Bill McWaters. It was the only way to keep the ball in play because the half was already over on the clock. The Rams couldn't understand what in hell we were doing, which might explain why McWaters went busting into the end zone for a touchdown almost unnoticed. Some of the Rams actually complained that we ran McWaters off the bench and into the game in the middle of the play.

You wouldn't want to, or couldn't, minimize Van Brocklin's role in making us competitive offensively. For a couple of years the most productive play we had was what we called a "swing-and-up," where we got the halfback or the fullback one-on-one upfield against a linebacker. It depended on the game situation and matching the call against their anticipated defensive charge, but nobody at the time had it perfected as well as Van Brocklin. Most of our innovative stuff in those years was strictly ad lib, with both good and bad results.

Once in a while The Dutchman, who was normally pretty orthodox, went really far out in the clover. We went to Los Angeles in 1964, and Dutch had a grand design. First, he was going to beat the Rams by running an offense without a huddle. Every play called at the line. Quick tempo. Keep the defense disorganized. It can be done, of course. Calling every play on the line is no big deal. The basic purpose there is to deny the defense time to huddle, and make it call its own formations on the fly. You can get arguments either way, but the fact that nobody really uses the no-huddle system except as a freak suggests that the other system is better and certainly more orderly. But, fine, we were excited to try it.

Then there was the second part of Dutch's grand design. The Vikings' public-relations people got it into the Los Angeles papers that both Tommy Mason and Bill Brown were hurt and wouldn't play. Mason did happen to be hurt. Brown wasn't. The Dutchman was going to run him into the game at the precise psychological moment when his appearance would demoralize the Rams. To carry out the fake, Dutch was going to withhold Brown the whole first quarter. What happened is we played the entire first half against the Rams with Bill McWaters and Darrel Lester as our running backs. Bill Brown spent the first half stirring around and wondering what he had done lately to break into the doghouse. We lost the game, but you can't say we didn't score a psychological breakthrough.

Van Brocklin and I never had any arguments about scrambling. And although he took shots at me in team meetings, he never roasted me publicly. Our differences didn't take that form. It was just an attrition. In retrospect, I think I'd admit it if I was the guy who was out of step. But Dutch has done this to every quarterback he coached in pro football. He did it to Bob Berry and Bobby Lee in Atlanta. And, of course, the people who love poetic ironies saw something positively lyrical in our reunion last year. All three of us were together on the same team in 1975 in Minnesota. The Dutchman isn't humorless. I think he would be amused, at this great distance in time, when he was out of coaching, that his name still recurred almost daily before or after the Viking practices. There were that many Dutchman stories, not many of them told with huge affection.

But as to quarterbacking style, he didn't bitch when I tried to salvage a broken play. Sometimes he complained to me that I created a broken play by moving out too fast, and I never argued much about that, because it was true. You can kill yourself with hindsight. The idea in football is to win. You try to win systematically, but winning doesn't have to be scenic or artistic. In the years when I scrambled most I was just trying to figure out a way to win. I didn't plot it. I didn't lie awake nights concocting some supernatural fakes and pirouettes. If I moved about better than most quarterbacks of that time, it was because I had good reactions, I could think pretty well on the fly, and I wasn't afraid of getting knocked on my can twenty yards behind the line of scrimmage if the whole thing went smash.

I never looked at myself as being gallant or pioneering. I had already played years of ball, from the sandlots to a major-college schedule. When I got out there, winning *was* everything. By any way that occurred to you. If I play differently now, it isn't because I've reformed. It's just that I've got a different kind of team to play with. I never *preferred* scrambling. If I had entered pro football as a quarterback with Lombardi's teams, I would have played about the way Starr played, I suppose. In other words, I refused to get straight-jacketed into any kind of style merely because that was supposed to be the accepted style or the most popular style. I tried to be Francis Tarkenton then, and I still do.

Your head gets cluttered with memories, pleasantly cluttered. Kids used to ask me at banquets, "What are you thinking about when you're running around back there twenty-five yards behind the line of scrimmage and Alex Karras is a half-yard behind you wanting to tear you apart?" I used to tell them in all truthfulness, "I'm thinking how bad it'll be for me if he catches up."

One night one of the networks did a football documentary and put together some horror film showing what happens when things go wrong. It was absolutely hysterical. One of them showed Eddie LeBaron, I think it was, when he got forced into a scramble and wound up looping five times crossfield, losing five to ten yards at a crack, and then finally going down from exhaustion. I talked about it with a reporter the next morning, and we agreed that it had to be the ultimate scramble disaster of all time.

Then we played the Lions that Sunday. Someplace in the third quarter I got involved in a scramble. I kept looking for Paul Flatley, but all I could see was Roger Brown, the Lions' tackle. He weighed three hundred pounds, and he was a terrific rusher. Every time I pivoted to come back crossfield, Roger Brown was two strides closer, and he had the angle on me. By the time we got thirty yards behind the line of scrimmage—and that's God's truth, you can look it up —all the rest of the Lions' pursuit had given up. They were lying on the field like beached whales, gasping and kind of bloated. But Brown must have made a personal crusade out of this play. For all of his weight, the guy had speed. He was blowing and snorting as he got closer, and he just scared the tar out of me.

Then I remembered the television strip a couple of nights before. I was retracing LeBaron's steps, exactly. I told myself, "No way are you going to wind up in a lump thirty yards behind the line of scrimmage." It was hopeless to throw. All my eligible receivers were so far downfield they were outside my range. So I started running down the sidelines. I was going to break it. It would be the most spectacular scramble play of all time. And then four freight trains hit me from behind. When I got up, I turned around to confirm that. It was Brown, of course. He's looking at me with huge, soulful eyes and he's saying, "Francis, don't you watch television?"

My offensive line eventually got conditioned to scrambling, but the other teams never did. We got into a scramble in Dallas in ninety-degree heat one game. It lasted so long Landry ran a replacement into the game for Bob Lilly, who was all smashed out. Nobody told the rest of the team the replacement was for Lilly. Four Dallas defensive linemen walked off the field simultaneously. All of them were convinced they needed first aid.

It was remarkable how the most brilliant minds in football actually believed some of those plays were rehearsed or cued, or something. When I was in the Pro Bowl one year, we finished our basic work on offense the first practice day, and Don Shula called out, very seriously, "Francis, we've still got time to work on your scramble series." Forrest Gregg of the Packers once asked Grady Alderman, also getting ready for the Pro Bowl, what kind of blocking he did on my scramble plays. Grady looked at him very thoughtfully and said, "A lot."

I did actually call a scramble play once. It was an incredible play and an incredible game. Van Brocklin always had us ready for the Packers, usually with an imaginative running game. As a matter of fact, he always took a very strong interest in the running game and coached it well. In this game, though, we were flat on the canvas with less than a minute to go. We had never beaten the Packers. We were a couple of points behind, and we were looking at fourth down and twenty-two from our own thirty-five. The Packers dropped a half-dozen guys forty yards downfield. The only thing that could possibly beat them was a long pass and a field goal because there just wasn't time for anything else, so they were going to prevent that by stacking a half-dozen all-pros between their thirty-five and the goal line.

I could see them peeling back toward the end zone as I was about to call the play. We just didn't have anything in our playbook that can cover a fourth and twenty-two against a three-man line. Nobody does. So I just said, "All the receivers go down about twenty-five yards. Pick a spot and turn around. I'm going to run around until I find somebody. Good luck. On two. Break." Just like that. Can you imagine? Supersophisticated professional football.

I got the ball and pretended to drop back, but I was really looking which way I should break, right or left. I headed right. Willie Davis was chasing me. When I got to the sidelines, nobody was open, so I turned and went the other way. I got someplace near the center of the field, way back, and I started diagonaling back toward the right sideline. I could feel Davis. I actually could, because on one swipe he got a piece of my heel. I looked downfield and Lord, there was Tom Hall open on the sidelines at about the Packer twenty-five. I had a lot of momentum coming upfield, and I just threw the hell out of the ball. It was right on the money to Hall. It was zooming in on him right at the numbers. But just before it got to him I saw a form come flailing into the line of flight: Gordy Smith, our tight end. I just groaned. I said, "No, Gordy, no." But up he went and he made a sensational leaping catch, ran another ten yards and out of bounds. Freddie Cox came in and kicked a field goal, and we won. Vince Lombardi just stood there. It was as though somebody just told him the Pope was Presbyterian.

A Letter of Intent

6

One of the popular diversions among jock celebrities is to arrange make-believe retirements at strategic moments in their careers, frequently at the point of impasse on contracts. Norm Van Brocklin was one of the leading exponents.

Francis Tarkenton's first announced retirement had no connection with contracts. But it did involve an impasse with, of course, The Dutchman. It occurred early in 1967 and in Tarkenton's mind was attended by considerable anguish. Anguish No. 1: Would it last two weeks or four weeks? Anguish No. 2: Which NFL team would rescue him from his self-imposed exile?

Apart from his liberation from Van Brocklin, leaving the Minnesota Vikings brought no pleasure to a twenty-seven-year-old quarterback whose football friendships and devotions represented an emotional investment of six years.

His loyalties were only part of it. His football experience by then had convinced Tarkenton that while he might score greater personal triumphs in the years ahead, no phenomenon he was likely to encounter would equal the Minnesota Vikings of the 1960s.

Where was he going to meet another Charley Ferguson? A tall and leggy flanker, Ferguson was traded to the Vikings by Paul Brown of Cleveland at a time when Brown was bestowing his largess on the Vikings, the only team in football that couldn't possibly injure him with his own evicted players. On a sunny afternoon in Chicago's

Wrigley Field, Ferguson lived for 2½ hours in the football player's El Dorado. Nothing he did before approached it in derring-do, and nothing he did afterward has been recorded. On this day, Charley was unstoppable. Early in the game he caught a twenty-one-yard touchdown pass from Tarkenton. Later Tarkenton stood on his goal line and lofted a ball sixty yards downfield. It was an act that confounded both Van Brocklin and Dave Whitsell, the Bears' left cornerback, neither of whom thought Tarkenton could throw that far. Ferguson, being more credulous than either, kept running full throttle. He speared the ball in midstride and rushed into the end zone to complete the Vikings' longest scoring pass then or since, eighty-nine yards. And in the fourth quarter Charley caught his third touchdown pass on a play that will forevermore memorialize that day as Black Sunday for the Chicago musicians' local.

As one of his rare concessions to the general comfort and amusement of his customers, Halas maintained a little civilian orchestra behind the ivy in the end zone grandstand at Wrigley Field. It had great sincerity and occasionally played on key. It consisted of several trumpets, a couple of trombones, a bass drum, and four reeds, including a hot-dog piccolo player. These irregulars played melodies deemed contemporary by Halas, which meant a diversified program that often began with "Oh, My Darling Clementine" and ended with "Nearer, My God, to Thee."

It was third and eight from the Bear twenty when Tarkenton called a pass play that quickly degenerated into one of those abandon-ship stampedes. Ferguson had been assigned a post pattern, meaning he was to angle toward the goalposts. When the play broke down and Tarkenton began scrambling, Ferguson swung toward the right corner flag, building speed as he observed the ball traveling in a general course toward the flag. By the time the ball reached the end zone, Ferguson had developed an awesome stride. The ball was high, requiring a great leap. Ferguson jumped three feet into the air, catapulted by the full impetus of his forty-yard sprint. He came down just inside the chalklines but in no condition to stop. Out of the end zone he bolted, over the low brick wall and into the grandstand, where the irregulars were arrayed in splendid oblivion to the oncoming scourge.

At the last moment the piccolo player looked up and saw Ferguson bearing down on his defenseless friends. "Look out," the piccolo player screamed, "here he comes." It was a brave effort, worthy of the signalman on the sinking *Titanic,* but it was much too tardy. Ferguson burst full bore into the musicians. Jagged pieces of trombone flew twenty-five feet into the air. Disembodied trumpets followed. The bass drum expired with a terrible rending and exhalation of air. No fatalities were reported, but the local maintained later it took the trumpeters two years to regain their lips.

"The worst thing about it," the bandleader said, "was that he hit us square in the brass."

Would there be another Bill Brown, and could Tarkenton foresee that some day they might be reunited? To Tarkenton, Bill Brown was The One, The Unforgettable Man in football. He had cowpuncher's legs, a crew cut out of a Prussian barracks, and a face that must have stood up to a landslide. In style and disposition he seemed to have descended from another football age. He should have been wearing armstripes with a big leather football sewn on the front of his jersey. He should have run without a helmet behind a flying wedge. He was fearless and destructive. Yes, he had much ability. He could catch the ball as well as any back Tarkenton had ever seen or would see. Brown blocked like a gatecrasher and ran the ball as though every lunge might be his last act on earth. To guard against this possibility, he refused to go down. He made the expression "second effort" the seal of his performance, and he would physically assault the trainer or doctor who tried to remove him from a game for injury. Everybody called him just "Brown." Even the ballboys. It was no disrespect. "Bill" seemed much too, well, precious for a man of Brown's playing behavior.

It made Tarkenton swallow to think of playing a football game without Brown.

Would any other football team in the world entertain a Palmer Pyle? A large-chested, girthy Chicagoan, Pyle was a man of much intelligence but unpredictable social habits and a yen for late-hours tippling. He played guard for the Vikings but reserved his best competitive efforts for the place where they were more urgently needed, in his living room and bedroom. For his beloved, Pyle had chosen a very attractive and headstrong Italian girl, whose several credits included the fact that she was the daughter of Anthony (Tough Tony) Accardo, usually described in the journals of the day as the No. 2 man in the Chicago Mafia. Palmer and Marie occasionally forsook the rapture of their union to pelt each other with harsh words, particularly when Palmer committed some social error, such as going to a party and forgetting to invite Marie.

"The guy," a teammate recalled, "was one of the all-time roamers. He would take off and have a few schnapps, and you didn't know if you'd see him again. He invited a lot of people over one Thanksgiving and was the only one who didn't show up. He went out to get the cranberries and just didn't come back, for two days."

His teammate remembered the night Bill Jobko, the linebacker, and his wife, Katie, were going to have some of the people over for a lasagna party. "It was right after the game, and everybody was supposed to go home and change into something casual. Palmer forgot to pick up his wife. Marie just had a hard time understanding this omission. She had gone home after the game and got herself all prepared and was waiting for Palmer to come for her so they could go together to the Jobkos' apartment.

"My wife and I were about the last to leave the party sometime around midnight. It was the last I saw of Palmer that night. He seemed to have a great time. He liked the lasagna so much that he took a whole tray of leftovers, made himself a big martini, and headed out of the Jobkos' place for his own, which was in the same complex. We last saw him sort of stumbling through this vacant lot.

"So he got home and knocked on the door. His wife opened it, and Palmer said, 'You should have been at the party, hon. It was great.'

"This teed her off something fierce, as you can probably imagine. Palmer goes into the kitchen and puts the lasagna in the oven and turns it up piping hot. He then goes into the bedroom and strips down and is lying there like King Tut. At about this point Palmer felt a driving hunger and he yelled, 'Hey, Marie, when that lasagna is done bring it in here.'

"He's still sipping on his martini awaiting the arrival of his devoted wife with the lasagna, but she stays out there in the kitchen waiting for the stuff to get really steaming hot. After fifteen more minutes she takes it out of the oven and brings it into the bedroom. 'Palmer, honey,' she says, 'here's your lasagna.' With that she dumps the whole thing on his chest. The guy nearly burned to death. He roared out of bed and started throwing that hot cheese and goop in Marie's hair, and I guess it was the wildest scene in the history of Bloomington, Minnesota. We got the story more or less that way direct from the returning hero in the locker room the next practice. Everybody used to rush the door when Palmer came in to get the latest news from the arena, like you call the newspaper office to get the wrestling results."

Would his new employers be able to uncover another Steve Stonebreaker? Tarkenton mused gloomily.

Stonebreaker was a seventeenth-round draft choice from Detroit. He entered the National Football League devoid of virtually all the conventional gifts of the professional football player except unflinching confidence. He was 6-2, weighed 220 pounds, enjoyed collisions, and frankly admitted on his first day in training camp that he was probably destined to be rookie of the year. He affected great maturity and football acumen, and was said to be the only rookie to enter the NFL claiming ten years' seniority. The problem with granting him immediate stardom was that none of the coaches could figure out where to play him. He had the disposition of a linebacker but insisted on playing his own defenses. He was finally installed at tight end, a position where he was compromised because of (a) a running gait that would have been spurned by a Clydesdale horse and (b) an inability to catch the ball. But he was very belligerent, which met Van Brocklin's first requirement. In addition, the regular tight end, Gordy Smith, broke his leg in the final exhibition game, leaving only Stonebreaker among his successors.

Stonebreaker had distinguished himself early that season by flooring a teammate, Paul Dickson, in a shower room fight. A few weeks later Stonebreaker got kicked out of a game for brawling with one of the Lions, proving his essential bispartisanship. Although he found Stonebreaker's pugnacity a redeeming part of his character, The Dutchman was never hooked on him as one of the most endearing personalities he had met. This attitude may have originated in a brief conversation the two had under the pines at the Bemidji practice site when Van Brocklin forced Stonebreaker to play one hour and forty-five minutes without relief at tight end. Stonebreaker decided at that point to call it an afternoon, and began walking off the field. Van Brocklin ordered him to stop.

"Screw you," Stonebreaker advised the coach.

"Screw you," the coach corrected.

They moved closer to each other to shelter their exchange of confidentialities.

"Screw you," Stonebreaker repeated, with heightened feeling.

"Screw *you,*" Van Brocklin replied, not wishing to be misunderstood.

Their relationship thereafter declined. It bottomed out one night when Stonebreaker, Roy Winston, and Tom Franckhauser chose the Cheshire Cheese Room at the Sheraton Ritz in Minneapolis as a civilized place for an evening of grogging. Stonebreaker always prided himself on being an innovator in these pursuits. Like many rooms of Old English motif, the Cheshire Cheese featured a custom called ale by the yard. The receptacle was a thin, graceful tube resembling a flower vase three feet long. At the bottom of it was a relatively large bulb or globe. Imagine such a receptacle containing not a yard of ale, but a martini three feet long. Despite the vigorous dissent of the bartender, Stonebreaker ordered and received this beverage, replete with forty-two olives.

By closing he had progressed no farther than a foot in his campaign to drain the stylish beaker. Franckhauser, a pioneer in the consumer movement and very precise in his reports, measured it at only nine inches. The point was largely academic to Stonebreaker. He keeled over on his way to the men's room.

When he failed to return in fifteen minutes, Winston and Franckhauser launched a search. They never did locate Stonebreaker, who, lucklessly, had landed on an upward-moving escalator. He was borne unconscious to the second-floor lobby while his friends fruitlessly combed all available crannies on the first floor.

It was the bartender who finally telephoned Van Brocklin. "We got one of your ballplayers here lying on an escalator," the bartender said.

"Is he alone?" Van Brocklin grumbled.

"He's alone and out," the bartender said. "I think his name is Stonebreaker."

"You're being generous if that's what you call him," Van Brocklin said, hanging up.

Roused, Stonebreaker found his way to his suburban house yard in time to wave good morning to the milkman from a bivouac under an elm tree. At the end of the month, Stonebreaker's bill from the Cheshire Cheese carried an extra assessment: five hundred dollars by Van Brocklin.

As a wee-hours operative, however, Tarkenton was forced to admit that Stonebreaker was a crude impostor alongside the squad's plumed cavalier, Paul Flatley.

For the first three years of his pro career, Flatley was the bachelor who won all the blue ribbons in the league's parlors and spas. People like Paul Hornung and Max McGee had the reputations. But it was Flatley, his contemporaries maintained, who retired the trophies. He was an articulate Chicagoan of worldly good looks and diverse appetites. As a collegian he played at Northwestern on Saturdays and in a variety of other environments the rest of the week. As a professional player he was a flanker, never with much speed but always with steady hands and wits, and a jauntiness that characterized his style equally in a crossfield pattern and in the night club. Yet much as he esteemed Flatley's touchdown statistics, Tarkenton was more vividly impressed by his recitals of his nightly explorations. Recognizing an appreciative audience, Flatley would weave his stories into a troubador's tapestry, sparing no detail or subtlety. As he did, the quarterback's eyes would widen, and he would finally exclaim: "Flatley, you dog."

"Why," Flatley would respond, "deny it?"

Before finally being domesticated, Flatley sculpted some of the enduring sagas of the NFL's great night crawlers. None surpassed the one in San Francisco when the purple knight decided a great city deserved his best. He declined to observe the 11 P.M. curfew the night before the game. He declined to return at midnight, which was usually his backup target. At 7 A.M. his roommate rose to greet the arriving sun and was mortified to observe Flatley's bed unslept in. Shortly before the team gathered for breakfast the truant showed up, moving uncertainly among the palm fronds in the Jack Tar Hotel lobby. Friends hustled him to his room. In the Viking locker room a few hours later Eason, the equipment manager, happened to pass within ten feet of the convalescing flanker and stifled a gasp. "God, if Dutch smells your breath, you're dead," he said. Eason then set about covering the aroma and restoring Flatley's sobriety. He poured quarts of black coffee into his somnambulent client, moved him around the dressing room, and in general tried to keep him upright. By kickoff Flatley was sober. But he was cadaverishy pale and barely able to clip the chinguard on his helmet, his fingers fluttered so violently.

"Do you think I should tell them I'm sick?" Flatley asked.

"You do," Eason said, "and it will cost you a thousand bucks. You better suck it up and don't even think of missing a ball all day."

Flatley gulped dismally and ran out for the introductions, nearly dislodging two steps that he didn't see.

It was a football game that did not wholly match the grand manner of the Colt-Giant sudden-death game and the sixteen-below Armageddon in Green Bay. But it might very well have been the most excruciating game of the decade, for the coaches, the bettors, and for Paul Flatley. And it represented the culminating stroke of the Van Brocklin–Viking alliance, when his personal thumbing at the odds and the team's reckless indomitability blended in their most extraordinary hour. The Vikings trailed the 49ers by three touchdowns at half time. At one stage in the second half the Vikings fell behind by 35–10. But Tarkenton threw bombs, puffballs, darts, and balloons—whatever he had to throw. And Brown and Mason ran their legs out, but there was nothing to match the panic-inspired miracles performed by Paul Flatley. He played the game in an advanced state of agony. His greening cheeks reflected the inner ravages of an all-time hangover.

Tarkenton threw to Flatley nine times. Once the ball was spiked to the ground by the 49er secondary. But Flatley caught the other eight passes, two of them sliding on his nose and one when he had to belt the 49er cornerback in the jaw before establishing possession. He totaled more than two hundred yards receiving and caught two touchdown passes. It was unanimously acclaimed to be the game of Paul Flatley's life, and he did it without a blink of sleep.

"Anything less," Eason said from his philosopher's chair when it was over and the Vikings had won, 42–41, "and you would have been dead."

"You can get rid of all of your tape and jock straps," Flatley told him, "but never lose your percolator."

Both as a collaborator of Tarkenton's and as a perceptive man aware of the personality interplay of those years, Flatley is uniquely qualified to evaluate Tarkenton the football player of that era. Flatley happened to be an admirer of both the quarterback and the coach. And he still assesses Van Brocklin as a genius despite his ambition at least twice in his career, once in Minnesota and again in Atlanta, "to walk up to him and rip him in the mouth for things he did and said to my teammates."

"The way Tarkenton impressed the ballplayer who huddled with him," Flatley said, "was that he was a take-charge guy who took advantage of everything anybody gave him on the field. There were a few people on the team who felt that sometimes he was more concerned with himself than he was about anything else. I never paid that much attention. You hear that about almost any successful person. And Tarkenton had a great desire to be successful personally. It surfaced in different ways, and it wasn't confined to the football field, of course. He was probably the first of the businessman football players, I mean guys who were serious about using their football careers as a springboard into business life. Nobody ever had trouble getting along with him. He was always a chatty and accessible guy in the locker room. But away from there he was more aloof from the guys than most ballplayers are, even the stars. Part of that was because he didn't have much of a role at beer parties, and part of it might have been that he just didn't care too much for mob scenes.

"The players didn't criticize his scrambling style. They knew what the problems were trying to win in the NFL with an expansion team, and they also knew that Tarkenton had abilities that were unique in a quarterback. Not everybody who played quarterback for the Vikings would have scrambled, with any kind of chance of reaching old age. Tarkenton and I never worked out any cues or plans for use when the play went into one of those playground routines. Everything was strictly on the fly. The only rule was that you tried to get on the side of the field where Tarkenton was headed, which sounds easier than it was, because he headed for several sides on the same play. All I did was try to pick out a spot he could see and then run that way waving my arms. You'd be amazed how many passes I caught doing that.

"The difference between Francis running around then, and Francis moving around outside the pocket today is that in those days he was really too young to know how to co-ordinate the routes his receivers were running with what the defenses were doing at the same time. Today Tarkenton knows right off the bat who he *can't* throw to. It simplifies things a lot. But he was smart even then. He really worked at it. And although he was young, by the time he was in his third year or so he was a veteran quarterback with a lot of mileage on him. He bossed the huddle, all right. I can't remember anybody ever confronting him. Every now and then somebody would do some yipping about this or that in the huddle, and Tarkenton would say, 'Hey, goddamnit,' and that was the end of it.

"He was a good guy to locker next to. He always had some chatter, something to kid you out of the dumps with if you were in that state of mind. And he was thoughtful if some guy really had a problem he thought he could help solve. He was never pushy about that. He just never intruded himself on a guy's personal situation unless asked. His close buddies were Alderman, Tingelhoff, and Brown. He didn't think he had to act as Perle Mesta for the whole team, although he changed a little there as that big soiree he had for the offensive line at the Super Bowl attested years later. He bitched and grumbled a little, like any normal person when he figured he had been abused at a squad meeting, but he never really made any anti-Van Brocklin speeches in the locker room. I knew he was upset when he came back from some of the quarterback meetings, and I'd ask him what was wrong, but he never really divulged anything to me. I thought he was actually a pretty good trouper that way. Dutch later said Tarkenton was stirring things up against him, but I went wherever the offensive team went, and I never saw or heard any evidence of it.

"I think Tarkenton is off the mark somewhat in believing Van Brocklin could have prepared us better for the changing defenses at the time. Van Brocklin played his whole career against man-to-man defenses. The zone started coming in the mid-1960s, although Baltimore used it before that. What could Van Brocklin teach us about the zone? He was learning about it like the rest of us.

"In a lot of ways I envied Fran, even at the top of my career when I was supposed to have the world knocked and I had the kind of life where every night was Mardi Gras. He gave you the impression he knew exactly where he was going. Most of the times his problems with the coach were piddling things, and he didn't really let it affect his outlook. He was going right to the top of pro football, and he had the nerve not to let his personality or his style of play be altered by this strong-minded guy who coached him and would like to have altered them. He had a good head intellectually, but even more than that, he had a lot of mental tenacity. You can call it drive or sense of purpose or discipline. The terms come and go, but you had to respect the qualities they expressed in Tarkenton."

Tarkenton had a lot to remember about the Vikings. For five years their graph moved upward toward what Van Brocklin told himself and his players would be championship contention, in the mid-1960s. They won only five games their first two years but equaled that in their third. By 1964 Van Brocklin had a football team that just failed to dislodge the Colts, Browns, and Packers but kept audiences in an uproar with its offensive volcanics and random anarchy. The blue-ribbon entry in this last category was a game against San Francisco when a sixty-six-yard sprint by Jim Marshall took him into the end zone. The play had style and suddenness. Unfortunately, it was the Vikings' end zone. Momentarily confused in midfield when a San Francisco pass and fumble moved the ball in several directions on the same play, Marshall ran the wrong way. Because he was a child of spontaneity, who found himself flung haphazardly into roller-coaster moods of glee and gloom, Marshall seemed fated above all people to be the victim of such harsh burlesque. It almost broke his heart. But his many gifts included the one of rejuvenation. Friends, Tarkenton among them, told him he would live to smile about it, and to forget it. This he did. And now that he has become football's Father Time, almost nobody remembers it.

The team's solidarity had deepened, partly in response to a practice-field accident that almost took the life of Tom Franckhauser, the defensive back from Purdue. He was a leprechaun, glib and popular, a practical joker. Late in the afternoon during an August scrimmage in 1964 he came up hard to tackle a reserve fullback who had broken through the line. The impact crumpled Franckhauser. Fred Zamberletti, the trainer, rushed onto the field and found quickly that the injury demanded immediate surgery to avert permanent brain damage or worse. Unconscious, Franckhauser was carried to a field-side van and taken to a Bemidji hospital, where for several hours after the operation he lay in danger of death from a massive hemorrhage.

Nothing in his football career so jarred Van Brocklin. He sat up all night in the hospital reception room, almost unable to speak to visitors. The team's defensive coach, Harry Gilmer, called the players together several times that night to inform them of Franckhauser's condition. The next day Tarkenton and Rip Hawkins, the two captains, sat together in a waiting room near the injured player's recovery room, symbolically declaring his teammates' presence in his gravest hour.

Franckhauser recovered without aftereffects. His football career was finished, however, and he left training camp within a week after the accident. The shared anxiety of the episode seemed to touch his teammates with a new sense of fraternity and buoyed them into the

1964 season. For the first time they climbed beyond .500. At 8–5–1, in just four seasons, they had reached a won-lost level surpassed that year by only three teams in the NFL.

"We're going over the hump," The Dutchman announced. His team had no doubt of it. The Colts were the Western Division champions in 1964, but the Vikings had beaten them, 34–24, in Minnesota. The Packers' won-lost record was no better than Minnesota's. And the Cleveland Browns, although the league champions, were hardly an immovable object.

To leaven his impulsive troupe in 1965, Van Brocklin imported such ripened reserves as Red Phillips, the receiver; Phil King, the fullbacking Cherokee; and Billie Barnes, another running back who was one of Van Brocklin's cronies on the Philadelphia Eagles. Barnes was judged to be an excellent ally in a brawl, but by now he was less than terrifying from the line of scrimmage. The Dutchman also imported Gary Larsen, a blond ex-Marine from the Minnesota potato fields who unaccountably had wound up in the employ of the Los Angeles Rams. Of all the Van Brocklin immigrants that year, Larsen was by far the most significant. Several years later, he would become the fourth member of the most powerful defensive line in football. But by that time Van Brocklin was no longer around to enjoy the harvest of one of his rare successes in the NFL bartering markets.

As a talent sleuth, The Dutchman was usually a catastrophe. He picked and signed players in accordance with the old locker room biases and slogans of his playing days. He was convinced, for example, that a black player from the South was amenable and therefore coachable, but a black player from California—presumably less submissive to the old white autocracy—wasn't. This attitude was hardly unique among the NFL coaches of the day, or among most of the white players for that matter. Nor was the country as a whole any farther advanced in its social thinking. In the context of the times, such mind-sets in a pro football coach did not necessarily constitute a shocking Jim Crow racism. The Dutchman also freely acknowledged being partial to the sons of the old Confederacy. Many of his playing buddies were natives of the country-and-western belt, and shared with him a lack of regard for Big Ten, Notre Dame types, whom they considered overpublicized and less congenial to the pain and sacrifice of the professional playing pit.

The Dutchman's burdens as the team's de facto personnel director were largely self-imposed. His frictions with Bert Rose contributed to the dismissal of Rose as the team's general manager in 1964, and his gradual downgrading of Joe Thomas as the personnel man was responsible for Thomas' resignation some time later. Thomas and Rose both were more familiar with college football players than Van Brocklin, whose job was to coach people, not discover them.

Yet the Vikings had enough wherewithal—Tarkenton, Mason, Brown, Carl Eller, Jim Marshall, Paul Dickson, Mick Tingelhoff, Grady Alderman, Paul Flatley, Freddie Cox, Rip Hawkins, Karl Kassulke, Ed Sharockman—to shoot for the championship in 1965 without apology. The Dutchman honed them crisply at Bemidji. No horror days now. They were young veterans who knew how to win. In the exhibitions they destroyed everything in sight. Their sweep included a 57–14 deflation of the Dallas Cowboys, who were then only two years away from playing for the league championship.

The Dutchman had them afire for the opener in Baltimore. He had prepared them for everything, in fact, except a Maryland heat wave in mid-September. Septembers in Minnesota tend to be frosty and sometimes sprinkled with snow. Baltimore confronted the Vikings with a windless ninety-five degrees and humidity dense enough to float the Atlantic fleet. The Colts might have won on their own devices. With the Jamaican weather, they won by three touchdowns.

The Vikings also lost their next game, to Detroit, when a fullback named Amos Marsh unhinged everybody on the field by running the wrong pattern and catching a touchdown pass in the final minute. But in their game against the Rams, Tarkenton brought them back from the crypt by taking the team the length of the field in the last two minutes, and Cox won it, 38–35, with a field goal.

The team's defense in 1965 could not have stopped a runny nose, but the offense played with an effervescence that turned every game into a carnival for the fans and an ordeal for the statisticians. The

Vikings scored forty-four points against the Giants, forty-two against the 49ers, and suddenly they were back in contention at 5–3. They would find out against the Colts in Bloomington, The Dutchman told them, whether they were man enough to go to the title. Unitas was ailing, and Baltimore put it up to Gary Cuozzo. Given the state of the Viking defense, they could have gotten by with Francis Scott Key. Cuozzo threw five touchdown passes, and the next morning Van Brocklin announced his resignation.

He didn't revile his players or the hustlers of Hennepin Avenue. He blamed himself for not being able to lead his team to a championship and declared, "I have taken them as far as I can."

The Viking administration was duly shocked, partly because Van Brocklin—with his typical hardhead independence—called his own press conference to announce the news. His employers heard about it from the reporters, and by that time the coach had already left his office, driven home, and taken the phone off the hook. Jim Finks, installed as the general manager the year before, saw that Van Brocklin was all twisted emotionally, clothing himself in a disgrace that was hardly warranted considering the condition of the Minnesota defense. With Bernie Ridder, then the team's most influential owner, Finks sought to marshal a task force that would talk The Dutchman back into combat. One of the first he approached was Francis Tarkenton. "For the good of the team," Finks said, "I think we ought to ask Norm to reconsider."

"For the good of the team," Tarkenton said, "I don't think we should. He's a big boy. He knows what he's doing. He keeps telling us you can separate the football players from the quitters, so now he walks out after we lose a big one."

Tarkenton understood that walking away from an untenable or infuriating situation is not necessarily the same as quitting, in the accepted sense of surrendering. It depends on who is doing the defining. Nearly a decade before, a young quarterback at the University of Georgia had walked off the campus because he was infuriated. And he probably would not have defined that as quitting. Nor would he so define his announced resignation from the Vikings two years later. Sometimes when you walk out you are making a statement of principle, or so you choose to define it. Or perhaps you are negotiating.

In later years Tarkenton would find time to ponder those tantalizing semantics. But in Minnesota in 1965 what he knew was that he did not want Van Brocklin back as coach. They were mismated. No appeals to team loyalty were going to change that.

The players gathered at the Midway practice field the next day, most of them bearing the half-staff eyelids that commemorated a long night at the Rand Bar in St. Paul. Van Brocklin walked in to reveal he had changed his mind and was still the coach.

Most of the eyelids fluttered uncertainly and drooped.

But Van Brocklin was down from Olympus now, having relinquished the cornerstone of his leadership, his prestige as the unsinkable man who would never yield. He was less believable now. They would fear him less, and follow him only when they chose.

The Vikings finished the season at 7–7 and sank to 4–9–1 in 1966. In midseason of 1966, however, Van Brocklin and Tarkenton produced one final piece of dual craftsmanship, a victory over Lombardi's Green Bay Packers. It was textbook football, filled with long drives, grinding line play, and tactical chessmanship that Lombardi himself celebrated as his profession in its purest form. Van Brocklin and Tarkenton beat him in the second half with two drives that each consumed more than eight minutes. In his sixth season, Tarkenton belonged with the best.

He was rarely viewed in that light by the media commentators of the time, however, or even by some of the coaches, who were still shackled to the orthodoxy that required great quarterbacks to be motionless quarterbacks. The distance the quarterback strayed from the pocket, therefore, was directly equatable with his distance from greatness. It didn't matter who he played with or what specialized skills he brought to the game. If he didn't lock himself seven yards behind the line of scrimmage, count to three, and either throw or accept obliteration, he was a rogue weasel among the great lions. As such he could be looked on with curiosity or amusement or even tolerance. But one does not honor rogues, does one?

In the Pro Bowls, yes. They needed curiosities. But when the all-pro selectors came to quarterback, they looked at the standings, and also the documents of orthodoxy. It was a kind of loyalty oath. The ones who cleared it were people like Bart Starr, John Unitas, and Sonny Jurgensen. But Tarkenton, on the day he quarterbacked the Vikings against the Packers in 1966, was their equal, as he was on other days that year. And as if to prove the mortality of all such quarterbacks, the following week he threw for five interceptions against Detroit.

The week after that, Van Brocklin played Ron VanderKelen at quarterback against the Rams, explaining that his team was finished as a contender in 1966 and he had to examine its potential for 1967. One week later, against Atlanta, he decided to examine Bob Berry.

It was a decision that irrevocably closed the gate on the Tarkenton–Van Brocklin relationship. Tarkenton saw it as a deliberate humiliation, the last he would accept from Van Brocklin. He played in the remaining games but told his friends he was through in Minnesota. It was a viewpoint apparently shared by the general manager, Jim Finks, who was now prepared to overhaul the franchise. He had no hostility toward Tarkenton but understood that his goals might best be served if both Tarkenton and Van Brocklin left.

In January the Vikings began to discuss trade possibilities with the New York Giants. Van Brocklin's status in that period was never clear. He still projected an impressive air of command among the owners and had been the centerpiece of the organization for so long that they curdled at the thought of firing him. The Politburo, after all, never really fired Joseph Stalin. The Vikings were disposed, however, to accept Van Brocklin's resignation if the thought occurred to him. Nor did Van Brocklin or Tarkenton themselves have the whole thing tracked. At this late date they were not completely estranged. They met once for hours while Tarkenton was en route to the West Coast. They talked about all the daffy times, the medium good times that could have been great times, how the Vikings were not that far removed from winning a championship, and how Francis Tarkenton and Norm Van Brocklin could together guide them to that grail of grails.

"He was a persuasive guy," Tarkenton said. "For a while we both yielded to the illusion that we had it back together, although I had made up my mind I wasn't going to play for him again. I was making my off-season home in Atlanta by then. We were raising a family. Angela, our first, was already a preschooler. I had some business interests there in the winter and spring and I was reaching a maturing stage in my life. I just didn't need any more hassles in a game that should have been fun to play but never really was while I was in Minnesota.

"But here was Dutch talking about some swashbuckling new future for both of us with the Vikings, and he got very confidential about how our personalities played off against each other. He offered a theory that mystifies me to this day. Religious guys, he said, needed people like him to anchor to—or something on that order. He may have been saying that the Van Brocklins are the strong, earthy leaders that give a sense of direction to those who are supposed to be more brittle and idealistic in their struggles with life. I don't know if the Dutchman qualified for his role, but I'm positive that I didn't qualify for the one he was trying to assign me.

"We parted amiably. It was a strange but interesting encounter, although it didn't materially affect my thinking about a future without the Minnesota Vikings. A couple of days later I heard new reports about a trade that involved me. So I sat down and decided to do something about a situation that was approaching a sort of unfunny slapstick. I told myself, 'Self, you are a very unhappy man in that career environment. You are going to play a lot more football but you are not going to play it in that situation. You have achieved enough so that you can make something happen. You are going to have to deal with this now.' "

Tarkenton wrote Van Brocklin a letter announcing his decision to disaffiliate:

Dear Norm,

After much thought, I have come to a definite conclusion that under no circumstances can I return to play football with the Minnesota Vikings next season.

Because of the events of the past few months and my feelings toward a number of things, it is impossible for me to return to the Vikings with a clear and open mind. As you know, I have tried to subdue these feelings and erase them from my mind, but it has been impossible.

Feeling as I do, I am sure this decision is the best for the Vikings, you and myself.

Norm, I sincerely appreciate your help and guidance during the early years of my pro career and I certainly wish for you, and the Vikings, every success.

I hope you and the organization understand that nothing can be done which would change my decision.

Because of all that the organization has done for me, I am writing this letter in the event that it might be helpful to the Vikings to know my feelings at this time.

Sincerely,

Francis A. Tarkenton

It was a statement intended to be definitive without being defiant or sour. Copies were sent to the Viking directors. They arrived at about the time a wire service dispatch from Atlanta reached the country's sports desks, summarizing the contents of the letter. Tarkenton had exchanged lamentations at Jimmy Orr's in Atlanta during the week with Lew Carpenter, a Viking coaching assistant whose ardor for the Dutchman had also dissolved. Atlanta newspapermen learned about it and Tarkenton's letter. They quickly shared all these saucy discoveries with their readers. Ridder and Finks telephoned Tarkenton in an attempt to arrange a meeting in Chicago. The quarterback gave them his regrets, explaining he was afraid the door was now closed. The sudden appearance of the Tarkenton decision on the press association wires riled the Viking executives, causing them to interpret the whole sequence as a Byzantine scheme spawned by Francis Tarkenton to remove Van Brocklin.

"How," the quarterback later asked, "could there be any substance to that? I just wanted out of the situation. I couldn't make it plainer. There was no conceivable way I could come back to the Vikings in 1967 after my statement became a matter of record."

Two days later, Van Brocklin himself disaffiliated.

The Tarkenton decision was the climactic embarrassment for

The Dutchman. It meant that one of his personal frictions had cost the franchise a valuable property, although Van Brocklin himself had a role in the trade negotiations with New York. If there is a certain lack of logic there, it should be condoned. Coaching and quarterbacking insist on that prerogative.

The Vikings' owners were not unanimously heartbroken when Van Brocklin made his decision. To discourage any afterthoughts, they offered him nearly a hundred thousand dollars in balm—for resigning as coach. It appeared to be a gesture of both genuine esteem and relief.

And in New York not long afterward, Giants' owner Wellington Mara announced the acquisition of a quarterback he hoped would rescue his disintegrating football team and recover some of the big city's old-time ardor, now transferred to the Jets and the whiskey-sipping, wenching, touchdown-throwing Joe Namath.

The Giants told Francis Tarkenton they would require him only to throw touchdowns.

The Quarterback

7

New York City may be bankrupt and dirty. It is a hard place to catch a thief and an impossible place to govern. But to me it sings. The greatest, most exciting town in the world.

I didn't really plan to play there, or rather to maneuver my way there, as it was alleged by all the financial experts who write football columns. If my own priorities mattered, I would have been traded to Detroit or Chicago, which were potentially winning situations where a good, experienced quarterback could find a home. Those two were my preferences. But obviously it didn't plunge me into mourning when Finks traded me to New York for a lot of draft choices. There are very few professional athletes who blanch at the thought of playing in New York City, with all its electricity and its frank love of show biz.

But then there were the New York Giants. We played them the year before and blasted them. I thought they were the worst team in football then, and when I got there I found out the material was worse than I imagined. I really am not being haughty about that. I'm a very fallible guy who's had plenty of bad days. But admitting that doesn't alter the Giants' situation in 1967.

I don't think it's quite accurate to say I envied Joe Namath. But I was very impressed. I certainly didn't envy Joe his girl friends or his ability to function on short sleep. Any way you defined it, Joe was in the saddle, quarterbacking a rising football team that would play

112

in and win the Super Bowl. I didn't resent Joe being a Super Bowl quarterback. I wanted to be one myself, to have that stature. We met a few times in my early years there, and I liked him. I still do, and I consider us friends. We've both become entrepreneurs, I suppose, but in different settings. Joe has merchandised the strong public image he established, the star aura. He arrived with it. Sonny Werblin, who made the deal for Namath originally, did a masterful job promoting that—the whole four-hundred-thousand-dollar contract bit, which was a phony figure but had tremendous appeal to the sports public. It just so happened, of course, that Joe had some good years as a quarterback, and when he climaxed all that by quarterbacking a Super Bowl championship, he was set for life. Nothing he did before or after that made any difference. He was invincible in show biz as a sure-enough legendary figure. When his personal performances and those of his team subsided, Joe no longer felt the need to keep his private life geared to all that razzmatazz, and he became what he is now, a really decent guy who seems happier being quieter.

Most of my connections in New York were not with football but with the business establishment. I was a regular at the 21 Club, and I enjoyed it. The business establishment is where my long-term world is. I found people there I could relate to, not on the jock-to-wealthy-fan basis, but as a young businessman meeting other businessmen. Now, that might be a hard gulp for a football fan who lives with his images of Frank Merriwells spending all their waking hours concocting a way to win the big game in the last thirty seconds. The professional football player's career is full of games that are won and lost in the last thirty seconds. It conditions his competitive life. But that is football. And I had another life.

I may as well unload my lecture here. A lot of people in professional football will smile at the so-called goer, or convince themselves he's greedy and lopsided because he tries to maximize himself—to discover what life has in the way of gratifications and rewards. And it isn't all spelled money, please believe me. But there are all too many football players who delude themselves into thinking that somebody is going to take care of them the rest of their lives. When they're playing and in the headlines, influential people invite them to lunch, the golf course, even set them up with good jobs in the off-season. And somebody is always going to come by with a deal that will make tons of money. Most of the time it doesn't, but sometimes it does. It's very easy for the football player to get a false security. It's very easy for us to translate the prominence we have as football players into a permanently giddy ride in the clouds where people fall over each other trying to make us comfortable and wealthy.

It's that kind of life for many football players for a while. I was enticed into that state of mind myself. And then I remembered some of the things the preacher said, and I also saw dead ends ahead in this coast-along mentality. So I decided to work at other careers. I wanted to get myself involved, informed, to make use not only of my celebrity but also of whatever brains and energy I was born with. I'm not unique by a long way. I think of people like Andy Russell of Pittsburgh, Merlin Olsen of the Rams, Grady Alderman of the Vikings, a lot of others.

But let's look at the pitfalls facing the athlete. He comes out of high school as a football star. What does that mean? It means he's taken out to dinner, taken to college and pro games by the big industrial leaders of his community. Colleges recruit him and tell him the campus will disintegrate without him. It's impossible for him to look on himself as anything less than Alexander the Great. He might get money under the table. He might not feel unclean about that at all because he knows others are getting it, so it's part of the approved system, endorsed by the legislature. He gets the idea that the world revolves around his being a football star, because good things suddenly fall on him. He gets boarded and fed at college. The essentials are all taken care of. Everybody caters to him. Free tickets are made available for everything from wrestling matches to fish fries. Girls are not exactly remote—in fact, they may wear him out. Everybody caters to him. He gets special privileges and special discounts. He not only gets these favors, but he observes that people actually feel honored to give them.

Is that the real world? Of course it isn't, but why should it end for him tomorrow, or next month, or next year? I have buddies in pro football who are convinced it will *never* end. They are indestructible. Never mind the actuarial tables, which in pro football are called the waiver lists. The pampered athlete has a hard time believing he might find his name there next year. The year after maybe, but never next year. In the meantime he is drawing good money and getting a lot of adoration. Important figures in finance, who would slit their throats before humbling themselves to a competitor, freely salaam to the famous jock. They do it because he has achieved in that great never-never land of big-time athletics. The businessman-patron might have dreamed about that when he was a boy, achievements that make his own seem very humdrum.

Now, all the athlete's blissful state of affairs depends on his playing football. He is making more money than any of his old high school or college pals. He comes into the locker room, and his uniform is waiting for him. Clean socks every day. Waiting for him. When he arrives at the airport, he might not even have to go through the lobby anymore. A bus takes him up to the plane. When he gets on the plane, attractive stewardesses start bringing him fruit trays, his choice of beverage, reading material if he feels cerebral, pillows if he feels sleepy. His baggage is taken care of.

For most pros, of course, all of this begins in earnest at the advanced age of twenty-one. At that point, millions of other twenty-one-year-olds are just beginning to learn a job. There's a difference between a pro football player learning his job at twenty-one and an insurance salesman learning his job at twenty-one. When he's thirty or thirty-five, the insurance salesman is in full command of his trade. If he's got energy and abilities, he can be moving toward the top. Big horizons open up.

The football player, when he's thirty or thirty-five, may be washed-up.

Bear in mind that the football player started at a salary the average guy hopes he may be making twenty years from now, if ever. From the age of fourteen, when be began being a football star, he's lived his teen-age life, young manhood, and adulthood where he's gotten everything he wanted by being able to block, run, or tackle. And he convinces himself that all his admirers and patrons really do like him for what he is, and that this pleasant sensation will continue after his playing days. One way or other, he will be taken care of because, well, he deserves that consideration, doesn't he?

Then one day the coach calls him into his office and tells him, "You've done a lot for this organization and for me, but I just don't think you can help us this year. I wish I didn't have to say that. Maybe I'm wrong and you can do it for another team. I'll do my best to try to place you."

That's about the way the conversation goes. But he probably isn't going to be placed. He's out of football. Maybe somebody will give a testimonial dinner for him, but probably not. Maybe he's done some sales work for a company or tried insurance, and maybe not. One of his old admirers may hire him, with great fanfare and a press party, because his name still means something.

But it won't mean a damn in a year or so if he can't produce in accordance with what they're paying him. If he goes into sales, his name will help for a while, but after that it's work and resourcefulness and contacts and knowing the business. If he hasn't worked at it, he's competing with people who are ten or fifteen years ahead of him, and he's just a rookie. His speaking appearances drop, and he gets less money for them. The endorsements drop, too.

There are also more subtle changes in his lifestyle, but ones that perhaps depress him more. He may have been a member of an athletic club. They loved to have him. Who's more athletic than a professional football player? He might have had a complimentary membership, or maybe he paid only a token fee. Six months into his retirement he gets a letter saying: "It has come to our attention that you are no longer an active player in the National Football League, on which your reduced-fee membership was contingent. Effective January 1 will you kindly remit $40 a month instead of the $12 you have been charged? We regret this inconvenience. There is no alternative open to us under the club's bylaws."

Is there any more devastating way to tell a guy he's an athletic has-been?

You can't blame the athletic club, of course. But what it all adds up to for the ex-pro football player, suddenly and rather mercilessly,

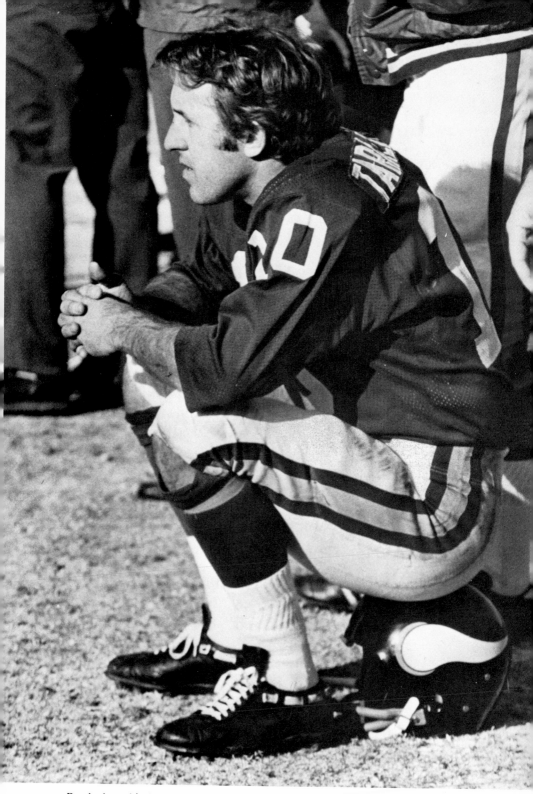

Perched on his helmet in what has become his most familiar sideline posture, Tarkenton views the battle between offensive series.

Tarkenton achieved a milepost in 1965 Pro Bowl, where he quarterbacked for the West team with Johnny Unitas (*left*), the hero of his high school days. (*Wide World Photos*)

John Gilliam, fleet and shrewd, was the receiver to whom Tarkenton looked in the critical situations for the four years of their Viking partnership from 1972 to 1975.

Chuck Foreman conducted a two-front war against Viking opponents in 1975, gaining more than 1,000 yards on the ground and catching 73 passes. He also scored 22 touchdowns, making it a season unequaled by an NFL running back in recent years.

Mick Tingelhoff's endurance and consistently high plane of performance made him one of the finest pro football centers of the era.

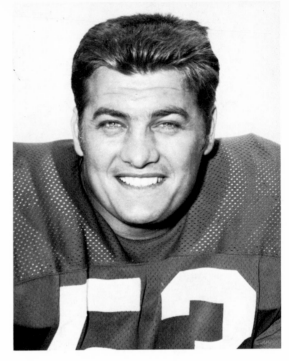

The bedrock of the Vikings' defense in the years they overpowered the NFL's Central Division and won three National Football Conference titles. From left: the defensive line's Jim Marshall, Alan Page, Carl Eller, and Gary Larsen.

Grady Alderman was Fran Tarkenton's closest friend in the ten years the two played together with the Vikings. He competed in the 1973 Super Bowl despite the knowledge of a cancerous condition that was removed two weeks later.

rry Burns' feisty wisdom and terror crawly animals make him a provoc-ive character for the Viking offen-e team he coaches.

Tarkenton views from the sidelines with Bud Grant.

While a restless Norm Van Brocklin licks his fingers, Tarkenton stares pensively awaiting a return to action in 1962, Tarkenton's second season with the Vikings.

Eyes probing downfield and arm cocked for delivery, Tarkenton wheels crossfield in the maneuver that made him notorious in his early seasons and ultimately a trailblazer in quarterbacking style. The fans and critics used to call it "scrambling." "What he's doing," says Coach Bud Grant today, "is buying time." Tarkenton's description: "You do what you have to to win."

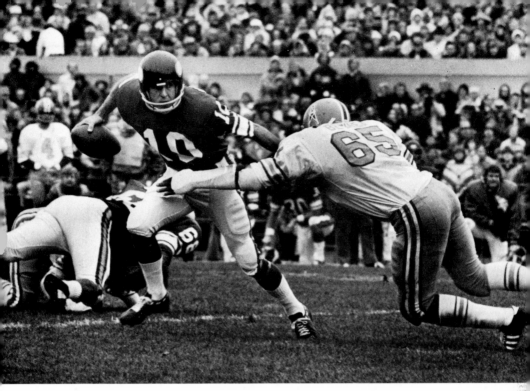

Pivoting, twisting, Tarkenton fights to escape from a Houston tackler.

Old pals Fran Tarkenton and fullback Bill Brown (30) embrace after a Viking touchdown against the Houston Oilers.

Always the referee's most enthusiastic adviser on goal-line plays, Tarkenton signifies a Viking touchdown against Green Bay.

The best of the season, as recognized by the Touchdown Club of Washington: Fran Tarkenton as Player of the Year, 1975, and running back Mike Thomas of Washington as Rookie of the Year.

The late Rev. Dallas Tarkenton, Francis' father, speaking to a group. His death while watching the Vikings' 1975 playoff game with Dallas on television was the climax of the toughest day in the quarterback's life.

Fran and Elaine Tarkenton's wedding, December 1960.

Elaine Tarkenton and the masked quarterback admire their first-born, Angela, who arrived weighing slightly more than nine pounds in November 1964.

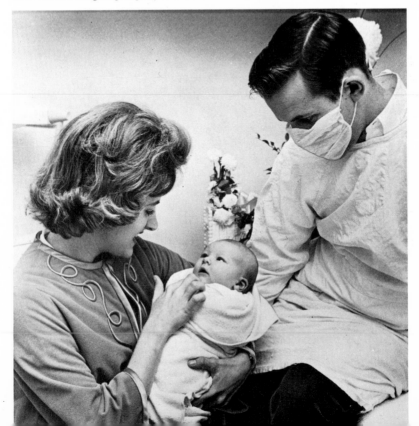

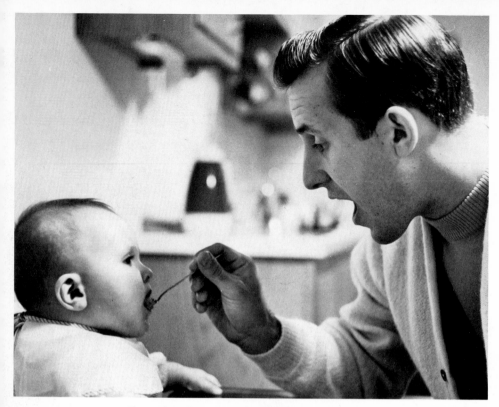

Fran takes time out to feed his hungry daughter.

Fran and Angela, age two, with the family's German shepherd, Duke.

Grant and Tarkenton plot the next offensive series on the sideline while Foreman watches the play.

Tarkenton, in another characteristic sideline pose, watches the Viking defense as he waits to go back on the attack.

is reality. One of my very best friends in football prepared himself for his retirement as methodically as he could, so that he could step immediately into a full-time job, paying good money. But when the athletic club announcement came, it was still traumatic. It hit him like a bolo punch. The emotional shock is that heavy when a guy leaves the happy fishbowl he's been playing in all this time. Now, take that condition and compound it ten and twenty times by a sudden drop in earning power, and the sudden discovery by the formerly catered-to celebrity that at the age of thirty-five he's got to get up at 7 A.M. to go to work—and work his rear end off *just to learn a business.*

Well, it's a staggering adjustment. A lot of guys aren't prepared to make it in a way that will give them anything close to the satisfactions they experienced as athletes. But they could have even more if they built carefully and intelligently on their football careers.

Why do I dwell on this, when such problems don't affect more than a fraction of 1 per cent of the people? I dwell on it because (a) millions of people lavish an enormous and, I'll admit, a disproportionate amount of attention on that less than 1 per cent and (b) I have been denigrated here and there as a capitalist.

I admit being a capitalist. I'm a capitalist without apology. I believe the so-called work ethic can be distorted, but by and large it is very defensible and very much at the heart of what makes a country like the United States an exciting place in which to live.

I am not obsessed by money. But I don't find the making of money either sinister or irrelevent when it is a reward for effort, risk, legitimate capitalization, or ingenuity. A long time ago I decided I wanted several sources of income, some of them not related to football, and none of them dependent on each other. This would both broaden my life and make me less vulnerable to the accidents and flukes of a football career.

I envisioned another ten years of football, but I was never going to make that an end in itself. I shuddered to read Mickey Mantle's testament to the remembered joys of a life gone by and irretrievable. Mickey was one of the great ballplayers of all time and a worthy person, I know. But I just can't agree with his "I sit and dream about being in Yankee Stadium hitting home runs; it was the best part of my life, and it's over." The words may not be exact, but I think that was the sentiment.

I say "No!" The best part of the athlete's life, at least the most important part, should be ahead. He may have made more money as an athlete, had more pure fun. But what he does with himself thereafter should be a measure of his *response* to a bigger and more demanding world. All right, maybe the home-run slugger will use the same putdown on my perception of life beyond the locker room. And the fan might say, "Tarkenton isn't typical." Correct. I have received more attention, made more money than the average athlete, had more opportunity. I have tried to use it creatively. A prominent name can put you in front of a television camera. But it won't keep you there indefinitely unless you try to understand the business and work at being informative, entertaining, or whatever it demands.

And so it was not a coincidence that I began diversifying myself as a businessman after I got to New York. The whole environment was alive, not only for that but also for the athlete ready to embark on a new phase of his career. I suppose to me initially it was the whole aura of the town. It's huge and in constant ferment. It has great buildings and the full spectrum of humanity's moods and behavior. It's unpredictable and arty and vast and wealthy, ugly and poor, greedy and generous. And it has Yankee Stadium, the one stadium in the world that had any special meaning to the kid who collected bubble-gum cards.

Playing in that stadium every Sunday was an occasion in itself. The crowd was special. It was aware and responsive. It expressed itself wildly and profanely and even proudly. There was more pride than a lot of detractors are willing to admit. And after the game a limousine downtown, the restaurants, the most exciting in the world. You might sit down and Lee Radziwill was at the next table and Bobby Kennedy was over there and Teddy a few chairs away. It was meeting people that certainly were no better than people I grew up with, but people who were doing things on the world's platforms and in its arenas. Is there any reason why quarterbacks shouldn't be excited by that, any less than tourists?

I can't imagine any place as the world's capital except New York in fall. The shows are opening, the new fashions are in, the vacationers are back, and the football season is on. I come back to the fans at the ball park. They are as memorable in some ways as the ball games. I think the New York fans are more demonstrative than any fans I ever played for. If you do anything worthwhile, they shake the stadium with their noise and their appreciation. You can't walk down the street during a football season and accept the stock portrait of New York as a coldhearted town. Truck drivers and garbage collectors yell to you, "Hey, man, we're with you Sunday." Just like Gopher Prairie before the ball game Friday night. And this is supposed to be rockhearted, soulless New York City. There's a real and enduring warmth in New York that the ballplayer needs, an outpouring of the honest emotion that he lives on in a very emotional game.

Then there are the glamour people, of course. The high-profile guys in the communications business. For the athlete, that's supposed to be the bottom-line virtue of New York, the exposure he gets to the media powerhouses. There's certainly opportunity there, although the "star quality" doesn't need New York to thrive so much now with television blanketing the country.

New York as a world communications center means a fellow like Howard Cosell. My relationship with Howard has always been good. We con each other pretty well. I figured I had to do something like that in self-defense. In our first interview, Howard came on with something like "Tarkenton, they say you can't throw, they say your legs are giving out, they say your wife is going to leave you, your kids don't like you, and you can't win. What do you have to say to that?"

Well, I began to feel pretty sick. But I figured if I fainted, Howard could always claim he raised the dead, which would have been a network first but not necessarily a first for Howard. Anyway, that was pretty much how he came on, and I know millions of people can't hack him, although they wouldn't think of missing Monday night football. But I've always found the picture of the overbearing, sarcastic Howard Cosell to be mostly a front. To me he's a great dinner companion, very human and stimulating when the façade falls away. He digs into the ballplayers now and then, yes. But most of the time I don't think it's very damaging. I think he understands communications as well as any announcer. I think he knows what sells. He has a style and rhetoric that are unique, and he knows that is important in his business because too many guys in the trade sound like the next one, saying the same things. He has a different style of interviewing, different not only in the questions he asks—more pointed, sometimes offensive—but also in that different voice, which a lot of people can't stand but remember anyway. So you may get millions of people saying, "I can't stand Howard Cosell," but he's one of the few they talk about. I'm speaking of television announcers who are full-time, purely professional announcers. You also have a lot of jocks in the business, like Fran Tarkenton of NBC. Some are good, some not so good. And I better stop right there.

But I do think a guy like Cosell, who is controversial and a turmoil-stirrer, broadens the fan's interest in a televised football game as an occasion, a couple of hours of entertainment. Howard doesn't really know much about the strategy of the game, for all his erudition. Most of the former-jock announcers, in fact, don't know much about the strategy of the game if they've been out of it for three or four years. Because almost all of them have other jobs, they can't stay current. Many times they're guessing just as much as the fans, and when they get to that point they might use terms like "Well, that pass lacked precision."

How would any announcer know what constituted precision on that play, unless he knew every route every receiver ran, and what the defense was doing as distinct from what it seemed to be doing? Also, if he's not careful, he might completely overlook the fact that a big, hairy tackle just about disemboweled the quarterback as he was releasing the ball.

It's a trap I will probably run into myself somewhere down the line. The microphone is a demanding and risky instrument. It insists on instant wisdom and it is not always patient with moderation. But whatever other problems he has, the technical expert on a football telecast certainly can give the viewer insight. And if he can do that and bring the fan into the game, not only with his knowledge but also with his enthusiasm and his command, he performs a very worthwhile service. The best I've seen by those definitions are Joe Garagiola and Bill Russell. I think they have added an enormous amount to any game with their style and presence.

In any case, New York brought me in contact with the network and syndicated people, the movers, the show-business royalty, and the business heavyweights. I don't think they altered me or turned me into a Broadway or *Social Register* character. I simply enjoyed the excitement, the conversation, both serious and jocular, with people like Kurt Vonnegut, George Plimpton, John Glenn, Neal Walsh, a New York commissioner, and so many others.

And way beyond that, I enjoyed playing football with the New York Giants. It was a totally different environment for me. Wellington Mara's teams, of course, are very much all-in-the-family teams. It's a sociable organization, not the best managed, by any means, but one with a great deal of humanity. The locker room before a game, for instance, was a whole new structure for me. The place usually was crowded with ten or twelve priests, official family, and miscellaneous greeters. Lord knows what all. Good people, mostly. I never minded them, and I enjoyed a lot of them. The whole atmosphere was relaxed. No yelling, no screaming, gnashing teeth, or name-calling. For the first time in my professional career, I actually felt joy going to the ball park.

I don't suppose the Giants expected me to convert them into the colossus of football in one season, or even five. We nearly made it to the division championship in 1970. But I think the most demanding critic would agree that the Giants did not have the wherewithal to win championships in those seasons, no matter what the quarterback did.

I also think that the most critically bad decision the Giants made in the 1960s, at a time when they were in the upper echelon of pro football, was to trade away Sam Huff, the middle linebacker. You get several schools of thought in pro football about Sam. He was among the first of the glamorized defensive players. "The Violent World of Sam Huff" business and all of that. Partly for that reason it got to be fashionable to call Sam an overrated football player. I'm sure he never was. He was an outstanding football player, and he was magnetic for the fans and a catalyst for the team. I think the Giants' decline began almost exactly on the day they decided to trade Sam to the Washington Redskins.

The year before I got there, the Giants finished 2–12. Their assets in my first season included some very distinguished football players who were close to retirement and either in eclipse or nearing it. People like Jim Katcavage, Del Shofner, Vince Costello, and Darrell Dess had done big things in the National Football League, but you can't do them forever. There were three good offensive linemen: Greg Larson, Pete Case, and Willie Young. Joe Morrison wasn't a very picturesque running back or very big or very fast, but he had a tremendous will and adaptability. Whether he had to grub or squirm or roll, Joe got the yardage. Tucker Frederickson was a big back of great potential who couldn't escape injury. Aaron Thomas was a competent pass receiver.

And then there was Homer Jones. Homer was the fastest guy I ever saw in a football suit, without question. An Olympic-class burner. I don't know how many years he knocked around in pro and semipro football, but by the time we got together, the program listed him at twenty-nine. He admitted to me once he was thirty-six, and I actually believe he may have been closer to forty. He was 6-2 and weighed 235 pounds and ran like Secretariat. He didn't have much refinement as a receiver, and sometimes he missed the easy passes. But if he ever got a step on a defensive back, you couldn't keep him in the stadium. I lived on Homer Jones that first year. We finished 7–7, and he scored thirteen touchdowns. He didn't have particularly good hands, and if he wasn't the obvious receiver, he tended to get lazy. He'd take a step off the line and stop. But if he ever caught that little out-ball on the sidelines and the cornerback missed him, he was gone. Pfft.

He was also a delightful character. We were playing an exhibition against the Redskins in Raleigh, North Carolina, and I started scrambling. Homer ran his pattern two or three times, then stopped to watch me run mine. I spotted him and waved him to the right sideline. He ran to the right sideline. I couldn't throw because I was under pressure, so I waved him to the left sideline. When he got there

I had to dodge again, so I waved him a third time, toward the center of the field. Homer just stood there, waving back to me. It was like we were saying good-bye at the depot.

A little later Freddie Dryer came along. Freddie was and is a defensive end. He is now employed by the Los Angeles Rams, where he has reluctantly taken on some respectability. Somebody called Freddie the football hippie, which he never protested. They have also called him a genius, a vagabond, one of the world's great mimics, and the Emmett Kelly of pro football. I think he admits to all of them. The fact that he is also one of the best defensive ends in pro football seems academic to a lot of people, including Freddie. When I knew him, he never wore anything but a T-shirt and jeans. In my last year with the Giants I was spending Christmas Eve at home in Atlanta with my family when the telephone rang about midnight. I picked up the phone and the guy says, "Hi, Tark." I was thinking who on earth would know my telephone number, but the operator interrupted by telling the guy, "Will you deposit sixty-five cents, please?" So I hear "Boing, boing, boing," and the guy comes on again and says, "Hi, Tark." Naturally, it's Freddie.

"Freddie," I said, "Merry Christmas, how are you?" He says he's down the road fifty miles, and do I mind company? Freddie goes everywhere in his van. He used to live out of it, even when he moved to supersophisticated Los Angeles. I tell him, "Come ahead, you can stay here." So at 1 A.M. in comes Freddie Dryer. I've got the house all decorated for the kids, and Freddie walks in majestically with two other guys. I said, "Bring your bags on in, Freddie." He said, "Tark, I'm traveling light. This is it." He came with a T-shirt and a pair of jeans, and he stayed a week.

Attempted Miracle at Yankee Stadium

8

All the man said about the New York Giants' football audiences was that they were responsive and passionate. He never said they were especially kind or even smart.

What would a nice and knowledgeable crowd be doing singing "Good-bye, Allie" in four-part harmony in the summer of 1969? Or hanging Francis Tarkenton in effigy a couple of years later?

"I just characterized the Giants' crowds as great," Tarkenton said. "I didn't claim they weren't misguided."

In the make-believe gallery of his private shrine, the football fan will switch a light on this portrait or that. A flashing caption will zing through his head, explaining the hero's right to such veneration. If the light falls on Gale Sayers, the fan will recite instantly: "Most dramatic runner of his time; tremendous acceleration and command of the field." If the light trains on Gino Marchetti, the fan (the middle-aged fan) will react with Pavlovian predictability: "First of the great pass-rushing ends who glamorized defense."

And when the beam settles on the Prince Valiant coiffure of Francis Tarkenton, how will the fan read the portrait? "Record-setting passer," he will say. "Pioneer among the moving quarterbacks. A man who gave you the impression there was no situation in football he hadn't seen, or couldn't find some way to salvage."

Yankee Stadium, and the other playgrounds where the New York Giants were required to perform, provided that text. With the

Giants, Tarkenton became the central character in a soap opera, caroming from crisis to crisis, manhandled by fate and a cast of sandbaggers that changed each week. He learned new responses and refined old ones. He discovered what a defense might yield to him on a wet field that it might not on a dry one. He developed an unwritten book on rival players, a glossary of frequencies and tendencies. It might be valueless for entire games. But someday, in a moment impossible to forecast, it would leap out at him with some clue or instruction to produce a first down or spare him annihilation.

The process slickened him and toughened him. While Tarkenton gained new admiration each week for the principle that winning teams tend to create great quarterbacks, his sense of self-reliance deepened every game. His recognition of defenses was now instantaneous. The rush of bodies downfield had long since ceased to be a blur of disordered color and clashing purposes. He could cut up the field now, ignore whole sections of it, ignore both the friendlies and the hostiles who just wouldn't figure in the play. He gambled and he grubbed, he could throw deep three straight times and then lob a balloon ball and all but float it to a flaring halfback. The play might have looked off-balance and clumsy, but usually it got a first down. Like the enduring politician, Tarkenton learned the art of the possible, the tactical compromise.

But because he still insisted on moving with the football, creating opportunities where none existed, or trying to, the watchdogs of football decorum kept calling him names. He was still a scrambler, a .500 quarterback, exciting but a nonchampion. It was a reputation he sometimes attacked with ridicule, sometimes with strident logic. Later he just deflected it with vaporous contempt. How much did he have to worry about name-calling and the judgment of cocktail-party purists? He had arrived in New York as a $50,000-a-year quarterback. Five years later he had expanded that to $125,000, and he did it by quarterbacking as many victories for the New York Giants as any quarterback had a rational right to, up to and possibly including the watershed year of 1971. It was then that his frustrations—did somebody use the term arrogance?—led to a contract dispute and his second term in Minnesota.

To the Giants he brought his wits and a maturity beyond his six years' experience. Yet he willingly acknowledged a debt to Giants' coach Allie Sherman for hastening the process. Despite his near-championship successes of the early 1960s, Sherman was unpopular with the New York football public and most of the press when Tarkenton arrived. No coach who experiences a 2–12 season is going to be unanimously idolized. Yet Sherman's situation had deteriorated to the point where he was in serious danger of losing his job. Tarkenton could feel that stress in his daily encounters with the little man who had the appearance and sometimes the scholastic manner of a geography professor. But he taught Tarkenton more technical football than he had learned at Minnesota. From the beginning, Tarkenton liked him, and respected his intelligence and devotion.

Over his fifteen years in pro football, five men have struck Tarkenton as belonging to a presidium of supercoaches, the ones who could enter into any coaching situation and within a couple of years make winning a permanent property of their stewardship. They were Vince Lombardi, Paul Brown, Don Shula, Bud Grant, and Tom Landry. Sherman obviously fell short of that group in impact and quality, but he was a big-league coach, all right. What Tarkenton admired most about him was his decency as a human being in a situation of stress. Every week during his first 2½ seasons with the Giants he would meet with Sherman at the coach's home to frame a plan for the coming game. They would review film and discuss personnel, their own and their opponents'. In his most pressing hours, Sherman never undermined another person in his quarterback's presence. Sherman made errors in generalship on the sidelines, and certainly he made errors in evaluating personnel. And while a family-conscious Irishman and sentimentalist like Wellington Mara gave him as much loyalty as he could expect, there was no way Sherman could survive the catastrophe of an all-losing exhibition season leading up to the 1969 season.

That whole summer was a congress of misery. The Giants had mediocrities at most positions. Organizationally they were reduced to skulking around their own hometown because the toasted gallants in New York in 1969 were the Jets and Joe Namath. The Jets were the football champions of the universe, but even more importantly, New York City. And one day in New Haven the Jets and the Giants met in an exhibition. Under the circumstances that prevailed then, it was a game that almost had to be scheduled by Howard Cosell, or NBC, or whoever was the most influential patron of the old American Football League and the Jets. The Giants were reduced to bungling, amateurish foils for the main-eventers, the role the Washington Generals play to the Harlem Globetrotters. At that, the Jets may merely have exposed the condition rather than created it. The Giants played another exhibition in Montreal, and it was worse there. For the first time, "Good-bye, Allie" was rendered in French.

By then the team's morale had pretty much bottomed, partly as a result of some bizarre staff moves that reflected, in Tarkenton's eyes, the most grievous weakness of Mara as a football executive.

"He's really a decent guy," Tarkenton said later, "a man with a very strong Irish temper but a man who really loves football and has concern for his players and coaches. He has taken care of them to a fault. That was the problem. I don't think he has realized it was a fault, but it has hurt his organization because it has meant the accumulation of just a lot of dead wood. When I joined the Giants, some friends who love to mix their metaphors said, 'Just keep your nose clean and don't rock the boat.' And I guess that was about the situation in essence."

Neither Tarkenton nor most of his teammates could quite keep pace with the hysterics involving assistant coach Jim Trimble, who has a sizable number of friends in the game but did not have a great many on the Giants' team in 1969. Trimble had been the offensive line coach in the mid-1960s. But after Jack Patera left the defensive line coaching job to join Grant in Minnesota, Trimble was installed as his replacement.

"He was preparing our team for a game in the Yale Bowl against Namath and the Jets," a Giant player recalled. "Bob Lurtsema was our best defensive lineman, and that year we had a big rookie lineman from Princeton named Tim McCann, a free agent who never played at all. We were in the locker room before the game, and Trimble comes up to talk to the defensive line. 'Lurts,' he says, 'I'm not gonna start you today. I'm gonna start Timmy McCann. I'm giving Timmy McCann the nod.' And he nodded. Then he said, 'The reason I'm doing that is because, as you may know, Timmy played for four years at Princeton and here we are at Yale and Timmy knows the terrain.' "

The news failed to touch off any teamwide jubilation. So Timmy McCann knew the Yale Bowl terrain. Well, that just might give the Giants a huge psychological advantage over Joe Namath, Matt Snell, Emerson Boozer, and Larry Grantham. But if the Giants were overwhelmed, the bookies weren't.

Trimble resumed his pregame motivational. "I've been watching that rascal Namath," he said. "So I'm gonna start Joe Szczecko at the other defensive tackle because of his speed."

This announcement was evidently intended to dissolve all remaining anxiety in the locker room. Szczecko was acquired on waivers from the Atlanta Falcons. He stood 5-feet-9 and weighed 240 pounds. He had the general contours of a fifty-five-gallon oil drum and seemed to have comparable mobility.

"I've been watching that rascal Namath," Trimble repeated, "and every time he jabs his right foot forward and takes the snap, that's when I want Joe to jump between the center's legs and grab it!"

The strategy failed to achieve total success, the Giants falling behind by four touchdowns in the first twenty minutes. They did not improve substantially thereafter. Tarkenton's best recollection of the afternoon centered on his team's mathematical quirks. The Giants lined up with ten men on the field five times and with nine men once.

When they lost to the Steelers in Montreal later in the exhibition season, Mara decided to remove Sherman. In this situation it was the human impulse for a troubled owner to look for a replacement popular enough with the players, the press, and the masses to silence the pelting ridicule the Giants had been taking for weeks.

The anointment fell on Alex Webster. He had been an immensely popular fullback with the Giants in the 1950s and 1960s, a man who would run through exploding shrapnel to get an extra yard. He was bulky and guileless and straightforward, and everybody loved old

Alex. Although an assistant on the Giants' staff, he would not have been your basic first, second, or third choice for head coach in any guessing pool. According to all accounts, however, the most difficult obstacle in appointing Webster was locating him to break the news. It took some research in view of his pastime of splitting a few ales at the more genial pubs after the ball game. Mara's first telephone call to Webster's house was promptly misinterpreted by his wife, Louise, who had heard about the dismissal of Allie Sherman. When Mara called and identified himself, the lady broke into tears. As a long-standing Irishman, Mara was not completely foreign to emotional scenes. He calmed the lady with great gentility, assuring her nothing bad had happened to her husband or was even contemplated.

Mara's field scouts finally located Webster and informed him he was wanted for an audience with the company president. Webster shaved, changed clothes, and presented himself. Like his wife, he was prepared for eviction.

"Alex," Mara said, "I want you to be the head coach of the New York Giants."

Webster pondered Mara's words with a clear and honest stupefaction. He had never visualized himself as head coach of the Giants, a viewpoint shared by most of his associates. Alex was a red-blooded football man, no doubt, with a good mind. But when you saw him as an archtype, you thought about the gnarled field sergeant willing to take on tanks barehanded. He was therefore beloved by all of the privates and corporals, who couldn't, and also by the commanders, who knew they didn't grow many like that anymore. You didn't think of Alex as the man running the war himself.

Mara repeated the news. "We had to let Allie go, you know, and we want you to take his place."

The coach-designee of the New York Giants now spoke.

"Mr. Mara," he said, "are you shittin' me?"

The president of the ball club assured him his fears were baseless.

Webster recovered in good time and began performing his first duties of command. He informed the coaching assistants, his beer-drinking buddies, of the passing of the torch. One of his first calls went to Roosevelt Brown, the great bruin of a man with whom

Webster had played for years. He was now the offensive line coach. "Rosie," Webster said, "I'm the new head coach."

Roosevelt Brown registered instant skepticism. "You're drunk, Alex," he said, and hung up the phone.

In the week prior to the opening of the 1969 season, the Giants enjoyed the same kind of expectations borne by the first inmates of Alcatraz. Their exhibition season had been a travesty. They were shaky at most positions. They were now coached by a man who willingly confessed to being a nongenius, and their opening opponent was the Minnesota Vikings.

Minnesota had won the Central Division championship the previous season, almost solely on the pulverizing line play of its defensive front four, now coached by the Giants' expatriate, Jack Patera. When they arrived in Yankee Stadium that week, the Vikings were reputed to be the next superpower of pro football, or at least the next superdefense, which amounted to the same thing in those years.

The Giants had recorded 7–7 seasons in 1967 and 1968 with Tarkenton at quarterback. It was certainly more than they had grounds to expect, given the arid state of their roster. And untold grief was forecast for them in 1969, beginning with the Minnesota Vikings. From the very start, the Vikings butchered the Giants' undernourished offense, forcing Tarkenton to adopt the techniques of a fugitive from the Inquisition. He ran most of the plays on quick counts, threw off-balance, on tiptoes, on the dead run, and a couple of times into the stands. Carl Eller, Alan Page, Jim Marshall, and Gary Larsen so depressed the Giants' offensive line it was one of the only games of his career in which Tarkenton honestly considered it a moral victory to get rid of a handoff. But in those years the Viking attack was a very bland instrument. Minnesota fans howled appreciatively when the offense left the field so that the defense could enter and get to the serious business of scoring.

The Giants thus trailed by only thirteen points heading into the final six minutes. With Tarkenton mobbed on every play, the situation clearly was beyond rescue. The Giants tried every protective device known to technology at the time, stopping short of bear traps and fragmentation bombs. Merely to throw the ball—let alone get it over the line of scrimmage—Tarkenton was forced to several extremities.

"In order to get a pass off," he remembers, "I would tell Greg Larson at center to double up with the guard on Page. I'd double on Marshall with the left tackle and the fullback. Against Eller I told the tight end to stay in and block with the right tackle. That meant I was doubling on everybody on their defensive line except Gary Larsen, who almost always stayed at home looking for draws. So I never sent more than three people out on pass plays—one back, the split end, and the flanker. Just three. And the Vikings are sitting back there with three linebackers and four defensive backs. In the meantime we've got six people assigned to block three of their defensive linemen. I've never seen anything like it."

It got worse. "It was almost hopeless in the fourth quarter," Tarkenton recalls. "It got to be third down and seventeen on our forty-three, some absurd situation like that, and we're behind by thirteen points. I stood there counting the cadence on that play and I could see Eller practically salivating he was so eager and ready to rush, and I said to myself, 'Your daddy was so right telling you to enter a seminary.'"

They shagged Tarkenton twice across the field before he planted his right foot and threw. He has never pretended aiming that pass. He has never denied Eller's allegation that it was impossible for Tarkenton at that particular angle and posture to see a man downfield. Eller was perfectly right, Tarkenton admitted later. He didn't see a Giant receiver, and he wasn't throwing to one. His target was larger. "All I saw was the stadium seats beyond the end zone," he concedes. "I just threw in that direction. I did that because I was scared to death of Eller. I honestly don't think he wanted to tackle me. I think he planned to eat me."

The ball came down fifty-five yards away in the vicinity of two Viking defensive backs. There was one other object on the field, Butch Wilson, a Giant receiver lying flat on his back and therefore powerless. Unhurried, the Viking defenders both batted the ball away, all according to the manual. The ball fell to the ground and onto the chest of the bemused receiver, Wilson. With nothing better to do, he seized the ball before it rolled off his chest, and was credited with a completed pass.

Having crumpled the Viking defense, Tarkenton produced a touchdown a few moments later on a pass to Don Herrmann, and the Giants had suddenly been exhumed. The sight so unsettled the Vikings they fumbled on the next series. The Giants recovered and, in the final minute, won, 24–23.

Knowledgeable Giant fans thundered their congratulations to Mara for his spasm of genius in hiring Alex Webster.

For a while Mara might have been inclined to join the applause. Lifted by the new brotherhood and the tension-free atmosphere that flowed from Sherman's departure and Webster's disposition, the Giants won three of their first four. But they bombed out for the next seven weeks, during which time Webster and Joe Walton, the offensive backfield coach, overhauled the Giants' standard pro offense and installed a series of man-in-motion plays, spreads, rollouts, and I-sets in the backfield. These delighted opponents for a month or so by confusing the Giants even more than their opponents. Yankee Stadium galleries roasted both the Giants' offense and Tarkenton, very knowledgeably and very sincerely. But by the end of the year the strangeness had disappeared from the new formations, the Giants pounded St. Louis and Cleveland, both heavily favored, and concluded with a 6–8 record.

In three seasons the New York Giants with Francis Tarkenton at quarterback had won twenty games and lost twenty-two. The NFL classicists around the country nodded as though the numbers had verified their judgments. Tarkenton was a .500 quarterback, no doubt about it. Well, make that a .476 quarterback.

Better-informed voices, especially those familiar with the pre-Tarkenton Giants, maintained that he was worth the money Mara was paying him if he did nothing more than keep them respectable at .500, which appeared to be the long-haul limits of the Giants' resources. "In a couple of those seasons," said Greg Larson, the respected center, "we wouldn't have won a game without Tarkenton."

Before the 1970 season Mara dealt the suddenly aged Homer

Jones to Cleveland for Ron Johnson, a splendid young running back from Michigan, and Jim Kanicki, for several years a dependable on the Cleveland defensive line. The trade, with a few other personnel changes and the maturing of some of the young people on the team, transformed the New York Giants into a contender for the Super Bowl in 1970, although logic insists to this day it was all a statistical mistake attributable to some malfunctioning cogwheel in the computer. The Giants just weren't that kind of football team, the contrite computer now claims. If the record shows New York winning nine games in 1970, it had to be a mechanical error or a misplaced printout. But the record insists the deed was done.

And while the town never quite stirred itself to swarm Fifth Avenue with confetti and brass bands in honor of the quarterback, Tarkenton had nevertheless become a celebrity. His easy presence in front of a television camera made him the ideal talk-show host. If Namath merchandised his furs and teeth and libido, Tarkenton could peddle his cerebrum, which sounds terrible but does prove that television watchers are willing to be entertained by a smart young man using his brains. In his opening show, in fact, he surrounded himself with black athletes and spent a half hour probing the status of the black in big-time sports.

After ten years of locker rooms in the National Football League, Francis A. Tarkenton was also moving toward the board room—his own. He had real estate in Minnesota and Georgia, and endorsements all the way from spaghetti and starchy shirts to supersonic airplanes.He began capitalizing his own companies in the late 1960s. Some of the earlier ones were hothouse ventures, like a prospective fast-food restaurant chain. For several years he was seriously involved with a federally aided learning-center project for minorities and the disadvantaged. By then Tarkenton had five years of training in advertising and promotion with Batten, Barton, Durstine, and Osborne and the Coca-Cola Company.

"All of that was valuable," he said of his training experience with the advertising and merchandising giants. "It gave me a look at marketing opportunities I never knew existed and taught me about technique. But much as I admire the Coca-Cola Company, for example, I recognized that there wasn't much I could ever do to affect it in any meaningful way. It was just too big and too well programmed. So with other people who shared my motivation I moved in the direction of finding or creating the kind of business where I definitely could matter. And this ultimately led to the creation of Behavioral Systems, which has been retained by more than seventy business firms to improve their production by literally getting people to feel better about their work and company, and therefore doing a better job."

Tarkenton recognized the pitfalls of moving into the business world on his own. "The problem I have with life," he said, "is that I have more things to do and want to do than I have time to do. I spread myself around when I was in New York, but I never had the feeling of being harassed by outside activity. When it came time to concentrate on football, I blocked the rest out of my mind. The first thing I have to do in any activity I get involved in is to believe in what I'm doing, and to know what I'm doing. You can overdo endorsements. I know. I have. Capitalizing on your name and prominence isn't going to top your list of doing creative business. But it's money fairly arrived at. It's also an ego ride. It measures the credit you have with the sellers and with the public. You may say that doesn't sound particularly noble, and you are right. But it is reality. When I talk about actually doing and creating, I'm talking about a deeper involvement. You can get it on the football field, of course. You can also get it in a van I lived in for sixteen to eighteen hours a day several years ago, motoring around the South and finding out what assembly-line workers were doing and saying. As a big-league quarterback I might not have had to do that in the off-season. But I loved it. It put me eyeball-to-eyeball with people whose lives I thought I could enhance by building a closer link between them and their companies. And when we—the company I helped form—were able to do that and demonstrate that we were doing it, the feeling was every bit as exciting as anything I have experienced on the football field."

The gum-card collector never really lost the family evangelism, merely widened its parameters. When Tarkenton plunged, it was with a full percussion of exploding bubbles. Nothing tepid or half-way. He was zealous as the after-supper orator at kid banquets in the early 1960s, zealous twenty yards behind the line of scrimmage, and superzealous when selling one of his own visions—or selling himself, for that matter.

Onto this he grafted a new urbanity, a required garment for a quarterback-capitalist in the capitalist capital of America. His hair lengthened in tone with the times, his shoes bore Gucci labels, and he discovered that a man could enjoy a temperate Scotch without seceding from the society of the redeemed.

To spare him the damage of being permanently Easternized, a covey of Republicans from Georgia proposed that Tarkenton could best alter the course of humanity by becoming the lieutenant gover-nor of Georgia. Specifically, they invited him to consider running for lieutenant governor of Georgia on the Republican ticket, which is not quite the same as being the lieutenant governor.

Republican losers are not entirely unknown in Georgia. At the time, Tarkenton tentatively judged his chances of getting to the Super Bowl with the Giants to be better than getting into the Georgia statehouse with the Republicans, although this was hardly his sole criterion in arriving at a decision. Politics had tweaked him for years. The opportunity it offered to create an impact on the times appealed to him. He was also at the stage in his career when a public response to his work and his presence was still important to him—and if you can't get it from big-time athletics anymore, or decide not to, politics and entertainment are two of the very few alternatives. Two years before, in 1968, he had done a testimonial for Richard Nixon in his campaign in Georgia. But while Tarkenton was an economic con-servative, his social attitudes were more liberal, and he had no trou-ble from time to time supporting certain Democrats, which is not a hard decision for a young businessman in Georgia.

Although flattered by the Republican delegation's attention, Tar-kenton said he was inclined to turn down the offer, one of the unstated reasons being that he was drawing one hundred thousand dollars for five months of football.

He then received a letter from a prominent national Republican, accentuating the rewards of a life in politics. It was signed by Richard Nixon, the President of the United States. Not long after, the Georgia emissaries escorted Tarkenton into the office of the Vice President of the United States, Spiro Agnew, who added his witness to the fruits of a life in politics.

There was no question about it. The nation's two highest government executives thought Francis Tarkenton might make an excellent Republican politician. And Francis Tarkenton, being Francis Tarkenton, did not necessarily disagree.

In the long run, it boiled down to the system of rewards. With the Giants, Tarkenton could pretty well predict the size of his next payroll check, and the numbers were attractive. For a Republican politician in Georgia, the prospects were considerably less ripe. In addition, Tarkenton reasoned, one of the things Georgia did not need at that stage in its economic growth was a scrambling lieutenant governor.

He declined the invitation with thanks.

The football statisticians may not record 1970 as Tarkenton's finest year, but the professionals, and certainly the New York Giants' coaching staff, might. It was a team that had lost seven in a row in 1969, but a year later it came within the final game of the season of qualifying for the playoffs. Repeatedly the quarterback brought them back from defeat with his head, arm, feet, or brass. Tarkenton hardly did it as a solitary Captain Marvel. Ron Johnson gained over a thousand yards. Spider Lockhart was a great defensive back. Bob Tucker, forced to begin his pro career with Pottstown of the semipro league in a horrible miscarriage of the scouting systems, had become a Giant and caught passes in every conceivable posture. Tucker Frederickson played on days when he should have been under ether. Pete Case, Greg Larson, and Willie Young on the offensive line nourished the kind of attack that for the first time made use of Tarkenton's mobility in a calculated way. He was armed with rollouts and option patterns intended to give him maximum time to probe the defense. And his scrambles no longer attracted groans of heresy. Other quarterbacks, notably Roger Staubach in Dallas, were doing it as much as Tarkenton.

The infidel had acquired that ultimate stamp of respectability: imitators.

The Giants lost their opening games to the Bears and Dallas. Almost by way of displaying their versatility, they then lost to New Orleans, proving they could also blow them to patsies. Wellington Mara addressed the squad a couple of days later in Yankee Stadium. It was an adult talk, in which the owner of the team expressed his undiminished respect for his players, recalling their finish in 1969 and declaring they were good enough to win a championship. He neither threatened nor swung from the locker-room doors. It was the kind of talk that could sting a thinking football player in a positive way. Duly aroused, the Giants won six in a row, including a game in which they overtook the Washington Redskins in the fourth quarter after trailing 33–14. They lost to the Eagles but won three more and, in the final game of the season, faced the Los Angeles Rams with a chance to enter the 1970 National Football League playoffs.

It was that day of deliverance the small black print on the back of the Wheaties boxes had foretold for Francis Tarkenton twenty years before. It was also what Wellington Mara had told his downcast football team just three months before.

But somebody forgot to tell the Los Angeles Rams.

They buried the Giants and all of their illusions by a score too grisly to relate.

It was as close as the Giants had come to a title in nearly a decade. But, in ways then impossible to foresee, it marked the beginning of the end of the New York Giant-Francis Tarkenton partnership. The Giants in 1971 resumed their melancholy tradition of the carefully planned festival-turned-chaos. Tarkenton quit for three days in a contract dispute. Ron Johnson got hurt. The defense fell into disorder, and the offense was eccentric to bad. The Giants were playing in a heavyweight division with powder-puff weaponry. Yet there were some isolated hours of redemption. None was more vivid for Tarkenton personally than the day in Atlanta, where the heavily favored Falcons of Norman Van Brocklin prepared a ritualistic slaughter of the blundering Giants. It was not the first Van Brocklin-Tarkenton reunion since they jointly left the foundering Viking longboat by opposite ends of the gangplank. In The Dutchman's opening game as the Falcon coach in 1968, in fact, Tarkenton's Giants strutted into town with a four-game winning streak. They fell behind but were about to win the game in theatrical style when Tarkenton threw an end-zone pass into the accommodating arms of Lee Calland, with whom he had played in Minnesota. The problem here was that Calland now played for Atlanta, not New York.

In the postgame interviews that year, The Dutchman took the usual professional hard-balls line in dismissing any notion of personal revenge against Tarkenton. That's dime novel stuff, pure pulp, he suggested.

And Tarkenton's privates were no less stony on the subject. He too gave no thought to any Tarkenton–Van Brocklin feud, he insisted. This is a football game. Bigger than any two people. What happened years before belongs to history. That's dime novel stuff, pure pulp, he suggested.

Except, of course, that it wasn't. Tarkenton squirmed and brooded all the way back to New York in despair over what he later called the worst hour of his career. Of all the people to end the winning streak! And in his first game in Atlanta, before he even knew the plays, let alone who was playing.

The scenario flipped in 1971. The Giants were reeling, and the Falcons were the then-typical Van Brocklin football team, young, belligerent, moving up, fearing the coach, admiring him, cursing him, following him. They were favored over the Giants by at least seventeen points. The chroniclers asked Van Brocklin and Tarkenton beforehand whether they had any incentive to win beyond the stakes of the game itself. In other words, how would you like to stick it to the other guy?

To this The Dutchman snuffled contemptuously. Pro football is too big for that Hollywood junk. Tarkenton simply looked airy. When you've been in this league for eleven years, you just don't think about personalities.

How is General Motors doing on the Big Board?

Nobody really believed those clumsy charades. Sure, Tarkenton and Van Brocklin wanted to stick it, wherever it was least acceptable.

They would give their game salaries to do it.

The Giants were wounded. Ron Johnson was out. Tucker Frederickson was playing with two bad knees, which tended to balance his pulled hamstrings. Joe Morrison was playing in the backfield—good, durable, never-yield Joe, whose speed was now down so low the slow-motion camera had to be goosed to keep him in focus.

The game was a better match than the sages had predicted. And with nine minutes left, the Giants trailed, 17–14. From the Atlanta fifteen Tarkenton embarked on a drive. When it began acquiring first downs, a new anxiety struck him. What if the Giants should score too fast?

It had occurred to him many times in his five seasons with the Giants. Partly because of injuries and partly because of errors in player procurement, most of the Giant defenses of those years were variable. Sometimes they were bad, and the other times they were worse. The quarterback discovered that it was possible to be too impulsive in trying to score late in the game. This might achieve the short-term objective of putting the Giants ahead. But it led them into a trap dictated by the rules. A Giant touchdown with time still remaining on the board meant the other team got the ball. And that, given the Giant defense, always created a situation fraught with the potential for disaster.

Against the Falcons, Tarkenton resolved to (a) use up the rest of the clock, and (b) score.

Onward moved the Giants. But slowly. They moved off tackle and around end. When they moved through the air it was never more than ten yards at a time.

"If we hit one deep," Tarkenton told himself, "we're sunk."

This was no real disparagement of the Giant defense, merely a statement of statistical truth. What would Tarkenton be doing downrating the Giant defense? His own season, while all right mathematically, resembled Wall Street's in 1929 in terms of long-range growth.

Van Brocklin was pacing the sidelines when Morrison, sweeping wide to the right, barged into him. The Dutchman was knocked on his can and rose with a whole cornucopia of unkind things to say about Morrison.

As he was standing at the line preparing to call his signals, Tarkenton was distracted by one of the Falcons' defensive tackles, John Small. "You really are trying to beat him, aren't you? I mean, you must really have a hard-on for this guy."

To which Tarkenton replied, "Sure, wouldn't you?"

Twice the Giants stood fourth and one, and both times they pounded into the line for the first down to keep the drive breathing. The clock was now on the final swing of the second hand. Theoretically it was safe to score. The prospect seemed especially inviting because the Giants were on the Atlanta one-yard line with two downs to go. Tarkenton rolled out and lost a yard. One more play.

The Falcons would be looking for another rollout because it gave the quarterback the option of running or throwing. It was a standard goal-line play. Expecting it, the Falcons lined up their tackles wide. Tarkenton's intent was to slip the ball to Tucker Frederickson, who would hammer up the middle between the spread tackles. But peering into the Atlanta defenses as he recited his signals, Tarkenton was astounded to see the Falcon middle linebacker chasing the Giants' man in motion, Joe Morrison. It was a bungle by Atlanta. The outside linebacker should have been handling Morrison. Tarkenton was about to go "hut" for the last time when the full magnitude of the situation gripped him. If the middle linebacker was gone, who on earth did the Falcons have to handle the quarterback if he just slid behind his guard and headed into the end zone?

But if the Falcons nailed him, could they ever restrain The Dutchman in the postgame beer parties? "The little smart-ass thought he could beat me all by himself."

The quarterback actually imagined a conversation like that.

But it was too tempting to ignore. The final "hut" went up and Frederickson pounded for the line, creating a basket with his arms to receive the ball.

He never touched it. Tarkenton swung to his left and tore into the end zone without resistance.

"Did you get any personal satisfaction out of winning under the circumstances?" one of his old chums of the Atlanta press, Al Thomy, asked Tarkenton.

Tarkenton regarded the bait thoughtfully. "In this league," he said, "you've got all you can do to concentrate on the ball game. A man would be crazy to let personality clashes interfere with his judgment."

Just in case you had any doubts.

The Quarterback

9

The unions have a house anthem called "Solidarity Forever." I envy them. Solidarity is not quite as permanent in pro football. The Giants in 1970 came within one game of making the playoffs. It was a year of achievement and fellowship. There were mutual pledges between management and players to walk arm-in-arm into a beautiful tomorrow. Less than a year later I missed the first exhibition game in a contract dispute with Mara, who decided to retire me temporarily. Then I was unretired a few days later in what was called a "capitulation" by the management.

That year injuries and a breakup in the old togetherness arrived about simultaneously. Our team's best running back was disabled. The Giants fired one of their best defensive players three hours after he reported the owner's unpopularity among the players in a survey commissioned by the owner. And at about midseason Mara started negotiations to trade me. We had a miserable year. And a few weeks later I was gone.

I think that's a fairly accurate summation of the year's events. But in reciting them I would like to make it clear that I'm really not trying to attribute pettiness to Wellington Mara nor martyrdom or total innocence to me. Both of us believed we were being reasonable men, pursuing ends we thought could be equally beneficial to player, team, and management. But my bargaining position was weak, and I vowed then I would try to make my nonfootball business life

142

productive enough so that I would not be basically dependent on football income to maintain myself. That would toughen my bargaining stance and free me from the kind of juvenile sparring matches that characterize most contract fights in professional athletics.

Anyhow, I couldn't do it in 1971, not as a practical matter. Wellington and I had been discussing a contract prior to the start of the exhibition season. We had, and still have, I'm sure, a mutual regard. But it did not extend to the negotiating table in the summer of 1971. My thinking was this: The government was getting a big tax bite out of my football earnings. I was then receiving around $100,000. I had other commercial involvements, of course, and my total net worth was well beyond $1 million if you figure it the way the accountants figure it. There are a lot of legal ways you can save yourself tax money in the position I was in. I proposed to Wellington that the Giants make a loan to me of about $250,000 over a three-year period. They would also pay me a salary less than what I had been making, in the range of $75,000. I would repay the loan, obviously. It was a loan to me personally, not to my businesses. I reasoned that an arrangement like that would benefit not only me, by producing more actual dollars than a straight salary, but also benefit the Giants.

Wellington didn't agree with that view of economics. Coming up on our exhibition opener with Houston in the Astrodome, we still hadn't made any progress. I told Mara I was willing to play the exhibitions without a contract, which I hadn't done before. He said we would work something out. But we met two days before the game, and Wellington told me that the offer he had made two months before, for about $125,000, was his final offer. I said his plan wasn't acceptable. He said, "That's it."

I went back to my room, thought about it for a while, and then called Wellington to tell him I'd like to see him that night. He said that couldn't be arranged, because he was taking some people to dinner. I said right now would have to do then. I wanted him to understand my thinking, where I was coming from on this. I couldn't accept his contract arrangement. Several other prominent players in the NFL had loan provisions in their contracts, including Roman

Gabriel, John Brodie, and one other from the recent past, Fran Tarkenton. I had had a loan agreement in a previous contract with the Giants. The one I proposed in 1971 was for more money, but the principle was the same. Wellington balked, though. So I told him that I had agreed to play in the exhibition with Houston, and I would. But I wanted him to understand that after the game I would leave. I wasn't going to play in any further exhibitions without a contract.

Wellington said in that case I should leave now, the night before the game.

And I did.

I told him I didn't want any big controversy over my decision (which was rather out of my control, of course, newspapers and owners and huffy quarterbacks and fans being what they are). He said he appreciated that (without necessarily believing it, I'm sure). That's how we left it.

I flew home to Atlanta. I think Wellington was surprised the next day to discover I was actually gone. He appeared before the players that night and talked emotionally about his fairness in contract dealings and how he couldn't yield to my demands, and that he knew the Giants would deliver to the fullest in the absence of the first-string quarterback.

Dick Shiner played most of the Houston game at quarterback. For understandable reasons, the Giant offense didn't scintillate. That doesn't make me an indispensable man. It just means that the re-moval of the No. 1 quarterback right before a game does tend to disrupt an offense and, as Satchel Paige might say, roil up a bunch of people. I regretted that, of course, because the people who were roiled up were almost all friends of mine and men for whom I had great respect.

Houston, which wasn't reputed to be a powerhouse, bombed the Giants, 38–0. The next day I was listening to the radio in Atlanta and learned that I had retired from football, at least on the basis of an announcement from the New York Giants. That surprised me because I hadn't retired at all. I'm not sure what my status was. I supposed I was absent from training camp without permission, seeing to a private problem. And more or less at the invitation of Wellington Mara, I was going to be absent until the contract was settled.

I realize that by Mara's lights he was acting in a completely responsible, proper, and legal way. I was the renegade. I don't deny that description. I think you have to take risks, if you believe the end is right and you are acting without jeopardizing the rights of others or violating a trust. And by this definition I was acting responsibly. I know other words were used. Some of the media people thought I was being autocratic and selfish. They thought that I was threatening the welfare of the team and that I had no right to leave when I did. I'm sure a few of my teammates felt that way, too. Well, if we choose popularity as a criterion of everything we do, we are going to frustrate ourselves into a very dark corner, or wind up as cheerleaders for people we call our betters. I just have a hard time accepting that kind of behavior.

My bargaining position, though, wasn't the most enviable. Yes, I think the Giants needed me, but they could have played the schedule very well without me. Also, under the league operating rules, it *was* possible for the Giants to declare me retired in another few days. If they did that, I would be out of football for a year, which I didn't want to be. So I really didn't know how long I might have to sit in Atlanta.

After a couple of days I got a telephone call from Frank Gifford, a good friend to both Mara and me, and a former Giant. Frank said Wellington wanted to talk with me.

"Why doesn't Wellington call me, if that's the case?" I asked.

"You know Well; he wouldn't do that," Frank said.

It was part of the tableau some executives and personnel heads like to arrange in their dealings with their performers. Wellington would call it protocol. The games people play with words.

So Wellington wanted me to make the first call. I said, "Frank, you know back when I was in high school I broke up with my girlfriend. I was fourteen years old. I wouldn't call her because I wasn't going to make the first move. But I think I've gotten over those things. Does he really want to talk?"

"Yeah, he really does," Frank said.

So I called him. Wellington said he would like to see me, and I told him I had to be in New York the following day and we would have plenty of time to talk in the evening after I wound up what I had to do there. He said that would be fine.

We had a good talk. We came to an agreement on the contract. The main terms were for a salary of about $125,000, the figure Wellington had pretty much begun with, and a $2,500 bonus for each game the Giants won, a provision not in the original offer. You couldn't call it a crumb, because the Giants had won nine games the year before.

You can argue either way, incidentally, on bonus arrangements like that. I was usually opposed to performance bonuses, such as so much money per touchdown pass. These obviously make you vulnerable to suspicions of setting personal goals ahead of the team's. Team performance bonuses are better, but still flawed. In the first couple of years of my second tour with the Vikings after I left the Giants, I had a bonus arrangement if our team won the conference championship and another if we won the Super Bowl. But there, again, while they link your own work with that of the team, you are subject to forces beyond your control.

Anyhow, Wellington told his subordinates, and the press was summoned to inform New York Giant fans that the quarterback had been rehabilitated. But before I left to meet the gathering, Wellington said, "There's one thing I've got to ask you, Francis. I would like you to say you accepted the Giants' terms." I said, "Why not, Wellington?" So he was happy, temporarily. But a breach had been created. What I had done, in Wellington's mind, was to commit an act of disloyalty, to disrupt the unity of the family. It didn't matter how we were going to finish that year, Wellington and I were never going to be able to enjoy the amity and goodwill we had before. Please understand, I never contended Mara was anything but an honorable man. We just had an abrasion there that couldn't be completely healed. Also, I had one conception of what was happening in the organization; he had another.

I should add this as a footnote to our contract discussion. During our talks Wellington expressed the view that I was one of the three best quarterbacks in football at the time and should be paid on that basis. But I knew, from some of the players around the league, that five other quarterbacks were receiving salaries within five thousand dollars of each other, so obviously the owners talk about these things and act accordingly. They're not supposed to do that. I told Wellington I would be glad to accept his evaluation of my worth as a quarterback and submit the whole contract proposal to Pete Rozelle, the commissioner, and let him decide what would be a fair settlement. I asked Tom Joiner, my attorney, to talk to the commissioner, in whom I have a lot of trust. The commissioner agreed to help, although I know he had no intention of creating an awkward situation for one of his owners. It was all a sort of contingency plan, confidential at the time. But Wellington decided he didn't want to enter into such an arrangement.

During the year, and it was just an awful year, the Giants tried to trade me. They tried with Dallas and they came close to dealing with St. Louis. Nothing happened, and the season stumbled toward a 4–10 conclusion. There was speculation that because of my actions in the contract battle, I had lost some of my leadership. I didn't see that. We were having a lousy season for reasons that included Ron Johnson getting hurt, our opposition getting better, and our own personnel thinness, which we had managed to overcome in 1970 but began to show up a year later. I threw only eleven touchdown passes, the lowest figure of my career.

Not the least of our problems was the Bob Lurtsema fiasco. Lurtsema was a good defensive lineman and a popular figure in the locker room. He was also active in the players' association. My understanding is that Mara asked Lurtsema to survey the players in order to get a reading on whether he still had rapport with them. Lurtsema took his soundings for a couple of weeks and returned to Mara with some pretty negative ratings. Lurtsema tends to be direct. He told Mara he had very little rapport, and I know it must have injured him because the ball club has been his life.

Within three hours Bob Lurtsema was on waivers. Wellington later told him he was surprised and embarrassed; he wasn't aware

Alex Webster had planned to make such a move. However it happened, Lurtsema was gone. The Vikings picked him up, and the poets triumphed again. Within a couple of years Bob Lurtsema was a pop hero in Minnesota, making thousands of dollars annually as Benchwarmer Bob on a series of television commercials for a savings and loan association.

The season was a bummer from every conceivable angle. And that wasn't only my opinion. One day Freddie Dryer came to me and said, "Frannie, you're not going to believe what'll be in the newspaper this afternoon." I told him the way the year was going there was nothing I couldn't believe. Then Dryer said he was so weary of it that he had gone to Larry Merchant of the New York *Post* and given him the whole story. Now, Dryer has a brilliant mind. And virtual total recall. So he pulled together all the disasters and bungles and player distempers, and Merchant collected them in a series called "Maranoia." Everything was in there just about exactly the way it happened, right down to perfection, as only Dryer could recall it and interpret it. The thrust of the whole thing was the incompetency of the organization. It was pretty explosive stuff.

Now, I happened to have a friend on the staff, a coach, who kept me informed from time to time on what was happening in the bureaucracy. When the series came out, the inside organization thought I was the source, the tipster. They wanted to believe that all their torment, the evil, was centered in me. Of all people. The bubble-gum-card collector. Can you imagine? Since I was the guy who walked away from the team in Houston, I had to be the agitator.

The consternation inside the Giants' organization and the team over the articles and all the losing was now pretty unanimous. In the last week of the season I decided I had to get away from the New York Giants. I wanted to be someplace where for once I could start out with an even chance of winning. I knew it wasn't going to be the Giants. I had the feeling I could finish out my career there, and be paid well, and spend most of the time losing. That was fine if you could be happy losing, which I couldn't. I was finishing my eleventh year in professional football. I knew my career was at a point where another move was mandatory or I was going to die with the Giants.

So I asked to meet with Mara and Webster and I told them, "I really like all of you and I've been happy, but I just don't think you've got the organization here, Wellington. And I don't think you've got the players to win."

Mara disagreed, of course, but because he had to make decisions he thought were in the best interest of the team, I told him he should know I wouldn't resist being traded. Which is a pretty precious way of saying that I really wanted to go.

I made the further point that I did not want to be traded to a noncontending team, which may strike some people as being a demanding attitude. But we're back to the free-enterprise principle. I think I had established enough in my eleven years in pro football, had built well enough outside of it. So I could afford to tell the owner of the club I played for that I thought not only the club's interests should be considered, but the player's interests, too. I don't think that is a subversive attitude.

If Mara did trade me to a bottom-drawer team, I said I wouldn't report. That was it for me. I'd had it with losing. I'd rather get out of football than have to put up with all of the aggravation from impatient fans, the flak in the media, all the unpleasantness that goes with it.

The season ended, and nothing happened for a month. I knew I was a property, and if I refused to play, Wellington would find a way to put me somewhere. I also knew that a trade involving a prominent quarterback tended to get complicated. When I came to the Giants five years before, for example, the deal finally involved four Giant choices in the player draft. And the Vikings eventually had a hard time concealing their satisfaction when the choices turned out to be Ron Yary, Ed White, Clinton Jones, and Bob Grim.

I finally called the Giants. My sources in the organization told me there had been offers. Oakland had made one, Baltimore another. But the Giants were afraid to deal with Oakland because they didn't want to get slickered by Al Davis. The inside man then advised me, "They're talking to Minnesota."

The mention of Minnesota, of course, had me throbbing. It was where my old buddies were. A place I always liked. Bud Grant was the coach there now, and he had it all together. They were winners. Imagine playing offense knowing that when the defense comes in, Eller, Page, Marshall, and Larsen are lined up there across the front.

I had watched the Vikings win the NFC championship in 1969, and I cried like a baby. "Lord, aren't you ever going to get into that thing?" I asked myself. Joe Kapp was their quarterback, a guy I had come to admire for the total fearlessness with which he played the game. That and the obvious emotional force he imparted to the team. He was a big, tough quarterback who was willing to stand up there and trade punches with the big defensive linemen who rushed him. It was some sight. And while I could respect another quarterback directing the team I had played with for so long, I was envious. I also remembered visiting the Vikings in their locker room at Tulane Stadium after they lost to Kansas City in the Super Bowl. It was a miserable locker room artistically, and there was a lot of misery in it emotionally. I don't think they really believed—after all they had done in 1969—that they were capable of losing that football game.

"Minnesota? Do I really want to return to the Vikings?" I asked myself. Does a drowning man welcome a rope?

If you drew a scale from one to ten, and ten was the tops, and you asked how I would measure being traded to Minnesota, I'd rate it at about eleven. Mara told me he had some conversations with the Vikings scheduled for the following week. But it didn't sound promising at that point because we were getting into the winter and teams were doing their planning.

If the Vikings didn't come through, I figured I had two alternatives. I intended to sit down with Mara and spell out the things I thought needed some reform in the Giant operations to make me feel comfortable about staying on as a player. Somebody had to initiate the action. Why not me? I had stake enough in it. If Mara didn't agree that some things had to be changed, I was just going back to Atlanta, buy a new briefcase, subscribe to the *Wall Street Journal,* and say good-bye to jocks and pads.

Two days later, Jim Finks of the Vikings called me and asked if I wanted to play with Minnesota.

I asked him if he knew when the next flight left for the Twin Cities.

He responded by offering me a big salary cut to play in the great Upper Midwest.

"James," I said, "I dearly love Minnesota and all of my old teammates, and I think I could even grow to love you, but I do not love the sound of those numbers *at all.*"

He reduced the pain somewhat, but I still had to take a slight cut to play in Minnesota. And two hours later, Finks called back and said, "We have rescued your old No. 10 from the rummage sale and will have it laundered just to show our affection and delight at having you back."

In return for my services, the Vikings traded directly to the Giants my old pal Norm Snead, who had been a reserve quarterback that year with the Vikings; Bobby Grim, who had caught a lot of passes that year; and a reserve back, Vince Clements. They also gave the Giants a No. 1 draft choice that year, who materialized as defensive end Larry Jacobson of Nebraska, and a No. 2 the following year, who turned out to be Brad Van Pelt of Michigan State, a defensive back. But one of the men the Giants really wanted and failed to land was John Ward, the young Viking offensive lineman. By 1975 the only player left with the Giants of that group was Van Pelt, playing linebacker.

So for the second time in five years, the oppressed quarterback was liberated. You do understand I'm funning. At those prices I never considered myself an indentured servant. When I left Minnesota for New York, I wanted a new environment mostly to discover whether pro football could be enjoyed. I found that it could. I enjoyed almost all my tenure in New York. It was stimulating, profitable, maturing, even though it wasn't especially victorious. I think—I know—I gave the Giants all that was in me. But Minnesota looked something like the Garden of Eden. Since 1968 the Vikings had won the Central Division title every year, four straight. They had been to the Super Bowl once. They believed they could do it again with stability at quarterback, which they felt they did not have in 1971. So I was coming West to provide it. I thought a great way to start would be to let things calm down a little commercially, to ease off somewhat as an entrepreneur.

The first guys who met me as I stepped off the plane were representatives of a savings and loan association with a contract and pen for a television commercial.

Two Stars, Two Orbits

10

A few weeks before the restoration of Francis Tarkenton to Minnesota, the Vikings' Alan Page was formally honored as the most valuable player in professional football. The coincidence of the two events was one of those accidents of history that seemed—at least to Alan Page and his admirers—to be a sardonic comment on the odd spins of justice.

The best player in pro football, Alan Page reflected, was being ignored in Minnesota by the ad agency hustlers with their endorsement baubles. They thrust their affections instead on a quarterback who had been zealously avoided by the all-pro selectors for eleven years.

In the public prints, and to a lesser degree among the football audiences, Tarkenton's second term as the Viking quarterback was looked upon as the reaccession of some wandering prince. Having plied other lands and visited the oracles, he was coming back with much of the wisdom of his world and possibly the key to the Super Bowl vaults.

Page had no such Arthurian outlook. He reacted to the Tarkenton trade with a skeptical shrug and a cryptic fatalism, attitudes purely Page. The Minnesota Vikings, he contended, didn't need a savior.

If there was some mystical flavor in Tarkenton's return, Page wasn't buying. He grew up a black kid in Canton, Ohio, not a white

153

pageboy in Camelot. Like Joe Kapp, the Vikings' Super Bowl quarterback in 1969, Page did not believe in red-nosed reindeer or charming princes.

His admiration for Kapp's roughhousing leadership, in the three seasons the roustabout warrior quarterbacked the Vikings, might partly account for his indifference to Tarkenton two years later. It might, but only superficially. Page and Tarkenton had never been teammates before 1972, so there was no personal hostility between them. What bothered Page in his most private thoughts was the sudden materialization on the Viking roster of a man who was the embodiment of "the system," the same system that Page was convinced had denied Alan Page the deserved rewards of his greatness.

In the ensuing years, Page and Tarkenton would be civil and respectful toward each other as teammates and as colleagues in the superstar fraternity. Yet in their coexistence on the same football team, they represented—in ways largely unknown to the fan who admired both—archetypes who symbolized opposite and conflicting forces in the pro football society of their time.

It was almost as if the leader of the United Auto Workers and the board chairman of General Motors suddenly found themselves on the same side of the bargaining table.

As football players, both Tarkenton and Page were legitimate pathfinders of their era. Whereas Tarkenton had materially altered the technique of quarterbacking against the sophisticated defenses of the 1960s and 1970s, Page had changed the standards of defensive line play. The game was once played on the line of scrimmage with the same kind of strategic philosophy that led the French to build the Maginot Line, which was awesome, powerful, and stationary. The Germans wiped it out in one day by finding and running through a soft place and ignoring the rest. The conventional defensive tackle in pro football once weighed 270 pounds, had the disposition of an outcast Kodiak bear (and sometimes the breath to match), and could not run thirty consecutive yards without risking death by natural causes.

Page weighed between 245 and 250 pounds. He had both the straight-ahead speed and dexterity of a running back. At his best when he was a free-lancer, he played within the framework of the designated defense, but he was also at liberty to adjust. He was, and is, allowed to break off his rush of the quarterback to head laterally crossfield in pursuit of the pass receiver. Nobody in pro football performs that maneuver with as much acceleration or authentic passion as Alan Page. He brought a new set of qualifications to playing defensive tackle. The tackle must now be big enough to grapple with the behemoths across from him, but also fast and nimble enough to run with the ball carriers. And he must be persistent enough to hound a play across the field, or downfield, and overtake the ball carrier. The tactic has always worn the label of "pursuit," but Page gave it a more elevated and dramatic meaning.

In the late 1960s and early 1970s when he had full command of his speed, strength, and agility, Page was one defensive lineman who was capable of changing the course of a football game all by himself. In his street dress and sometimes during a game, he gave the appearance of a cool dude wrestling with oppressive forces that he viewed as some form of personal penance. These included football officials, offensive linemen who held him at the line, and what he called "the management system."

Aroused, Page could be a man of churning, violent intensities. Angered by two consecutive penalties against him in the Detroit game in 1971, he reduced the Lions' offense to hash and helpless discord. He caused fumbles, destroyed the Lions' passing game, induced a safety, and so controlled the game that on that very day he won all the ballots he needed to become the first defensive lineman ever to win the Most Valuable Player award.

And so if the Vikings had Alan Page and one of the strongest defenses in football, and enough offensive wherewithal and competence at quarterback to win twenty-three of their last twenty-eight regular-season games, why did they need to be saved?

The "savior" label became a kind of ammunition; it appealed to Tarkenton critics. That it was neither fair nor accurate didn't make it any less quotable. Tarkenton plainly did not regard himself as an instrument of destiny, and the coach who approved the trade, Grant, was much too involved in the here and now to dream about being guided to a football hereafter by missionary quarterbacks.

So what really troubled Alan Page?

The equation looked like this to him:

Francis Tarkenton was a good, imaginative quarterback who had played for eleven years in the National Football League. But he had won few if any of the prestigious awards, and his teams had won no titles (although none had been remotely favored to, and at least three of them violated natural law every time they did win). Tarkenton was a quarterback, white. Page was a lineman, black. Tarkenton was drawing in excess of one hundred thousand dollars. His team was 4–10 the previous year. Page was more than twenty-five thousand dollars short of Tarkenton's salary despite having won the Most Valuable Player award and being annually chosen to the all-pro team. He was one of the principals on a team that had won four straight divisional championships and played in the Super Bowl.

Yet at the pinnacle of his career, when he was recognized by his peers as the best in the game, the advertisers disclosed no hot-pants fervor to sign Alan Page to an endorsement or personal-appearance contract. As the months rolled on after his selection, Page chafed in the face of the skimpy harvest his award had attracted. He even yielded to the embarrassment of being quoted to that effect in the newspapers.

He held the Viking management partly responsible for not promoting his availability for such windfalls, although an outsider might argue that the Viking management couldn't be expected to control the merchandising policies of American industry. Yet it was these policies for which Page reserved his deepest bitterness. The Most Valuable Player award, which he probably overrated as a potential bonanza, netted him next to nothing.

Francis A. Tarkenton, on the other hand, deplaned at the Twin Cities International Airport a few hours after his trade was announced and was met at the ramp by two agents for a savings and loan association that sponsored the Viking games. They offered him what they described as an impressive figure to do a series of commercials. Tarkenton was more bewildered than impressed, since he was barely out of the airplane and still buttoning his coat. They negotiated briefly, and the contract was signed for seventy-five hundred dollars. Less than a day later, just a few hours after the press conference that marked his formal inauguration as the second-term quarterback, a commercial appeared on Twin Cities television showing Tarkenton as the savings and loan's newest customer.

It had been filmed, processed, edited, and canned in record time. The sponsors twittered within the ad trade over this sonic-speed coup, and the viewers were duly astounded. But it cost the incoming quarterback far more than he received.

The old adage of exploitation advertising is "Nothing succeeds like excess." Tarkenton was on the screen almost daily, selling loans and inviting deposits. He was also visible under other sponsorship, selling a sizable part of the nation's inventory, from macaroni to snowmobiles. His teammates, even Alan Page, accepted this as legitimate profit-taking of a type all of them sought. So they didn't resent it, but they did envy it. And a few of them wondered archly what Tarkenton's dollar flow would look like if he started winning.

The television campaigns had been orchestrated months before the season, in the expectation that the Minnesota Vikings and Francis Tarkenton almost surely would electrify the world. But by November, with the Vikings headed for a 7–7 season, Tarkenton pleaded for some merciful retrenchment by the savings and loan association.

"When I signed their contract, I thought it was a justifiable spinoff of being in the football limelight," he said. "You get both benefits and grief from that. I didn't realize they were planning that see-it-now breakthrough the very first night I was in town. And I didn't dream that they planned to air those things eighteen thousand times during the season. I asked to have them curtailed because they were getting embarrassing, and they were curtailed."

The round-the-clock commercialization to which he submitted himself that year brought Tarkenton to a decision. If you really believed in the capitalist system, all of this could be defended. But if you also believed in taste, it couldn't. He would do commercials after that, but only on a selected basis, and low-key commercials at that. The Tarkenton treasury could afford the restraint.

An interested witness to these ethical gropings was Alan Page.

Page had never been embarrassed by an overkill of his commercials on television. He did not have to ward off program chairmen offering thousands of dollars per speaking engagement.

In the years that followed, however, both Tarkenton and Page would reap the kind of money and fame that a kid growing up in Canton and another in Richmond would not have dared to imagine in their most secret reveries. Both had the esteem of their teammates as football players unexcelled at their positions. Both had bold appetites to make it big, in football and elsewhere. And both were headed irrevocably for football's Hall of Fame, yet neither regarded that as an ultimate.

"The game isn't fun anymore; I want out," Alan Page could say in 1975. "I'm playing it now because it will finance me while I get my law degree."

Tarkenton had no such disenchantment. Football in 1975 remained a pleasure and an expanding bounty. But he could say at the season's conclusion: "Football just can't be an end in itself. I love the game, but I want to be able to do just as well financially without it. Football is one excitement in my life. There have to be others."

Did these similar urges unite Page and Tarkenton as matching personalities?

Hardly.

Tarkenton was ebullient, happy with whatever piece of the world he happened to stake out on a given day, a man with a politician's gift for sunny conversation. He also had a broker's eye for a good deal and a preacher kid's willingness to get up early in the morning if it meant making a dollar or converting a faint heart. He also was a national football institution, white, southern, and a quarterback.

Page had conflicting ambitions and attitudes that pulled him in opposite directions. He liked the comforts and stature that being a pro football star gave him. But he warred with the oligarchs of the football establishment because he saw it as essentially a feudal white society despite the big money it gave to some of the blacks. He shared the enmities and aspirations of black America, but his efforts to make it as a black capitalist failed, and he found himself better off as an integrated Alan Page, including an integrated Alan Page as the husband of a gifted white woman. Although pleasant and articulate, he projected a subsurface fermenting anger. He felt constrained and slighted by white society, as an athlete and as a human being.

The law, he decided, would liberate him from those strictures just as the destruction of football's Rozelle rule and reserve clauses would liberate athletes generally. In the meeting halls of his team and the league, he signed in as a banner carrier, a front-line soldier of the players' association's militant movement. In some of the meetings he fulminated against people he called hypocrites who, he said, took the benefits the militant players had gained for them but shunned any participation in their strike threats. He did not mention names, Tarkenton's or anyone else's.

Many of his teammates were infuriated by what they regarded as Page's clubhouse demogoguery and grandstand public statements. His attendance record at the national players' association meetings was erratic. And he came away from those he did attend, one of his intramural critics maintained, "without knowing a helluva lot about what was going on, and able to explain even less. He got quoted and got his picture in the paper carrying a picket sign, but he never did much more than bitch and sound wounded and betrayed."

Tarkenton's attitude toward Page as a players' association leader and spokesman for the conscience of the professional athlete was cool and a little irritated. "Alan," he would say, "does a lot of talking. Some of it makes sense. Some of it doesn't. Sometimes the team listens to Alan. Sometimes it doesn't."

It was an evaluation most of Page's friends shared. They admired his willingness to talk publicly on player-management conflicts, but they did not always follow his logic or agree on just who the players' most consistent menace was—management, Commissioner Pete Rozelle, or the sword-rattling executive director of the players' association, Ed Garvey.

Page distrusted management and Rozelle with equal energy, and considered Garvey's aggressiveness the only practical buffer against both. Tarkenton saw the commissioner as an enlightened, independent thinker who kept his options open and was more qualified than anybody on earth to make a right decision in compensating a football team (as he did before federal court intervention in 1975) for the loss of a player who wanted to sign with somebody else.

Page considered it an outrage that an employer-appointed commissioner could determine the future of football players. In Page's mind Rozelle functioned not as a neutral party in player-management disputes but as the owners' agent in a conspiracy to keep the players trussed to the clubs that signed them. They were objects, in other words, to be used, discarded, or swapped at their owners' pleasure.

It incensed Alan Page to think that anybody had that kind of power over him. He was convinced that the NFL's standard player contract was an exploitation and a remnant of an age of bondage. Some of the players, although not the judges, smiled at this notion. Most of the fans smirked, taking note of the players' average salary of forty thousand dollars a year.

Tarkenton had no such conception of the working conditions of a pro football player. All right, not every player in the NFL is a headstrong quarterback who could force a move if he chose. But Tarkenton believed that even under the old structure the large majority of players could move to another club if they really wanted to, and in many cases to the club they wanted to play for. He further believed that the logical end of unrestricted mobility for pro football players was a lopsided league or no league at all.

Page disagreed. But if it meant a lopsided league, let it all hang out that way, he maintained. The law means what it says. It says there shouldn't be a restraint of trade. The owners argued that some artificial system—the draft and reserve clause—is necessary to maintain competitive balance in professional sports and thus preserve its existence. If that couldn't be done under the laws of the land, Page said, either change the laws of the land or change football. But let a professional athlete have the same freedom of choice as the bricklayer who builds the stadium and the vendor who sells beer in it.

Like other high-priced stars, Tarkenton did not need the militancy of the union to grant him mobility or to upgrade his contract. He believed that its militancy had grown out of medieval employer attitudes by the owners, but he never burned candles to the memory of the union founders.

"I think the sad thing is that unions ever had to happen," he said. "They happened because of bad management, because of management being insensitive or inadequate to the needs of its employees. I suppose to maintain a balance of economic power, unions had to come. I'm just sorry that the profit motive has been so powerful that management in the past lost sight of other things equally important. So now we have a union in pro football, which is too bad. And we have a widening breach of trust between the owners and the players. And at the very time I was trying to sympathize with the owners' problems in handling the court challenges and the escalation of their costs, they came and really tried to rub their boot into the players' association when the threatened strike early in the 1975 season didn't materialize. They had a chance to be progressive. They could sit down with the players and settle a contract. In the process they could have done something constructive about the reserve or so-called Rozelle rule that the players could live with. But they just sat by themselves, convinced they could outlast the players that way. And then more court decisions came, and it got to be a mess.

"On the other hand, I don't have any time for Garvey. You measure an employee by results. Garvey is an employee of the players. His attitude in dealing with the owners has been so unrealistic that over that bargaining table, at least, the results were terrible. I'm not really very wise about the player-management dilemma. I don't know anybody who is, except maybe Rozelle. And I tend to agree with Rozelle's logic on it. Maybe pro football has to get hurt, really hurt, to decide where it's going."

Page would be stunned if Tarkenton brought any other attitude to the problem of player-management relations. The system, whatever its drawbacks, may have been okay for a black lineman, but it was super-okay for a white capitalist quarterback.

But aren't the Alan Pages—meaning the proud dissidents— likely to find obstacles everywhere, because they are very difficult people to please? They are. And they are also sometimes very difficult to figure out. While making full allowances for his virtuosity as a player, Page's teammates were sometimes puzzled and annoyed by what they viewed as his self-centered conduct. Late in the Super Bowl game with the Steelers, for example, he declined to return to the field with the defensive unit. The explanation was never clear.

The fan might ask another question here. Aren't Page and Tarkenton teammates rather than corporate rivals?

They are, and they are therefore entitled to make judgments of each other, athletically and personally.

"With Francis in there," Page says, "you don't have to doubt the quarterback knows where he's going. His knowledge is what makes him the outstanding quarterback he is. I don't think I would give him great grades as a motivator, I mean when you compare him with a guy like Joe Kapp. Kapp got involved in every way. He revved up the team. I'm not saying Francis should have to do it. Certainly he's respected. He's a first-rate quarterback. He can move a team. But just as it isn't only a front four that builds a defensive record for a team, it isn't only the quarterback that moves the team. I think on many teams in many games the running backs and pass receivers are equally or more important as individual reasons why a team moves."

And what, despite their philosophical frictions, is Tarkenton's view of Page? Grown men, Tarkenton maintains, teammates, can disagree on what's best for themselves and pro football without personal enmity. He also believes it is stretching taste and fairness when players blame each other for a defeat.

"I understand his pride and his resentments, I think," Tarkenton said. "The matter of color has somehow gotten mixed up here in earning power and opportunity. In the case of pro athletes in the 1970s, I don't know how much validity that has. I see a lot of black players expanding their earning opportunities, being highly popular with the viewing masses and as a result being much in demand. I know it would be much better for humanity if all of us could walk in everybody else's shoes for a mile, or however long it would take to understand the tones of that person's feelings. That isn't possible, so we try to be more sensitive than we used to be. We don't always succeed. Like everybody else who is white in this country, I think I'm a better person in that respect. Black players and I never have trouble getting along as people. I think they will tell you that, and I'm not going to say any more in a self-serving way. I think black players as well as white have to make it largely on their own when it comes to capitalizing on their football prominence. The player should build securely, prepare, and not just pretend he's preparing with PR work in the winter or a sales job that makes use of his name. I think I know. I've gone both routes.

"As a player I look at Alan Page the way the fan does. I'm off the field when he's on, so I see him in that focus. He's been a tremendous player—motivated or not. Maybe we should motivate each other. Lordie, I thought I knew something about motivation, but I see Alan is not persuaded. I really do not know how a defensive tackle is expert on what or who motivates an offensive team. They're never on the field together, the defensive tackle and the offense. Maybe Alan has pervasive vision. As a quarterback, I envy that, just as I envy hindsight, which is very closely related to pervasive vision.

"Whatever differences we have philosophically just don't affect how either of us plays. I have never seen Page when he wasn't ready. I've played with and against a lot of great linemen, but I don't think I've ever seen anybody come off the ball as fast as Page. That and his incredible pursuit. Those are the things you notice about Alan Page. But for all of his greatness, I don't think Alan's year-in and year-out contribution to the Vikings has been any more decisive than that of Carl Eller and Jim Marshall, and I think Page would agree with that. Individually he may have burned brighter, because he does very dramatic as well as effective things on a football field. I have one regret about him. He's an interesting guy, and I wish I knew him better."

Tarkenton seems authentically bothered by that now in the retrospect of their long competitive association. The clicks and chemistries of people fascinate him. He is a gregarious person. Although he is a high-echelon star drawing well into six figures in salary, and playing a glamorous position, Tarkenton has never lost his adolescent delights in the game, the fellowship, and even much of the tomfoolery laced into it. In his two tenures with the Vikings he has found no football player with whom he could not hit it off, and very few have spoken of him with anything approaching dislike. His inquisitiveness about people—not only his teammates, but also random acquaintances—may explain his success and wealth in football as much as his durability and his shrewdness as a quarterback. Although he is instantly recognizable to millions of people, he has kept his willingness—eagerness, in fact—to listen to what another person has to say. For all the attention he has received, he is daily impressed by how much more he has to learn. It is not a realization that occurs to everybody who owns Cadillacs, but it might explain why he does.

The departure of the rollicking Chicano, Joe Kapp, did not lessen the Vikings' September-to-December dominance of the National Football Conference in 1970 and 1971. But where they had crashed the Super Bowl in 1969 with Kapp at quarterback, they failed in their first playoff games the following two years. Grant privately assigned much of the blame the second time to instability at quarterback. He opened the season with three—Gary Cuozzo, Norm Snead, and Bobby Lee. Nobody ever really seized the job, or was allowed to, depending on your perception of the weekly rotation. The unsettled conditions did not bother the Viking defensive front four of Page, Marshall, Eller, and Larsen, who controlled most of the action in the years when they were supreme. It also did not seem to bother Grant. He maintained that the quarterback is not necessarily the most important man in the offense and that a team could win with a journeyman performance at the position as long as the man was competent, erred only rarely, and stood properly at attention for the national anthem.

But in the 1971 playoff game against Dallas, what may have been the strongest of all Viking teams defeated itself with an interception and other second-half futilities. The defeat recast Grant's thinking. The one regret in his acceptance of the Viking job in 1967 was the exit a few months earlier of Francis Tarkenton. When the Vikings learned he was available five years later, Grant told Jim Finks: "He is the one quarterback in football I want for this team."

Tarkenton came back to the Vikings with no pronouncements. It was a winning team. There was no reason to believe it was going to stop winning because of or in spite of his presence. He met that proposition with the usual Tarkenton throwaway line. "My object," he said, "is just to be around when the Vikings win another title. I'll try not to be an obstruction."

So there were no marching bands to drum him to the Viking training camp, shifted to Mankato, Minnesota, in the mid-1960s, and nobody called a sensitivity meeting to decide how his old playmates ought to react. He slipped into his old hard hat and purple decor without MacArthuresque stances. He came back like the grateful and wiser politician who may have campaigned in bigger wards but was more relaxed with his first constituents. At thirty-two his face was fuller, his hair more profuse. But with the unspoken prudence of any immigrant entering a Bud Grant training camp, he had restyled it to accommodate both his helmet and the coach. There were seams in Tarkenton's face now. His expressions, although as spontaneous and droll as they were eleven years before, reflected a mature and distinguished athlete still in quest of a higher satisfaction.

He was wealthier by some very stunning numbers. But the locker room of a pro football team is no resort for returning maharajas. Jim Marshall flung some appropriate shafts, and the welcoming ceremonies were quickly done. The momentary awkwardness vanished, replaced by the trust and assurance generated by people Tarkenton knew and believed in—Alderman, Marshall, Brown, Tingelhoff, Eller, and others. His popularity with his old teammates was not unanimous. Page had his reservations. So did Lonnie Warwick, the middle linebacker who was an old hunting companion of Van Brocklin's, and Ed Sharockman, the defensive back. They weren't necessarily antagonistic. They did wonder about Tarkenton's deeper loyalties and his flair for finding new employers. First it was Minnesota to Broadway, then back to a championship contender when Broadway might have lost some of its allure and did not produce all-pro offensive linemen.

Tarkenton sensed some of that, but it was never very serious and nothing that could not be resolved by day-to-day fraternity. That and winning. His acceptance was warm. Grant himself did not try to hide his high regard for his new quarterback. And to the rookies in camp

the quarterback might have been a lofty figure with all of his experience and remarkable football mind, except that Tarkenton had no
interest in playing that role. Whatever the raps against him, Tarkenton was never a protocol man on the football field or in the locker
room. His runabout style as a young professional was as much a
product of his temperament as it was a response to the inadequacies
of his offensive line. That style, of course, had modified by the time
he returned to the Vikings. He had once played the game like a
gnome liberated from the workshop. It was a form of behavior that
concealed an important quality most of the discerning professionals
knew was there: his ability to move a team consistently and conven-
tionally, if it was the kind of team that allowed such virtues. The
Vikings of 1972 were such a team. He would still scramble now and
then. Did Fred Astaire ever give up dancing? Only now he didn't run
around the chicken coop. When he did roam from the pocket, Grant
had an explanation for it that was so startling in its clarity it ended
for all time any lingering complaint about scrambling.

"He's buying time," Grant would say. "The more time he buys,
the better chance he has of completing the pass."

The computers proved it, although every once in a while you
could buy so much time a Jethro Pugh or a Cedric Hardman would
stop the sale with a thud.

As the self-designated new boy in camp, Tarkenton made most
of the required sounds, and he meant them. "There are a lot of good
things to say about the organization the way it is set up now," he
said, "especially about the coach, his staff, and the stability here. But
I don't really want to labor that. All of it was true before I got here.
My saying it now isn't going to make it any more true than when
other people said it before me."

Yet it wasn't as stable as the surface readings suggested.

Three of the Super Bowl veterans—Gene Washington, Charley
West, and Clint Jones—had negotiated their contracts jointly. Finks
was troubled by that, and bitterness developed. None of the three was
filled with brotherhood for the Viking organization when the dispute
was finally settled. Page injured his leg. There were other hurts
involving important players. And in the opening game of the season

the Vikings had Washington beaten, only to let it grease through their hands in the fourth quarter. In defiance of the laws of probability, they did it again the next week against Miami, when the Dolphins needed a fourth-quarter touchdown and Garo Yepremian's fifty-one-yard field goal to win. The Vikings won some, lost some. They fumbled and blew audibles in ways Grant teams rarely did. In Chicago they scored an apparent winning touchdown in the fourth quarter but lost it, and the game, because Ed White was allegedly downfield when the pass was thrown. St. Louis beat them in the fourth quarter on a pass from the Viking castaway, Gary Cuozzo. They were blown down by Pittsburgh and Green Bay, and committed the capstone futility by losing the last game to two 49er touchdowns in the last five minutes.

The Vikings finished the season at 7–7, as Van Brocklin undoubtedly predicted. With a Super Bowl contender and one of the most expensive quarterbacks in football, they bombed.

Nobody with knowledge faulted Tarkenton. Even his critics credited him with a superb season. So did the fans. With a week remaining, they voted him the team's Most Valuable Player Award. He stood at a microphone and spoke of his chagrin.

"I've done a lot for this team," he said in a self-rebuke that was intended as a piece of pained buffoonery but got heavier as it went. "It was 11–3 last year, and now we're 7–6. I'm the quarterback who was supposed to provide leadership, help this team win the Super Bowl. I don't want to belittle the award, but the only award that's meaningful is the one they give after the Super Bowl. This has to be my biggest disappointment of a lot of disappointments."

The defeats, the wrangle over the commercials, and the re-emergence of all the old derisions of Tarkenton as a 7–7 quarterback made 1972 the most stifling kind of personal defeat for him. He took some of it home with him and found himself being remote and sometimes uncivil where he had never been before.

"I just don't think, though," recalls John Beasley, "that anybody could see how Tarkenton himself could have handled the season any better." Beasley was one of the unbuttoned elves on the team, a Californian who played an acceptable tight end and spread much merriment and unsolicited wisdom on his confederates.

"With Tarkenton coming back we all had this unconscious feeling that we were just going to walk onto the field and everybody was going to concede us into the Super Bowl. We really looked on ourselves as world beaters. As the season wore on, it was 'Migawd, what's happening?' After that some of them were saying, 'Christ, let's get it over with.'

"I remember walking into the steam room in the middle of the season, when we were still in the running, and hearing one of the best linemen in football say, 'I wish this goddamned season was over.' And there were still seven games to go!

"I was pretty shocked and a little teed off, because I thought at that point he was living off his all-pro reputation. It was that kind of season with us.

"But the big guy for us then, and in the seasons that followed, was Tarkenton. When he first rejoined the Vikings I was ready not to like him. Football players gossip a lot. Sometimes they get pretty sloppy with the truth. I heard from guys with the Giants that Tarkenton was a pretty hard guy to talk to, he was kind of selfish and just wanted to run the show.

"I matured in pro football at the time when Joe Kapp was the Viking quarterback, and I unconsciously compared every quarterback's style with Kapp's. He was a piece of work. Big, blustery, fearless old Chicano Joe. I'll never forget him coming back to the motel the week we played in the Runner-up Bowl in Miami in 1968. He rolled in about two or three hours after curfew, beating on my door. He looked like he had run off-tackle against a hurricane. His shirt was ripped off, and his pants were mangled. 'Somebody on the highway,' he said, 'called me a goddamned Mexican.' He figured that was explanation enough for his unusual appearance, and I guess it was.

"Tarkenton obviously was a different kind of guy. But I liked him almost from the first day. He was in a bind, coming back to his old team. It wasn't going anywhere when he left, but while he was gone it became one of the best, year in and out, and they were giving him the ball and saying, 'This is a winning football team. Everybody knows it. How about 13–1 this year?'

"He never let on, but he had to feel the pressure of that. He came across very friendly and content, like he meant it when he said this was his football home. There weren't any real problems in camp. He had leadership, all right. He was just a terrific head. You had confidence that one way or another the play he called was going to work. It was also reassuring to have him in the huddle. Most of the time he seemed to be enjoying it. In the huddle Tarkenton gives you a funny little look sometimes. He'd call a play and wink at me and say, 'And we got Beazer over the middle.' It sounded like something a kid would say in the playground huddle, and Tarkenton seemed to be spoofing all of the technical jargon he's been spouting all these years. You had the idea he was totally in command of the offense because there wasn't any situation in football he hadn't faced."

When they added up all of the figures for 1972, they showed that Francis Tarkenton had completed nearly 57 per cent of his passes, led an offense that outscored the 1971 Vikings by fifty-six points, and had reduced the Viking interceptions from the previous year by eight —and the team still finished 7–7.

There was the same baleful symmetry to that figure. It hovered over Tarkenton's head like a biblical judgment or a slogan dreamed up by some braying critic: fifty-fifty with Francis.

He had managed his career as carefully and independently as the rules allowed. He was willing to walk a lonely road in his dealing with football management, trusting to his instincts and nerve to head him in the right direction. But 1972 was his walk in the graveyard. They opened the gates to a football team that had won more than 80 per cent of its games for five years, and it didn't matter who played quarterback, Joe Kapp, Gary Cuozzo, Bobby Lee, or Norm Snead. So here was Francis Tarkenton, the sophisticated head who had called and run every football play imaginable in his eleven years in the business. Join the club, Francis, they said. On this team everybody who plays quarterback is a winner.

Considering the heraldry, what happened had the general impact of Neil Armstrong taking one giant step for mankind and landing on his head.

Tarkenton graded his own performance as sound. He realized that the point was inconsequential. One of the truths of leadership it had taken time for him to learn was that football teams are not built for the glorification of quarterbacks. Moreover, Grant had it in perspective. The quarterback calls the plays and handles the ball and throws the pass, but there is no particular reason why the game *necessarily* rises or falls on the performance of the quarterback. More so than any other player, he is in position to shape the outcome of a game, positively or negatively. But he doesn't always influence it that way, or even in a majority of the games. His position, like anybody else's, assumes a certain level of competence. If he fulfills it, he is meeting the requirements of the job. If he doesn't, the game and his job are in jeopardy. But the quarterback is the trigger man of a football offense, the fulcrum of all the action. He is the most visible of all players and therefore the one who is likely to receive disproportionate acclaim when his team wins, and unwarranted scorn when it loses.

He is also usually highly paid and profits externally. So Tarkenton never asked the fans or the writers or his teammates to spend their vesper hours mourning his fate.

"Grady," Tarkenton asked his friend on the return flight from San Francisco the night of the last game, "do you really suppose somewhere the Lord decided: 'Tark, you will have a number of good things in your life and you will meet many wondrous people and sights, but it is just not going to be your lot to play on a championship professional football team.'?"

Alderman pondered this harsh proposition. "I don't know what your brethren think," he said, "but Catholics don't figure the Lord would do such a thing to a Methodist."

Tarkenton brightened. He told Alderman he could certainly understand now how the Catholic Church, with that kind of faith, had lasted two thousand years.

The Quarterback

11

Television inadvertently has claimed a lot of victims. You think of network radio and popular magazines. You also think of Bud Grant.

Bud is still flourishing as a coach, of course. I was thinking more of how the television camera has shaped the American football fan's conception of him. I'm trying to avoid the word "image." Grant is suspicious of images. If he thought I was trying to define his image, he would turn me into a defensive back, which for quarterbacks is a fate worse than being turned into a frog.

I don't have to draw a picture. The camera comes in close on Bud Grant. He stands there in his purple cap and headset, as solemn as the North Wall of the Eiger. He is motionless and unfathomable. Years ago when the city of Bloomington put in a few blue laws to police stadium conduct, some people said they were afraid Grant would be arrested for impersonating a monument. Somebody started a campaign to rename Metropolitan Stadium Grant's Tomb. One year he evicted Don Meredith from the Viking dressing room, which is off-limits to everybody before games, including television announcers. Dandy Don got his revenge the first game of the next season, a Monday nighter. He said they had a popularity contest involving Tom Landry and Bud Grant, and both finished second. It took years for Howard Cosell to convince Minnesota fans that it was Meredith and not Cosell who said it. A friend of Cosell's tried to impart that information to Grant. He waved the man aside. He said he was amazed when either Meredith or Cosell bothered to see what was on the screen.

A good share of America views Bud Grant as some bloodless automaton who stands there impervious to noise, touchdowns (ours or theirs), falling bodies, or falling safes. He is like the guy wearing a white suit in the middle of a pie-throwing battle. He must be unreal because everybody else is covered with gunk and thrashing around, but Grant is anchored to the sidelines, motionless, untouched and oblivious.

That may not be a bad caricature, but it is not really Bud Grant. Let me say first that any quarterback talking publicly about his coach may have a credibility problem. But I also ask you to believe that at my advanced age of quarterbacking I really feel no urgency to go around lobbying with or for a head coach. Grant just happens to be a special kind of coach. I actually believe that if he went to Europe to coach soccer in the continental big leagues, he could win with Luxembourg after two seasons. If you gave him three, he could win with Monaco.

When he came down to coach Minnesota after winning for ten years in Canada, he shocked my old playmates in his first year. They had been playing five or six years under Van Brocklin, and the psychological change when Grant came in was numbing. The management should have given them a year to handle the withdrawal symptoms. It was like going from Napoleon to Calvin Coolidge overnight.

A lot of my buddies couldn't handle it. Bud started putting in some Rules. He never considered those as Mickey Mouse gadgets, but the players did, of course. He didn't like smoking in the locker room except for designated places, you had to have your hair cut reasonably, and you had to wear a tie when traveling with the team. Halfway through his first season in 1967, when the Vikings had a lot of problems, he cut out beer drinking on the road on nights before games. He explained it by advancing a revolutionary idea: He said professional ballplayers went on the road to play a football game, not to have a good time. Some of the guys really gasped at that. My friend Paul Flatley never completely recovered. He went into

Grant's office to enter his objections after the first season. He said he could see nothing incompatible in having a few drinks on Saturday night and then playing football on Sunday. Bud listened to him courteously, and pointed out that they probably had a philosophical difference there. He said he would try to resolve it, which he did, by putting Flatley on waivers.

Grant also thought it was a good idea for the players to wear their white oversocks at a uniform length. Furthermore, when they played the national anthem, it would promote orderliness and show proper respect if everybody stood at crisp attention, in a straight line on the field or sidelines. He devoted half of one entire practice in Mankato to having three linebackers demonstrate the prescribed posture and how to dress the line military style, after which the entire team practiced.

My buddies could not believe it. They didn't have their blocking in for the St. Louis blitz the coming weekend, but they already led the league in knowing how to stand at attention for "The Star-Spangled Banner." For days when Bud walked out of the training room heading for the field you could hear thin little bleep-bleeps from the players. They thought the guy had to be from Mars. They figured he should be walking around with green cheeks and antennae.

In all seriousness, they put very little credence and practically no faith in what he was trying to do. It seemed that foreign to them. All it was, of course, was an effort to achieve some form of standardization. To young America today that can be an ugly word. Regimentation, conformity, all that business. Grant understood you couldn't demand any Spartan conduct on an athletic team in the 1960s, and he never got close to basic-training chicken. What he was reaching for was consistency in the way the team conducted itself, the way it looked, and ultimately in the way it played.

If Grant has anything close to a professional beatitude, it is this: The consistent shall inherit the titles. The teams with the emotional and technical ups and downs are the losers. The ones who play at an even plane, again assuming a certain level of competence, the ones who play under control are the ones who win. Which then explains why Grant asks his teams—why be polite?—why Grant *tells* his teams—that some uniformity in how they look to the television audience, and how they look in the hotel lobbies, can influence their conduct on the field. This in turn is why you will see Bud Grant teams almost always looking in control of themselves and therefore very often in control of the game. Exceptions? Yes. Not even Grant can always enforce restraint, and I suppose I am the last man to have to cite examples.

I'm sure there is some military overtone to the way Grant arrives at a disciplined football team, but he's low-key about the stuff. He never really stops being Bud Grant, no matter how many horse laughs there might have been in the dormitory rooms when he first came in. He pursued ideas like those because he had seen them work and he knew they would be accepted when the team started winning. He moved about quietly and stolidly, and I guess it took a whole year for the guys to figure him out. None of that bothered him much. It was not that he was insensitive. I never met a coach who was more aware of what was gnawing at a football player or troubling a team, or more perceptive about the emotionalisms, both the volatile and subtle ones, that affect a team's performance. His method of contending with those, or making them work positively, is to make damned sure *he* is viewing the whole thing with a cool mind if nobody else is.

Because he is in command of himself, he can evaluate a football player honestly and incisively, and that means he can build football teams of stability. He knows they have to have that because there are forty or forty-five people on that team, all of them different. He's dealing with individuals who are competitive, egotistical, intelligent, and ambitious. Out of all of that he has to wring a willingness on the part of the players to elevate team goals above their individual goals, and at today's salary levels that isn't easy.

Yet he hasn't relinquished his own priorities or values. Grant is a football man, all right, second to being a family man. I honestly believe he could walk away from the football field tomorrow, if he decided he had coached as much football as was in him, and never look back. He could do that because he has found other values in life.

His first is his family. But he also gets it in the duck blinds or up there in the bullrushes around Gordon, Wisconsin, where he disappears when his work is done and not even the FBI could reach him.

He told me once he walked into his office on a Sunday in the off-season to pick up something he forgot, and ran into one of the executives. The executive was up to his eyeballs in work. Grant said he admired the man personally and respected his work, but he simply could not understand a person being so consumed by his occupation that he had to be down there seven days a week, feeding on it, letting some very precious time drain away that he might better use to let his life balance off. A time for work, a time for relaxing, a time for family, and a time just to breathe and walk among the high reeds at sunrise. Grant can do that. He is a compartmentalized man. I think the greatest strength Grant has with his players is their knowledge that he sees those things, has his values in order, that he is a moral and ethical man who also happens to be one tough rock to beat.

We talked for four hours about football in our first meeting. We talked about his philosophies, and then he put me at ease about the remarks Alan Page had made when the trade was announced. He said he was sure Alan had meant nothing personal, that he wanted to win as much as any player the Vikings had, and how torn up he had been by the loss to Dallas in the playoff game that previous season. He touched on his use of the three-quarterback system the previous year, when the Vikings had Cuozzo, Snead, and Lee. Grant fully expected Snead to take control of the job. But he said Snead never seemed to really come to grips with it in training camp. His arm had some aches, and he never took charge. So Bud rotated the job among the three, finishing with Bobby Lee as the starter the last month or so and in the playoff with Dallas. Basically, he said, he was a one-quarterback man, and that was the reason I was back with the Minnesota Vikings.

From the very beginning I felt at ease quarterbacking for Grant. The public sees him as a very austere guy—forbidding, I suppose you might say. But there are no tensions in his practice. Actually there is a lot of laughter. He teaches some, but the assistants are paid for that. Mostly he presides. He moves around without much visibility.

Once in a while he's sharp, but he is never cutting. I've played under Grant for four years, and I have never seen him strip a football player of his dignity. It's man-to-man stuff. He lets you know very early what is expected of you. He will go out of his way to tell a rookie that he doesn't have to go in there and win the ball game by himself. He will be very precise in what he expects the rookie to do. If the rookie doesn't do it the first time, he is going to have a chance to do it again. If he doesn't do it the second time, he should seriously consider barbering, because it is not likely he's going to play for the Minnesota Vikings.

There are two things Bud Grant does not want on a football team: dumb players and bad guys. A man would have to be at the upper level of all-pro quality to be either one and still play for Grant. He has indulged one or two of that variety in the years I've been with his teams. Grant may be a man of principle, but he's no idealist. If he has to play a bad guy, he will find the appropriate language to explain away the inconsistency. He will do it simply by denying there is any inconsistency. So-and-so isn't really greedy and self-centered, you understand; he merely appears to be.

All of that comes under the heading of realism, and no man ever coached pro football for twenty years without being a realist or a saint. As far as I know, only Vince Lombardi combined the two. While he is very careful not to make a public display of it, Grant does not treat all players alike. If a man's track record with the team warrants special consideration, he will give it, because that is a football player he is going to need. In this he parts with some of his colleagues, who maintain rigid codes that give them no maneuver. Some coaches make a spectacle of that. They force a confrontation. The management has to support either the coach or the star player. One way or other the team is going to lose. Grant avoids confrontations wherever he can. He obviously is not a timid guy. What he is is a very secure guy. He knows that if it came to a showdown he would have the support of management. But why bring it to that?

Grant is one of those leaders with the sense to know when a stand has to be made and when it can be sensibly postponed or avoided. He doesn't believe in making decisions until he absolutely has to.

Would you call that procrastination? I don't think so. The kinds of decisions a coach has to make often are best made on the last day or the last hour. Why decide who goes on waivers Monday, for example, when you can do it on Tuesday? On Monday afternoon two guys might get hurt. The decision might very well have been made for you, and you have saved yourself a lot of embarrassment as well as anguish. When all the information is in, Grant will act right now and not look back. Hindsight has killed off more coaches than interference from the owner's office.

Now, all of that requires a great amount of focus and orderliness and concentration, qualities that tend to obscure Grant's competitiveness. Television very often likes to personify competitiveness with closeups of George Allen agonizing or Ara Parseghian pacing or Woody Hayes ranting. I'm not low-rating any of those. But Grant's competitiveness seems, if anything, more animalistic. He's the guy in the jungle. Staring. Patient. Driven but careful. You get the feeling that one way or another he will get what he came for. We joke about it in the locker room. You remember the book *Alive,* about the South American rugby team that went down in the Andes Mountains? To survive, the passengers had to resort to cannibalizing the bodies of those who did not survive the cold or privation. Some guy in the locker room spoke up. "Wouldn't you hate," he said, "to be the last guy with Grant?" Well, he wasn't reflecting any on Grant's chivalry. What he was saying was that if it ever gets to be one-on-one in the jungle, Grant is the guy who will walk out.

They pulled that on Grant a little while later and he smiled, ever so slightly.

The TV cameras can make a cartoon of his impassive face on the sidelines, but the ballplayers in the NFL know this is a guy who will treat them right. He's traded players away from the Vikings in midseason, moves that cost them Super Bowl money. Still, you don't hear them ripping him when they're gone. And it certainly isn't because of any sentimental attachment they have for him.

I'll never forget the story John Beasley told when Grant called him into his office in the middle of the 1973 season. It was a Saturday morning after we finished practice for the week. You should know a little about Beasley to understand the interplay here. He was a tight end who sometimes sounded like one. I mean, he was one of those untroubled spirits who just let his good nature and emotion hang out. He was an intelligent guy and extremely popular, a veteran of seven years on the team. He got himself a huge amount of attention nationally and some prospective wealth when a prospector by the same name heard about him and gave him a share of a silver mine out West. Anyhow, John had labored honorably all these years, but after five games of the 1973 season Grant decided his team was supremely qualified to get to the Super Bowl without him. Beasley's presence on the roster behind Stu Voigt was retarding the development of rookie Doug Kingsriter. John also was displaying some symptoms of extremely original thought and behavior. So exit Beasley.

Grant gave him the news in his office. It was not exactly an emotional bath. Grant had planned a normal fall Saturday afternoon. One coach might go home and sweat about the big ball game. Another might rush to the TV to watch the college games. Grant goes down to the river bottoms to shoot ducks or quail or grizzlies or whatever he shoots on Saturday afternoon. Beasley walked into the office with his usual California gusto, to discover Grant stuffing shotgun shells into his jacket. There were old smudges of blood on the jacket from cleaning things, and he looked like The Deerslayer instead of a high-paid professional football coach who had just finished preparing his high-paid football team for the Detroit Lions.

I'm not sure whether John expected Grant to speak or squeeze off a round. Most newspapermen who deal with Grant daily will tell you he is actually an articulate and highly informative guy in a straightforward way, but in these end-of-the-road scenes he is never much of an orator.

"We've put you on waivers," he told John. "If nobody claims you, we'd like to keep you around. If you're claimed, good luck."

Good-bye seven years.

Beasley told us about it later when he had recovered his teeth and his good humor. "That guy," he said, "spoke to me three times all year. The first time he told me to trim my hair. The second time he told me to trim my mustache. The third time he trimmed *me.*"

Beasley was claimed and spent the rest of the season flourishing with the New Orleans Saints, which was a very tough status to achieve, given the Saints' won-lost record.

But even after he left town, Beasley was never owly about Grant. John recognized that when Grant finally had to make a decision to change the squad, and the decision involved him, nothing was served by turning the departure scene into a soap opera.

Still, within broad limits, he allows his players and coaches full expression of their personalities and attitudes. You take Jerry Burns, for instance. He is the offensive co-ordinator, the guy I have most of my dealings with. Grant distributes a lot of authority. I think he believes the most crucial decisions he makes as head coach involve the people who assist him. He will go literally for years without filling a coaching vacancy on his staff rather than fill it without being sure he has picked the best man available to him in terms of teaching ability and compatibility with the team and the rest of the coaches. Well, Burns is a shrewd, noisy, weather-wrinkled little guy who keeps a practice buzzing. Some of the things he does and says are beyond belief. He's chattering all the time, profanely, wisely, any way that rolls off his tongue. He can coach a guy for years and have trouble remembering his name. One of the more endearing things he'll say to a veteran fullback whose name he has temporarily forgotten will be "Try that block a little lower to the ground, big nuts."

I nearly flipped the first year I was back. In the third week of practice he yelled out, "You dropped a little deep on that, uh, No. 10." Twelve years of quarterbacking in the NFL! It could have been worse. He could have called me "big nuts."

One of the first things Grant did when I rejoined the Vikings was to schedule a meeting involving himself, Burns, and me. We were going to look at the whole Viking offensive scheme, and I appreciated that. I wanted them to know where I was coming from on quarterbacking a football team. I told them what I thought I could do well, what kind of plays I liked to run in certain situations. They did the same. They showed me the Viking offense. Some of it I liked; some of it was, well, narrow. I told them I would like to see more rollouts, more man-in-motion series because I thought that sort of offense maximized what I did well on the football field. It gave me more options. That was important because if I had any value over another quarterback, part of it was my experience. I wanted the widest possible range of play selection to exploit that experience in combination with whatever individual skills I had and the skills of the rest of the offensive team. I was going to work with Jerry, and I wanted to be sure he knew what kind of offense made me feel the most effective. That didn't mean I wanted to engineer the Viking offense. I was simply conveying what I consider the first principle of the effective play-caller. He's got to believe in what he's calling.

The three of us were together on that. In fact, in all the years I've worked with Grant and his staff, we've never had a problem being unified on how we approach a football game. There've been plenty of disagreements in the planning for some games, certainly. But we've always come up with a consensus we all can live with. Bud asked me to be frank, and I appreciated that. I said if they told me to do something I didn't believe in, I'd let them know and we would talk it out. I had to share their commitment to a play, or I didn't want to call it. I don't think an inexperienced quarterback would take that position. On the other hand, no coaching staff with any kind of maturity and good sense is going to let a seasoned quarterback function as an automaton and try to jam its playbook down his throat.

Even so, I readily admitted a seasoned quarterback can learn a thousand things each year he gets older in professional football. And I've learned much from Jerry Burns. When I'm not instantly overwhelmed by his logic, he knows I can be convinced. Listening to Burns is always a thrilling adventure anyway. His conversation sounds like a project in a chemical lab. It plops and bubbles. He uses technical lingo and barnyard words in the same sentences and with the same conviction. But he's got a very adroit, imaginative mind, and he has been the catalyst in a lot of games we have won.

His other great value is serving as a sort of Convulsion Factor in the practices and squad meetings. People who watch him in action for a day or so come away convinced he is a terrible, unbearable person with his constant practice-field snarlings. A week later the same people will classify Burnsie as a delightful and effective guy, which he is. Most of the times when he seems to be chewing on somebody he's actually talking to himself. He gets a release that way. It's a helluva dialogue, I'll say that.

People who make jokes about Grant standing stationary on the sideline in rainstorms and blizzards don't know the half of it. What he's hearing in those earphones is Jerry Burns from up in the press-box. Grant is standing there without a word, and Burns is screaming four-letter words a mile a minute about all the goddamned screwed-up officials or what is Tarkenton calling now or that last block by Tingelhoff or White looked putrid. He's just carrying on like a mad-man.

The way Grant takes it all in without moving a muscle makes it look like the head of the Strategic Air Command is on the other end of the phone, not this howling little guy with all the bad words. Grant must have some kind of scanning device in his brain that lets him filter out all that verbiage to get at the usable wisdom that's in there someplace. I don't want to give the impression that Burnsie's presentation over the phone is disorganized. It's just done at tremendous velocity and is highly colored with his judgments of some tackle's ancestry or his lovemaking tendencies.

With those characteristics, he has to be a patsy for the ball club's comics. Burns is afraid of animals and insects. I think he'd run away from a butterfly. In training camp people start collecting dead insects and little critters, and when the time comes, they put them in the movie projector, which Burns has to open. Somebody put a rubber snake in there once, and when Burns opened the machine he just went white and speechless. He shook so bad he had to sit down, like it was the beginning of a heart attack.

One day in the projection room at our practice field in St. Paul we hung a rubber spider from the ceiling with a cord that was practically invisible. Ed White sat in the back row of chairs slowly lowering this big, ugly rubber spider from the ceiling. We had it rigged so that the spider would descend exactly where Burns nor-mally stands. Down it came, until the spider suddenly dropped right in front of Burns' nose, hairy legs and all. Burns nearly choked. He shrieked and knocked over the projector. Just floored it.

But you've got to be able to develop a relationship with a guy like that, expecially when you respect his active mind, which is always probing. We have had no problems working together. We discuss every play thoroughly going into a game, and we are together on the things we want to do. We have winnowed out everything we think doesn't belong in there, and we are in accord.

It is one of the strengths of Grant's coaching that he is able to merge contradictory personalities—a sputtering, restless, dynamic guy like Burns; an intense, analytical, and psychologically perceptive man like John Michels, the offensive line coach; and a quiet and cool personality like Neil Armstrong, the defensive co-ordinator. None of them is a prima donna or lets his ambitions horn in on his judgments or his loyalties. And because each of them has a kind of solidity of his own, I think it has helped Grant bridge this huge transformation in player attitudes of today compared with what they were twenty years ago. I'd be willing to bet there isn't a day passes when some coach someplace in the country isn't being quoted in some version of this: "The athlete of today just doesn't have the same values as he did years ago. He's rich, independent, and selfish. You can't convince him it's in his interest and the interest of the team to work harder. He talks today about things like self-expression and being his own person, and all that is a lot of self-indulgent manure that we keep piling up by paying them or giving them everything they want."

Is that an overdrawn statement of a coaching state of mind in the country today? I don't think so. You don't hear it, of course, from the Grants and Landrys and Shulas and Paul Browns. Each of them learned his values in an older era when it wasn't tough to enforce discipline and when players were routinely dehumanized to achieve the goal of unquestioning obedience to the coach. Yet each has made himself believable to a different type of athlete, the one who may be wealthier, yes, but more importantly the one who will not buy all of the old b.s. that tried to make robots out of the players.

Grant has done it mostly on the soundness of his character and his willingness to practice his own dogma about submerging the individual ego for the benefit of the team. He doesn't have to be an up-front guy to experience the gratifications in coaching. He gets that out of winning. He isn't lifted to the stars by winning today and then dumped into catatonic shock by a defeat. He goes home every Sunday to eat dinner at seven o'clock with his family and play pool with his kids and watch a movie on television.

Despite all the exasperations of the 1972 season, I found myself at least being a whole football player, and it was satisfying. I had the experience, the skills, I was in an environment where I *knew* a championship would follow, and I remember pausing now and then driving home to try to locate myself, where I had been, where I was going. And very often this search would take the form of measuring myself for the right to belong with some of the great football people I had played with and against. It wasn't really daydreaming. Maybe it was the veteran athlete's version of the parlor games of my childhood. So I would allow myself a reflective look at the years. I wasn't congratulating myself on having come this far, but reminding myself to taste the full measure of the excitement of this time of my life, before those thoughts became the old jock's nostalgia.

Dick Butkus' face always jumps at me at times like those. Butkus, with his mustache and that black, ugly Chicago Bear hard hat. I think Dick Butkus is the greatest football player I have ever seen. Certainly the toughest. He was honestly tough. You hear about middle linebackers eating fullbacks and spitting out bones and thigh-pads and all the old gruesome deeds of the violent world. Butkus was the main man, and all the pros will tell you that, when it came to linebackers who combined fierceness with technical brilliance. He didn't have to put on a show, and he never did. He was so great he could take a group of average football players around him and make them play better than they knew how to play because they respected him so much they were scared of what he would do to them if they didn't play.

Butkus loved to play football, and he played it with incredible intensity. Whenever you played the Chicago Bears you were aware of Dick Butkus. You weren't aware of the over-all defense. You were aware of Butkus because you knew that any time you ran or passed successfully you would somehow have to escape him. He was going to make an interception or he was going to chase a play forty yards. One way or another he was going to be involved if the Bears did something right. He kept his team in a frenzy every game. He was the most dominating single player I've ever seen in a football defense. He had the kind of temperament that made him want to engulf the whole offense by himself.

You will hear the term "animal instinct" used to describe Butkus' disposition, but that is really inadequate, because most people playing in a physical kind of sport have to have that. Butkus took it a step beyond. He just reveled in the collisions, the tumult, maybe even the pain. He was a sight. He snorted and cursed and looked like Godzilla's brother crouching there in front of the center. Tingelhoff told me that when Butkus retired it added three years to his career and restored him to good standing with the insurance companies. Butkus was no unthinking brute, although he might not object to being portrayed that way for the benefit of his testimonials. Butkus not only had instincts but also a good head for the game. When he retired, I sent him congratulations and the little white flag I used to carry around in my helmet in case I needed it when we played the Bears.

Some of the younger fans of today don't know about Gino Marchetti. He was one of the guys who stood ten feet tall with me when I was a kid watching television, and I remember how much I respected him when I played against him my first couple of years in the league. Then we played together one game, in the Pro Bowl after the 1964 season. He was thirty-nine and it was the last game of his career. Cleveland had beaten Marchetti's Baltimore team by three or four touchdowns in the NFL championship game that season, and according to the way we got it, the crowd came onto the field with thirty seconds left and started to tear down the goalposts. The referee went to Frank Ryan, the Cleveland quarterback, and asked him if it was all right to let the clock run out right there. Ryan is supposed to have refused. Obviously it was okay with Marchetti, who was the Baltimore defensive captain. When Ryan supposedly asked for another play, Marchetti groaned. That was rubbing their faces in it, he figured.

A few weeks later Ryan was one of the Eastern Conference quarterbacks in the Pro Bowl. In his low-key way, Gino told us several times before the game he was going to make it up to Ryan. You hear a lot of that in football. But Marchetti sounded as though he meant it. Late in that game Ryan went back to pass. A guy sitting next to me nudged me and said, "There goes Gino." Marchetti beat his man and just threw himself into Ryan. I could think of a few million people I would rather change places with at that moment than Frank Ryan. Marchetti piled into him legally. But I don't think that was much consolation to Ryan, because when they finished examining him, the doctors said it was a shoulder separation.

Deacon Jones of the Rams stood right up there with Marchetti among the greatest linemen. The guy weighed 275 pounds and used to outrun Carroll Dale in the fifty-yard dashes in the Rams' camp, and Dale was a sprinter. Deacon covered the field from sideline to sideline and was a frightening sight coming at you on the pass rush. Which brings me to Mean Joe Greene. The first time I played against him was in 1969 when they were singing "Good-bye, Allie." Mean Joe Greene just stood up there on the line and said, "Nobody can block me, brothers."

And he was about right. We played him again in New York, and he took a swing at me on the sidelines, for what reason I don't know. He landed, too, but I took most of the impact on a pad. Otherwise, he would have put me in a coma. They threw him out of the game, which tended to ease some of our blocking problems and made the world safe once more for Methodist quarterbacks.

Then when I got back to Minnesota we played a game against Pittsburgh. I called one of those Public School 28 reverses where everybody winds up in front of the ball carrier, including the quarterback. The play called for me to peel back and block on targets of opportunity. The only available target of opportunity for me was Mean Joe Greene. With all the gallantry I could muster I hurled my 187 pounds at Mean Joe's shoelaces. I don't know whether he was seized by terror or didn't see me. One way or other he tripped over me and took himself out of the play. When he saw who the blocker was, he pulled off his helmet and laughed until the referee had to tell him to go back to his huddle.

Bob Lilly of the Dallas Cowboys may have been the best defensive tackle I ever played against or saw. He was just an unbelievable football player, whom I remember with special pain because in one Pro Bowl he smashed my face mask, mangled my lip, and gave me a ton of stitches. Nothing personal, he's just that strong.

You think of Alex Karras in the same breath. As far as I'm concerned, there was an underrated player. Because he's something of a clown on football television, people have forgotten or never realized what a great football player he was. And when you talk about memorable characters, you have to put Bill Brown of the Vikings right up there at the head of the billboard. You could call him Billy Football, I guess. He had those runty bowlegs and that World War II crewcut and that busted-up face and that hoarse, raspy voice. In some ways he looked like he came out of a Sergeant Bilko squad formation or a Bill Mauldin cartoon. But God, he was tough! And a tremendous football player, just the best all-around fullback in pro ball for years.

I'll never forget an exhibition game when Brown was playing the wedge on the kickoff team. After all his years as a starter, and being the most popular player in the history of the Vikings, he agreed to be captain of the suicide teams—and he even did *that* job better than anybody ever did. In this game Ed Marinaro kept telling Brown he didn't want to play that wedge position (Marinaro was the backup there) and it was all right with him if Brown kept it the whole game. Brown needled Marinaro all the time anyway, about being a greenhorn from the Ivy League. So Brown said, "Don't worry about it, rook, don't worry about it."

In the second quarter Brown came in for an offensive series and I called a screen pass to him, which figured, because he was the best pass-catching back I ever played with. But the rush screwed up the timing and I hung him up long enough for the linebacker to give him a terrific shot. Just busted up his ribs. Brown couldn't get his breath back. He groped around on his hands and knees for a few seconds and then actually crawled off the field.

On the sidelines he just sat there gasping and gurgling. I was sure he was about to go into his death shakes. And so was Marinaro, his young protégé. Marinaro came over to Brown and said, "Oh, no." What grieved Ed most was that on the next kickoff he'd have to replace Brown in the wedge, and the man the fullback was assigned to block was the biggest rookie on the other team, 6 feet 7 and 270 pounds. Marinaro sidled up to Brown and said, "Must hurt like hell, Brown, I don't suppose there's any chance you can take the next kick?" Five minutes later we scored. When the kickoff team ran out, there was No. 30, Brown, standing in the wedge, hunched up a little and breathing like he's about to drown. The two teams collided at the twenty-five-yard line and Brown just buried that 6-foot-7 rookie. Knocked him right out of the ball game.

Everybody loved Boomer Brown. Even the Viet Cong. He went to Vietnam in the off-season with a bunch of jocks, touring the hospitals. They were staying in a hotel in Saigon. Everybody had strict orders to stay in his room because bombs were going off all the time. Finally somebody decided they would be safer if everybody on the floor went into the same room, so an emergency order was put out, announcing all personnel should proceed forthwith to the designated room, carrying their mattresses. The order caught Brown by surprise. He charged out of his room carrying a mattress and wearing not one thread of clothes. Even fully clothed Brown is a gripping sight, so you can imagine what he looked like bolting into that brightly lit room with his bowlegs, bare everything, and a mattress on his back. They tell me the fifteen women in the room could not believe it.

Brown was a classic. We could always get a laugh sticking it to the Boomer. But I never saw a man who did more for a football team in the locker room or on the practice field. He was chattering, hustling, chewing out, philosophizing, burning rookies, hazing Burns, always something. We timed Brown once, actually ran a test on the practice field to see how long he could keep quiet. The watch showed two seconds.

Boomer was close to retirement. But he was still around in 1973.

Most of the old crowd was, too, and for all of the grief of the 1972 season, I knew 1973 had to be written in the stars for us. This was still the Age of Aquarius. And the quarterback was born on February 3, an undeniable Aquarian.

Super Bowl, 1974

12

Jimmy (The Greek) Snyder's jewelry had the unbashful quality of an antiaircraft searchlight. Even in the lobby of a Houston hotel it commanded respect.

The Greek wore his Super Bowl week ensemble, a four-hundred-dollar gray suit with silk tie and alligator shoes, and all the luminous accessories. In ascending order of candlepower these consisted of a gold bracelet with The Greek's name embossed in letters a half inch high, a gemstone stickpin, and a ring with the sociable girth of a plump tangerine.

The Greek could have been outfitted in an Egyptian tomb.

As he walked, he clanked affably. His smile was generous, but The Greek was no prima donna. Although he was one of the fully notarized Super Bowl spectacles, he acknowledged that his act had some competition. Among the distractions this January of 1974 were the Minnesota Vikings and the Miami Dolphins.

Accordingly, The Greek paid a midweek courtesy call on the Minnesota press delegation in the lobby of Houston's Sheraton Town and Country Inn. He carefully avoided glad-handing Francis Tarkenton and Grady Alderman as the two strolled by. The Greek was pure, but form had to be observed. The commissioner would approve of such restraint.

The Greek's processional of Las Vegas swells moved noisily through the lobby, giving all the rubbernecking guests from Min-

nesota a decent time to be amazed. A few anxiously inquired about
The Greek's prophetic reading for the game. He rendered his verdict
with regrets. "It's still Miami by six," he said. "Notice I did not say
'the spread' or 'odds.' That's gambler talk. I don't give odds. I give
figures. You may think that's splitting hairs, but it keeps me out of
jail.

"Miami is just faster than you people," he went on to explain.
"I mean, the linemen and the linebackers. Also, their defensive backs
are better. Nobody in football is as good as Jake Scott and Dick
Anderson. Then there are the field-goal kickers. . . ."

The Greek seemed genuinely anguished to have to break the
news in this fashion. His processional then vanished into the armada
of expensive cars parked in the driveway.

One of the lobby oglers was a tall, spare man wearing a flopping
jacket and lounging slippers. He seemed misplaced in the chichi
decor, and might have been mistaken for the janitor. He arrived late
and, although standing on tiptoes, was able to catch only a few
flickering carats of The Greek's retreating radiance.

An acquaintance sidled up to Harry Peter Grant, apologizing for
stepping on his slippers. "Did you ever meet Jimmy The Greek?" he
asked the coach. "Not a bad guy. Strictly a created institution, a
snow job on the public, cashing in on some vague old recognition of
'Nick The Greek.' Does his presence in this hotel bother you?"

"I never met him," Grant replied, sounding heartbroken. "No,
it doesn't bother me. Meeting important guys like Jimmy The Greek,
you know, is one of the incentives for professional football people to
make it to the Super Bowl."

Among the people infinitely more important to Grant in Houston
that week was the Vikings' rookie running back, Chuck Foreman. In
their preseason promotion the Vikings attributed to Foreman a wide
variety of superhuman qualities. He was alleged to be as fast and
spectacular as the northern lights, as powerful as Paul Bunyan, and
as hard to capture as a Minnesota walleye. This created some doubt
whether Foreman was animal, vegetable, or mineral. It also caused
broad skepticism among the Minnesota Viking veterans, who had
heard rookie running backs so described the three previous seasons.

None of them had approached these specifications, let alone the Viking roster.

As though recognizing this tradition, Foreman threw up on the first day of rookie camp in his first official act as a Viking.

But by the second week of summer camp he had convinced the veterans. By the third week he had convinced Grant, an extraordinary deed in view of Grant's long-standing conviction that playing rookies was a sin against nature. Foreman ran with strength and dedication. He was willing to take a blow, but he had in hand a dozen ways to avoid one, including straight-ahead speed, lateral speed, reverse speed, three-quarter speed, spins, half spins, aborted spins, knees, arms, and elbows. He could catch the ball deep, catch it flaring, catch it in front of him, and catch it out of the ear of defensive backs. He was a real, breathing wonder boy, and the only thing certain about his future was that although he was great as a rookie, he was going to be out of this universe in a couple of years. He was coachable, intelligent, proud, and willing. He was polite to his elders, and he hit like an avalanche.

Very little of this was lost on the probing eyes of Francis Tarkenton.

The Vikings had the all-purpose superstar running back they had been pining for. A couple of days before the team opened the 1973 season against Oakland, Tarkenton nudged Carl Eller in the shower room. "Hey, big Carl," he said, "make no plans for January that don't include Houston, Texas. I think we got an appointment there."

"I been thinking," he said, "in those terms, Francis."

It was the kind of measured, matured confidence a team experiences when it understands its strengths and can put a failure like 1972 in perspective. It wasn't age that had turned Minnesota into a mediocrity. The fans and the analysts worried about the imminent obsolescence of players like Marshall, Brown, Eller, Krause, Winston, Hilgenberg, Alderman, Tingelhoff, and Larsen. They didn't worry about the quarterback, who belonged to the same geological period. Antiquity is one quality not scorned in a quarterback. But one person who didn't worry about anybody's age was Bud Grant.

"Age alone doesn't end the career of a veteran ballplayer," he said. "There are thirty-year-old players who have had it, but there are thirty-six-year-old players who can still go because they have cared for their bodies and are willing to make sacrifices, and they can win with their heads as well as their legs. Someday Jim Marshall will have to step out, but I guarantee it won't be in 1973."

For Marshall and the others, 1973 became a football player's Shangri-la. They swept through the exhibitions, rolled back Oakland three straight plays on the goal line, and won nine in a row. At that point Norm Van Brocklin—in a deed that might have been decreed by a hunchbacked sorcerer rather than by simple justice—stopped them in Atlanta. But they were moving irrevocably toward the playoffs. For Tarkenton, the vindication of it was not so blissful that he could overlook the stings he had acquired en route. He was never going to win in the pros or rise above .500. Wasn't that it? If he now acted surprised that it was actually happening, or even seem impressed, it was an admission that the old slogans he scoffed at had some substance. So when people kept asking, he was ornately calm. "A satisfying season," he would say. Sometimes it was hard to detect his intramural wink.

And what a season! Never mind the myths about having to prove it by wearing a Super Bowl ring. For the first time in Tarkenton's professional life it all blended: the fraternity of the field and dressing room, the burgeoning excitement, the anticipation of the playoff season, the triumphant tone of the crowds. The country was watching. Football was just a little nobler now. It had taken a dozen years for Tarkenton to feel it. Putting on the uniform in the big leagues always gratifies a man. But somehow, winning seems to sanctify all the sweat and struggle.

It wasn't without grief. Karl Kassulke didn't make it to Houston, or to training camp. There was a motorcycle accident the day before the start of the summer season. And suddenly, the guffawing, rampaging hunky, with his unshirted zests for living and his great heart, was crippled for life.

And in late season there was an interlude, little noticed in the community but disturbing to the team, when Brent McClanahan's problems led him to escape to chemicals. The Bible-reading young halfback had to be removed from the squad for hospital treatment, to return a season later in the kind of comeback that only the pro athlete can truly understand for the discipline and nerve it required.

Tarkenton's instincts and football migrations told him the Vikings of 1973 had more quality and better direction than any team he had been identified with. He marveled every time he saw Jim Marshall slip on a jersey. Marshall hadn't missed a game since 1960, yet he was still a rollicking playground sprite in the locker room, and oblivious to pain and the mounting years on the field.

Marshall's fantasy lives were receding somewhat now in his football senescence. For years he had been an unquenchable role player, imagining himself the Count of Monte Cristo in death duels with the dark-hearted baron, or the balloonist Montgolfier hanging onto his gondola over the stormy Channel. He had a sweet-sad gift for reaching to the stars and tumbling into an awkward heap, but his buoyancy and gnomish mimicry always rescued him from any lasting downers. He was hospitalized once for a week because he swallowed a grape incorrectly. He survived a blizzard in the mountains on a cruel night when a lighthearted caravan was torn apart, and a companion died. He shot himself in the side accidentally one year, allegedly guarding a large sum of money in his glove compartment. The report about the large sum of money surprised both his friends and his financial advisers. But he always recovered to laugh with the world, and now he had one final and climactic role, that of the football elder statesman.

On the sidelines Tarkenton frequently found himself gaping at the strength of Carl Eller and the gymnastic grace of Alan Page. The ball game had changed in the NFL over the past few years. The Viking front four didn't terrorize the league anymore because tactics had been revised; quarterbacks ran more now and wouldn't sit there and await demolition on a third-and-twelve pass play. And Tarkenton couldn't imagine what or who inspired the quarterbacks to behave with such impropriety.

However the press and the customers saw it, he did not bleed at all in losing to Van Brocklin and his oncharging football team this time. It was another great scenario, all right, the old antagonists meeting once more in the town where both lived. It had been described as the biggest pro football game ever played in the heart of the Confederacy. The Dutchman won, and the world continued to revolve. The critics the next day were generous about Dutch's preparations; and he deserved the recognition.

But Atlanta did not make the playoffs. It was a pity. The teams would have met in a December rematch in Minnesota, and it assuredly would have been billed as the biggest pro football game ever played in the heart of the icepack.

The Vikings met the Washington Redskins in the playoffs, and the Vikings almost strangled on their own tension in the opener. Eller saved them with a wrath-of-God half-time diatribe that climaxed when he sent an instructional chalkboard crashing across the floor. It was understood that whoever failed to deliver in the second half would have to answer to Eller, and there was nothing on the Redskin roster as punitive as that.

Their victory over Washington qualified the Vikings for the National Football Conference championship game with the Cowboys in Dallas. The immediate crisis was not Dallas but the Minnesota winter. How do you prepare for a title game in Texas on four feet of frozen topsoil in Minnesota, a condition aggravated by sporadic blizzards? Tulsa, Grant disclosed, offered a workable alternative.

The very thought of three days in Tulsa strikes some people with the force of biblical retribution. It was said that old-time priests gave penitent carousers their choice in the confessional: ten recitations of the Rosary or three days in Tulsa.

Grant regarded all these as crude fables and slanders. He is a man of modest artistic appetites. He prizes tranquillity, the uncomplicated rhythms of life, and the value of good vegetables in the promotion of the body juices. Coincidentally, all of these are available in fabulous quantities in Tulsa. And in addition to its noncombustible atmosphere, Tulsa offered firm footing for Grant's warriors and the probability of near-Texas weather.

On the Vikings' first day in this subtropical sanctuary the community was attacked by an ice storm.

It converted Tulsa into an uncharted glacier, paralyzing all vehicular traffic and intimidating pedestrians. The lone exceptions were the Minnesota Vikings, who fell upon the Arctic conditions ecstatically. It was a little swatch of home, to be treasured and cultivated.

They gamboled on the ice fields with schoolboy happiness, seizing yard-long icicles from the motel eaves to impress passersby with their skill as swordsmen. They also thought nothing of dismounting en route to the ball park to push their own bus when the driver refused to turn another wheel for fear of driving into a crevasse. It thawed enough the second day to permit the Vikings to conduct a full-pad workout in slush and running water. Except for the artificial turf, it was a faithful reproduction of Metropolitan Stadium in late season and further heightened the athletes' soaring morale.

To appease thrill-seekers on the team, Grant took them to a movie. And then, at the appropriate moment, he flew the team to Dallas. With satisfaction he observed the symptoms of rising passion. His only fear was that all their ardor would spend itself before the Vikings raced into the Dallas stadium to inflame their admirers on television by lining up impeccably for the national anthem. It was heartening to Grant to discover that his men had achieved a utopian happy medium eighteen hours before the game.

He found Mick Tingelhoff asleep in the Dallas motel lobby.

Grant silently applauded. He did not want his squad's emotional readiness to reach electric excitement. Tingelhoff's posture indicated that this danger had been safely avoided.

But nobody wearing purple horns was asleep that Sunday afternoon.

From its opening moments the game struck Tarkenton as a consecration of the entire season. It was a sensation he had not felt in football, and he had been at it for twenty years at all the levels. He couldn't wait to call the next play. The Viking misdirection offense worked in ways not even its architects could explain. He had played in scores of games where his team got all the lucky hops and calls, but this one seemed positively preordained. Every huddle crackled with the exhilaration of a football team playing its game of games. To the cool executive quarterback it was as close as he had ever been to Nirvana.

The Vikings seemed almost to change their personality and robes, removing the stainless steel of their robot suits for the flowing capes of raffish adventurers. They hoodwinked the Cowboys, directing them on futile chases by disguising their normal blocking patterns. They even ignored the laws of gravity by having Tarkenton throw a sixty-five-yard pass.

For these and other wonders, not the least of which was the 21–7 final score, Grant gave generous credit to the odd regenerative powers of the city of Tulsa. It wasn't the natural gas in the air, or even the salutary presence of Oral Roberts. What it was, Grant, insisted, was the quiet.

He mourned its loss a week later when the Vikings arrived for their Super Bowl confrontation with the Dolphins in the city of Houston, an unremitting foe of quiet.

Whenever Grant feels himself and his team slipping into the grasp of show-biz characters who live on the fringes of his football life—such as Jimmy The Greek, television impresarios, and National Football League administrators at the Super Bowl—he experiences a rush of sadness. He believes the Super Bowl has been captured by the ghost of P. T. Barnum. Grant is hardly an antisocial creature; yet his conception of the greatest football game on earth is one in which the contestants slip into the Super Bowl city shortly before the game and spend the night in a monastery. Uncorrupted, they then plunge into action without once being assaulted by relatives from Eureka or regiments of barefoot autograph hunters. Not once would a shaggy New Jersey journalist ask the tight end if he ascribed his role in life to an Electra complex coupled with latent tendencies to chase fire wagons.

Most of these outrages, Grant predicted, would happen in Houston. He grieved, because in some measure it meant that Events Were Out of Control, a condition that always jostled Grant's sense of tidiness.

Steadiness. Constancy. Stability. Predictability. Consistency. These words were chiseled subliminally in Grant's stable and constant forehead. Nobody hung them on the bulletin board. Grant didn't believe in bulletin boards. But to thrive they needed an atmosphere congenial to homely, Tom Swift–style football virtues. So to the other capital letters you had to add Routine.

In Grant's carefully arranged universe, Routine guarded against the deadly intrusion of Surprise. And Routine meant doing Friday before the game what you did last Friday before the game, and the Friday before that, and the Fridays of last year. And when you lump the Fridays with the Thursdays and the Wednesdays and the Saturdays, you get an awful lot of days that look familiar. So you were very comfortable on those days, and therefore almost always on Sundays.

The Vikings raised only one objection when sophisticates around the league jeered at them as squares from the alfalfa fields. Grant's system worked.

The problem was: Did Grant have enough players on the team who were worldly enough and carefree enough to adapt when confronted with Houston, Texas, twelve hundred reporters, the NFL impresarios, a hundred-thousand-dollar hoedown at the Astrodome, autograph-chasing multitudes, and Jimmy The Greek? By combining Super Bowl week with Houston, Grant reasoned, the NFL had found what the Red Cross had not—a disaster that could be predicted.

The first tremors developed on the opening practice day. Grant's football team arrived at its prescribed training-field quarters at Delmar School to find a locker room apparently designed for the East Dry Gulch Groundhogs. It was the first record-breaking statistic of Super Bowl week: the only locker room in Super Bowl history without a locker. In the middle of the room were tables, on which some of the toniest athletes in America were required to drop their pants.

Skivvies and drawers followed.

Of the fifteen shower heads in the bathing section, three revealed signs of activity. The others were arid. Two of them atoned for their derelictions by serving as nesting grounds for a pair of sparrows.

"Men," declared Jim Marshall, "consider yourselves honored. It is the first time we have ever showered in an aviary."

Among the trousers that dropped unmilitarily were those identified as Bud Grant's. Although the room was rude and claustrophobic, it did have a certain democratic charm: The coaches had to undress right in there with the kickoff-return serfs. This created no dignity gap for Grant, a distant man but never a ceremonial one. He did walk out of the dressing room, however, with the sternly set jaw of a Norseman who has just been shafted in the fjord.

Grant's public eruptions are outnumbered by floods in the Sahara. There is only one act that can tempt him into any kind of display more emotional than clearing his throat: He abominates unprofessional conduct.

So he decided to erupt. The National Football League was unprepared for it. Grant's relatives were unprepared. It was like an unscheduled appearance of Haley's Comet. All assembled in Houston gaped at the phenomenon.

Grant stood up at his first Super Bowl press conference and denounced the National Football League's lack of professionalism in assigning a Little League locker room to his professional football team. His players deserved better, and the sovereign state of Minnesota deserved better. He indicted the league functionaries for sloppy preparation and bad eyesight. From emotional coaches you expect detonations. From Grant you expect the pulsing drone of computer logic. Everybody quickly checked the condition of the coach's solenoid. The mechanical man must have taken some bad oil.

To the puzzlement of the NFL hierarchs, Grant did it again the next day. This time he held the head hierarch himself, Pete Rozelle, personally responsible for the Vikings' dressing room ignominies.

If it's possible for a man to look suave and sandbagged at the same time, Rozelle answered the description. He also looked slightly browned off. Word was promptly tossed into the press corps pipeline that the commissioner was solemnly weighing a fine against Grant for various felonies against the regime. Grant subsided eventually, explaining that he blew up for two reasons: First, he was honestly infuriated by the locker room episode because it seemed to downgrade a football team and the game itself; second, he decided to deflect the writing hordes from their usual scattershot coverage of Super Bowl week and the possible distractions it might cause his players. So he, the nonimpresario, would stage a little production himself. He would be the lightning rod.

"My basic feeling about the Super Bowl hasn't changed," he said afterward. "It's a showcase week for professional football, and I understand all the stops being pulled to make it an extravaganza. But as a general rule I don't think they can have both that and a great football game. You work for twenty-one weeks in a controlled environment in which the players are comfortable because they know what to expect. And then you put them into this carnival, and the record shows you rarely get a great or even good football game out of it. I talked to Don Shula the week before our game and he had the right bead on it. He said it was a circus, but what are you going to do?"

The commissioner knew what to do. When it was all over he fined Bud Grant fifteen hundred dollars for unprofessional conduct.

The Grant lightning rod didn't work for long, and the journalistic thunderbolts began seeking their natural targets, viz., Larry Csonka of Miami and Francis Tarkenton.

Csonka was a magnetic subject for what newspapermen call the in-depth profile. He had a massive head, and a broad nose that seemed to straddle his mustache. He could have worked in an underground mine and been instantly recognized as a relative by all the Balkan diggers. His face and carriage bespoke a primitive force. The more imaginative of the chroniclers drew a comparison between Csonka and the second most popular grilling subject in the Miami press conferences, tackle Manny Fernandez. Fernandez projected smoldering, weary hostility. He replied to some questions—such as "Do you find yourself slowly building a hatred for Mick Tingelhoff?" —with a salvo of silence. Another questioner built his interview on the bedrock cliché, "Is this the biggest game of your life, and how much emotionalism will there be in it for you?"

"What big game?" Fernandez responded, exhaling a breath of prolonged incredulity, the gesture of a man trapped in a room with contentious but harmless idiots. "Every game I ever played was a big game. What do I have to do to show that I'm emotional? Run onto the field with two rockets strapped to my ass?"

Csonka was as thoughtful at the daily press symposiums as Fernandez was disdainful. The ballplayers' behavior at these inquisitions depended on their tolerance level for humbug. What bothered some of them wasn't the intelligence level of the questioners (which was pretty high, after all) or the quality of the questions (erratic). What embarrassed all the participants was the regimented solemnity of it all. The writers would wire back to their public lightly contemptuous accounts of the Super Bowl scene. But when they found themselves cued by the public-address announcements in the press conference ballrooms ("Ladies and gentlemen, Mercury Morris has now entered the room and will be available at Table 8"), the herd instinct took over. They behaved as programmed. The Super Bowl was an extravaganza, and they all had walk-on roles. Supernumeraries. Once each day the league would parade the athletes, and the bit players dutifully laid on their questions.

Csonka was invariably polite. You always asked him what he didn't like about training ten-year-old kids to behave like Super Bowlers in the potato fields of America.

Csonka hated the Little League fixation of America. He recognized this as a heresy, but he made it palatable to the reading millions with thick overlays of reasonableness and sincerity. The reporters usually remarked about that. Csonka was a heretic with feeling. His courtesy and relaxed independence made him likable. It was also clear that he was a young man of his times, socially aware and committed. Hundreds of in-depth profiles streamed across the country. The thinking man's Neanderthal. Butch Cassidy, or was it the Sundance Kid, was alive and maturing. Although he tired of it, after the first seventy-five minutes of in-depthing, he made no scene-ending declarations. When they hired Larry Csonka, they hired his duff as well as his forearms. He also had history on his side. The Hungarians were accustomed to surviving plagues and intrusions. They had been doing it for centuries.

Which might explain, incidentally, why Miami coach Don Shula, one of the Magyar clan, flourished in the charivari atmosphere of the Super Bowl. Maybe the Hungarians had acquired a national trait of adaptability. If you can adapt to Bulgarians, Romanians, Czechs, Germans, and Greeks and still get along with Hungarians, you should not be terrified by the thought of Super Bowl circuses. You outlast them, humor them, and confuse them. So there was a difference between the Dolphins' reaction to the circus and the Vikings'. Shula had an easy style of bemusement in the face of the whirling ballyhoo and contrived significance. It wore better than Grant's studious attempts to counteract them. In their own style, all of the combatants sought some defense mechanism for the game's insufferable importance inlaid by the NFL and the horn-blowing TV and press.

"No matter how cool you play it," the Vikings' Gary Larsen was asked, "isn't something really on trial for the ballplayers as people and individuals?"

Larsen tried to be responsive. "Yes," he said. "It is probably the biggest football game of my life. But I hope you don't think I'm a wiseguy when I add one thing: We've sweated a long time for this, and a whole bunch of people will be watching on TV. But there are eight hundred million Chinamen who don't give a good goddamn about what happens in Houston this Sunday afternoon."

It had the force of a Confucian proverb.

The same could not be said, on the other hand, for 75 million American television watchers.

Overhearing Larsen's summation, Tarkenton could smile his endorsement. Yet he understood that the quarterback in the nature of things is expected to expand on the most minute tactical details of the approaching crisis as well as the enormity of the Super Bowl as a sociospiritual phenomenon.

Did it heap new pressures on the besieged quarterback?

Did it matter?

He loved it.

And he did it better than almost anyone else. He bantered and talked with discernment. He talked provocatively, spoofed the super-sober question, outflanked the embarrassing ones, and plowed into the allegedly tough ones. He bandied big names. He downgraded the role of the quarterback and elevated the role of the extra-point holder. He spoke reverently of Grant and respectfully of Miami. Any way they wanted it. He wore a horrendous hat given to Ed White by a friend. It was part Mexican sombrero, part Aussie campaign hat, and it had a big pheasant feather stuck in the brim. It was a kind of statement, declaring that the Super Bowl was intended to be fun rather than an ordeal.

For Tarkenton, Super Bowl week was as much a celebration of the heart as it was the preparation for a football game. The goblins of his career had been buried, whether the public was willing to accept that or not. Because he had never played on a championship team in pro ball until then, did that mean he wasn't a winning quarterback? If so, how do you explain the Georgia championship the last time he played with a contending team before his entry into pro ball? And even when he didn't win a championship, should he spend his off-season hours in contrition, vowing redemption in the next year?

That was one of the popular pictures of the professional quarterback, of a man on perpetual probation until they slipped a championship ring on his finger, a man whose soul was a hostage until he proved some mystical right to stand beside the mighty. Tarkenton deflated that picture on the slightest provocation. Pro football had been a zinging good time, he said, with or without championships.

But the Super Bowl did belong on another plane. A ballplayer sought certain surmounting professional moments. This was one of them. And Tarkenton was therefore obliged to find a comfortable emotional posture for himself on the eve of that quest.

"You don't want ever to put yourself on a cliff before any ball game," he said that Saturday night. "You can't be saying, 'This is the biggest thing that's going to happen,' because if you lose, you know that's a lie. If you win, someplace you're going to have to do it all over again. I have to say this: If winning the Super Bowl is the most important thing that's ever going to happen to each man on this team, then we have got our values tipped over. But I have to qualify that. I've never been so hungry, and I've never been with a team I thought was so ready. You have no idea what we have had these last three weeks. It's just like the feeling you get in a spiritual rejuvenation, standing up and singing in a chorus. It lifts you. You are standing there in the huddle, and you have it going, and you know you can beat them, and you just want to tell the world, 'This is our team, we've got it together.'

"If a whole football team committing itself to the season has any meaning and any reward," he went on, "we are going to win this football game. If Miami can beat this football team they've got to be super in every way, and I think they'd also have to be lucky. I want to jump right out of this room, I'm so ready to play this football game."

So the executive quarterback, of all people, was on a high. He was also loose. At the team table that night he passed out gag T-shirts with a slaphappy sketch of Bud Grant on the front. Even committed football teams needed pacifiers. Tarkenton couldn't imagine what Miami was using. Maybe Manny Fernandez was impersonating a newspaperman, interviewing Csonka.

But an hour before the game, the atmosphere was a little less relaxed. Ed White could tell it was a special day by looking down at the sweat socks he had just put on. You were supposed to put the long socks on first, then the sweats. Some nameless force on the day of the big game impelled White to put on his sweat socks first. It happened too predictably to be assigned to simple jitters. White prowled around the locker room, studying his playbook and growling. It was his style. Roy Winston was probably in the can, throwing up. You had to worry when he didn't. Hilgenberg was bitching to Jimmy Eason about *his* socks. Conditions normal. Page wondered how he was going to change in the broom-closet locker room without suffering contusions. The rookie Foreman sat by himself, cramming the playbook into his head every loose minute.

On television screens all over the country, choirs of analysts were falling over themselves talking about significance, and when the producers took over, seventy-five million viewers had no doubts. Their screens filled with the Goodyear blimp, the Houston skyline, before-the-battle close-ups of the warriors, all taut, all ferocious but controlled, looking like trench fighters waiting for the whistle.

They were back from the warm-up, and nobody thought about calm professionalism now. This was the golden chalice for the football player. The Super Bowl. If you didn't clutch up about it, you weren't human. There was even a momentary fellowship among opponents, because only the football player can understand the hunger and will it takes to carry a man from the playground to the Super Bowl. In the corridor between dressing rooms, Don Shula slapped Bob Lurtsema on the tail. They once had a player-coach relationship at Baltimore, and now Shula was wishing him good luck, although they were with rival teams. Between the lines he was congratulating a journeyman football player for having the nerve and faith to outlast the waiver lists, to deserve this culminating day.

In the Viking locker room Grant said a few words, and then Grady Alderman, recognizing this as an occasion in which even Grant would not object to some Knute Rockne electricity, began to recite the names of the defensive team that would start the game.

It was raw incitement, and it lit their frenzies. With each name the yelling and the intoxication mounted. Grady would chant, "Here's Carl; he's the man. Here's Wally; he's the man."

When he finished, they were soaring. They burst out of the room, and nothing on earth that blocked or tackled was going to stop this football team. White, on offense, hadn't even been introduced, and he was in flames.

They would try to disorganize the Dolphin offense with odd line-spacing and by working stunts involving the linebackers and the front four. Grant and the front four understood that Csonka, Mercury Morris, Bob Griese, and Paul Warfield weren't going to be stopped by tactics alone. They had the best offensive line in football ahead of them. Langer, Little, Kuechenberg, others. The important thing was not to let Miami run the ball at you and hold onto it. If Shula ran up a lead as big as ten points, his four-linebacker defense could dictate the Viking offense by forcing it into a short passing game and eventually smothering it. The first requirement was to score early.

The Vikings lost the coin flip. It may have been, as Grant reflected afterward in all seriousness, the crucial play of the game. The Dolphins came with Csonka. They shifted their own blocking patterns here and there and caught the Vikings looping out of position a couple of times. But what Csonka was doing to the Viking defense owed no debt to the drawing board. Griese's third-down pass to Jim Mandich in midfield opened the track. From there Csonka went sixteen yards, five yards, eight yards, and five yards into the end zone.

It took 5½ minutes to score the first touchdown and another 5½ to score the second. The honorable old front four couldn't figure out the Dolphins, and the linebackers couldn't stop them. The Dolphins also got a couple of heavenly bounces, and the officials seemed smitten by the idea that Miami was predestined to win. It had all the appearances of a conspiracy. The Vikings had to contend with Csonka, the 53 defense (named for linebacker Bob Matheson's numeral), the Dolphins' offensive line, unsympathetic officials, and possibly God.

Miami led 17–0 in the second quarter and Tarkenton surveyed the dilemma. The Viking offense had chronically horrible field position, or had to spend long stretches brooding on the sidelines. The Miami 53 was the worst aggravation. The Dolphins were staying in it practically every play, and the Viking linemen really didn't know whom to block because Miami put just three men on the line and had linebackers coming out of the stadium ramps.

Still, Tarkenton got the offense unclogged late in the first half. From the Dolphin four with one yard to go on fourth down and a minute remaining, the decision was to go for the first down. Tarkenton agreed with Grant on it. A field goal there wouldn't turn it around. He called Oscar Reed over Yary. There was a hole. Reed cut back, but Nick Buoniconti hit the ball. If he didn't fumble, Reed would have the first down.

But he did fumble, and the Vikings came away dry. Still trailing 17–0 in the third quarter, Tarkenton kept the ball in the air. Mostly they were nickel-and-dime passes the 53 was willing to relinquish. He got a touchdown himself, but there was no wallop in that because Miami scored again and the game was winding down, not with a roar but with a sigh, 24–7. Another Super Bowl turkey.

The peerage lauded Tarkenton afterward: He had played soundly, with spunk and dash. His arm was accurate, and his eighteen completions in twenty-eight attempts, as a matter of fact, set a Super Bowl record. Somebody mentioned that on the PA before the last gong. It didn't kill Tarkenton with embarrassment. Why should it?

But why should it be so lonely on the bench in the middle of a packed stadium?

Alderman and Tarkenton walked off the field together. They had been friends for thirteen years, and it was no coincidence that they were two of the last pioneers, the remnants of the scruffy tribe of displaced persons and apprentices who had collected in Bemidji in 1961 for their mutual protection.

Tarkenton put an arm on Alderman's shoulder. "We gave it our damnedest, Grady," he said. "We've won a lot of football games. You couldn't figure in 1961 we'd be playing in something like this."

"I don't know," Alderman said. "I do know one thing. The Dutchman is still mad we didn't make it the first year."

The press conferences did not intrude long on their postgame exodus. The probers were occupied with Csonka, Shula, Warfield, Morris, Yepremian, and anything else that looked green and white and self-satisfied. Even Manny Fernandez smiled and took questions without examining the inquirer for rabies.

There was a party for the Vikings at the Town and Country. Even in its early stages it displayed all of the convivial symptoms of the last reveille on Corregidor. Most of the wives were staying at the Ramada Inn nearby. Tarkenton drove over with Alderman and Tingelhoff to pick them up for the party. En route Alderman said there was something he probably should say.

Grady Alderman was a 240-pound offensive tackle, handsome and well liked, a man with a resonant baritone and a relaxed, confident presence. For more than a decade he and Tarkenton had been teammates and friends who understood each other's ambitions, strengths, and shams. They made each other's causes their own. They kidded each other's pretensions, admired each other's resolves. They were alike temperamentally. Both were optimistic, quick intellectually, adjustable to the shift of rhythms in their athletic careers and life generally. They became friends in the early Viking training camps, partly because they shared a preference for the less boisterous off-field pursuits, although both had extroverted qualities. As their friendship deepened they supported each other in critical times and fought each other's battles, especially during the mid-1960s when Tarkenton became a target for public criticism and The Dutchman's enmities.

Tarkenton always maintained that Alderman was the most underrated offensive lineman in football, coyly dismissing any suspicion that one bridge player may not be the most objective judge of his partner's ability to handle the pass rush. But there were coaches who tended to agree. Alderman was invariably outweighed and outpowered by the defensive ends he had to block. He became a front-rank lineman and later a star by perfecting technique, learning all the subtleties of leverage and parry, the arts of guiding the attacking lineman in a direction least dangerous to the quarterback. As an offensive lineman he was the supreme technician. He made it on brains and finesse. He also made it on nerve in the many times when he played in pain.

Tarkenton had seen him under all conditions and respected him more as their careers lengthened because he had seen so many players achieve so much less with far more strength and capability.

So they had no secrets.

Except in January of 1974.

Grady sat in the car and told Tarkenton and Tingelhoff he had been to see a doctor a few weeks before the Super Bowl.

He had been aware of something foreign in one of his testicles for some time. He thought nothing much about it, but he got sick one day and couldn't understand the symptoms.

A urologist told him the growth might be malignant.

He played in the National Football Conference championship game in Dallas knowing that.

Grady talked to the team physician, Dr. Donald Lannin, who advised him to consult other urology experts. Their judgment was that while it was impossible to know whether the growth was malignant, he could play in the Super Bowl without any real risk, and that his physical strength probably would not be affected.

But no absolute guarantees could be made.

When Grady told his wife, Nancy, they embraced each other,

consoling, strengthening. He said he would like to play at Houston because he was afraid of the impact on the team if he were hospitalized for a cancer operation so close to this game of games. In this, he might have been thinking more of his closest friend on the team, the man in the most sensitive position to affect the outcome, and the one who would be most deeply affected by the news.

With Lannin he told Bud Grant, who informed Jim Finks, the general manager. But he didn't tell Francis Tarkenton, nor, of course, anyone else on the team. He and Nancy were to fly to Mexico with Francis and Elaine two days after the Super Bowl for a week's vacation.

For Alderman, it would have to wait. His doctors scheduled his surgery for that week.

Nothing he did or said before the game in Houston, during all of the buildup, the practice-field routine, and the hotel lobby japery, suggested to any of his teammates, and particularly to Tarkenton, that Alderman was carrying one of the most demoralizing of all burdens.

He went to the movies with them at night, and clowned with them in the projection room when they got on Burns.

On the Friday night before the game he took his wife out to dinner with Francis and Elaine, Mick and Phyllis. He joined in the usual table talk, shutting away the whisper in his mind. His maturity and inner toughness prevailed over that. He felt no pain. Why tear yourself apart over the unknown? The doctors did not seem that grave.

With the others he roared laughing the Sunday morning of the game when big Eller rose at the team breakfast table, deciding to dissolve any hovering tension. "Be sure," he instructed his teammates with make-believe grimness, "you don't lose your pants out there today." Whereupon Eller dropped his trousers.

They laughed a lot. And a few hours later Alderman led the chant for the starting defense. He played the whole game at offensive tackle, walked off the field arm-in-arm with Tarkenton, and just before their car got to the Ramada Inn he said he might have cancer.

Tarkenton could not find words. He tried to frame some response, and then he closed his eyes. They clenched hands as tightly as they could.

In Elaine's room, Tarkenton threw himself on the bed and cried.

"All that burden for all these days," he said. "He carried it by himself so he wouldn't hurt the team."

"Didn't Grady tell anybody on the team?" Elaine asked.

Tarkenton raised himself to his elbow and looked at his wife. He wanted to express the pride a young boy feels at being the best friend of another, and he could only do it in the boy's language.

"If he didn't tell me," he said, "he didn't tell nobody."

They all went to the team party, and a few days later Alderman underwent a successful operation for a malignant growth. He was back in Mankato the next summer, weighing 240 pounds and needling Burns.

The Quarterback

13

The pro football player insulates himself from the emotional jolts of losing.

He tries to avoid taking refuge in easy alibis, but he knows there is just as much danger in letting himself get torn apart by a defeat.

He has a tonic to nourish him during the season: the next game. It's a therapy that almost never fails to restore him. But losing a Super Bowl game puts you a little beyond fast remedies. All the rationalizations on earth, all the clearheaded philosophizing once the emotional hangover is gone, don't quite fill the emptiness.

I remember standing on the sidelines in a time-out just before the Super Bowl game with Miami ended. I brooded about the might-have-beens of the game. No matter how decisively you're beaten, you can always pick out three or four crossroads in the game where you are certain the whole flow could have been changed. That never consoles you. You gnaw on it for a while and then drop it. I found myself doing that, but it occurred to me that this wasn't the kind of game that you could easily reshape and reconstitute to feed your frustrations. What did Larry Csonka and the Dolphins' offensive line leave for hindsight?

Try to imagine the sensation. The Super Bowl is an occasion a football team molds its professional life for. And now with a couple of minutes left we were standing around, staring at the ground, or staring at the crowd, which was trying to generate some excitement the last few minutes by watching the Goodyear blimp.

That's how the Super Bowl wound down. Csonka was pounding us into the ground, and the crowd was watching a gas bag.

So it wasn't so much what happened in the ball game as the wrong-chord ending it gave to the season. You couldn't really feel hostile about it because Miami on the day of that Super Bowl was as good a football team as I've ever seen.

It was just devastating—its offense, defense, special teams, everything it had. We were belted, but it wasn't the kind of defeat that embarrassed you. You felt drained and deflated. You know you've gotten that far, and then it's over and you've been beaten by seventeen points, and after all the buildup and anticipation you're left with a very lonely feeling walking away from it. All of a sudden nobody seems to remember the kind of season your team had, the challenges it handled, the peaks it achieved. You don't really want to cry about that, because professional athletics teaches you very early that you better not expect the gratitude of the crowd. Yet, you do find yourself left in the street trying to pick yourself up; and the next day more than forty people who lived so intimately and with such purpose for six months scatter and go their ways. It's not easy. You don't really go into mourning because you're big boys and are well compensated. The Super Bowl ranks a few levels below birth and death on the scale of significance, after all.

But you do live with the failure for a while.

I got back in my office a couple of days later in Atlanta and discovered I couldn't afford to live with it very long. The business was moving and didn't need the board chairman meditating on might-have-beens.

For several years I've been caught up in the excitement of moving people in positive directions: factory workers, technicians, anybody who holds a job. It's a service to industrial firms called Behavioral Systems, Inc. I founded it.

Years ago I was one of the circuit riders pitching motivation. The speakers ran to types—jocks, ex-preachers, soul-burning orators. Business would bring them in at high fees and marshal the whole company to hear them. We'd talk about pride, competitiveness, and all the beautiful corporate virtues. If you're good at it, and you know the appeals people will respond to, you can sense the empathy soaring in the room, and you tell yourself, "Man, I'm reaching them. It's wonderful. It's a great adventure. They'd go through the walls for the company."

And all that great motivation would last one day. After the twenty-four-hour surge of enthusiasm had evaporated, the company corkoffs were still the corkoffs, and the drifters were still the drifters. Nothing had changed. All you had done was entertain them.

It has to have more substance and permanence than that. Our organization thinks it knows something about achieving this end, stimulating people to be happier, more efficient, and more involved with their companies. We deal with more than seventy firms, selling them our system. The basic concept we give to our clients is that they can make substantially higher profits by creating a work environment in which the employees *want* to achieve for the company because it means more to their own lives.

Track me on this:

Productivity in this country has declined. It has fallen well below the levels of some poorer countries. The message to me is that here, where living standards and income are the world's highest, money can't mean everything to the worker. If he's not working close to his capability, it means he's dissatisfied about something. Usually he feels unrecognized and pretty well convinced that nobody in authority gives a damn about him.

The questions are: How do you stimulate him? How do you give him an involvement in the company's performance, instead of a reason to bitch about the callousness of his superiors and laugh at the posturing of management?

We think you can do this in a methodized way that can be measured regularly. You can learn the positive things to which each worker reacts. What makes him behave on the job in a productive way. You can reinforce that behavior by making it pay off for the worker with a system of rewards and acknowledgments—a different job, different ways of doing things, money in some cases, prizes, many things.

Some people want to call this bribery or manipulation, but you can waste a lot of time haggling over terminology. I don't call it manipulation. I call it management. You can do enduring, constructive things in industry if you create the right working climate, and you do that by getting inside the person or people, finding out what turns them on or off about their jobs, about the people supervising them, about conditions. You work together. You develop a new feeling of partnership and pride. Let a person know what progress he is making, find out what reinforcement he wants or needs, and then supply it.

I got into this with a clinical psychologist named Aubrey Daniels, who has been associated with the behavior-modification principles pioneered by B. F. Skinner. We began our partnership in a project to upgrade the education of disadvantaged kids. The federal government dried up the funds for that, which left us with some principles but no project. Daniels convinced me that behavior modification could work in factories as well as in schoolrooms and households. We tell companies with which we deal: "If we can't dramatically increase your profits with this system, drop us." And we're a going concern.

Now, would you believe you can use these principles to improve a football team? We did in Minnesota in the fall of 1975, and if and when the day arrives when I manage, coach, or partly own a pro football team—I really want to do all three—I'd like to give it a serious trial.

I sat down last year with Jerry Burns and John Michels of our offensive team and I said, "You and I have been saying these meaningless jab-'em-in-the-butt things for more years than we can remember. Things like 'Let's go out and we gotta be better offensively,' or 'We got to move the ball more, score more.' As managers we ought to know what the really important things are to concentrate on, so we can do better. Everybody wants to win. But how? How to improve? And as you're improving, how can you measure that and reinforce it?"

We wrote down twenty areas we thought were important for our offense to contribute to winning. You might call them standards of excellence. Things like averaging four yards a carry on running plays, no fumbles, no interceptions, making first down on third and two yards or less, scoring 100 per cent of the time inside the ten-yard line, 80 per cent of the time inside the forty, and no more than twenty yards in penalties. We kept a chart. We'd have squares beside each standard, and if we achieved it we'd block out the square and give it a certain number value.

Those number values determined each week how close we were to excellence. Each Wednesday we'd check out the charts. If we blocked out categories that we as individuals were involved with, it meant we met our goals. And when we did that, it puffed us up just like kids. There was a lot of chatter about it. You want to realize that these are pretty worldly pro athletes, averaging forty thousand dollars a year in salary. The rewards they got on Wednesdays had nothing to do with dollars. But the rewards had much to do with job satisfaction, peer recognition, pride, things like that. It wasn't any solemn observance. There was a lot of razzing and hooting. But there's no question that achieving those goals meant something.

Pro football's hold on the American public remains secure. But in important ways that deal with the quality of the product, we haven't made use of the technology available to us. Teams use computers to tell them the opponents' tendencies. But how about the system we use in evaluating college prospects? The scout tells you he wants a tight end 6 feet 3, weighing 230 pounds, and fast enough to run with defensive backs. Okay, find one. But that guy is not necessarily going to make it because it's the hard-to-measure things that determine whether he gets past training camp. What about competitive instinct? Do you have to guess at that, or are there indicators to enable the scout to make a reasonable judgment about whether this player has it in a strong way and that one doesn't?

I think those indicators are present, if we research them.

Take a hundred players we know have been successful competitors, at all levels, the ones who really excel. I don't mean just the players on winning pro teams. Some of them might be benefiting from strength around them. I mean the ones who have done it everywhere they played. What things do they have in common?

Small things might surface, but they might be present consistently. Habits as a boy, for example. The player's interests in childhood, his versatility as an athlete. I'm just speculating here. But our technical sophistication is such that there have to be ways you can predict professional football stardom way beyond the present scouting methods.

Pro football is also deficient in, of all things, teaching. There just isn't much systematic instruction of the young player. Where there is, you see results. Paul Brown won wherever he went. You know it wasn't a coincidence, and you know he wasn't smothered with talent everywhere. Brown organized. He methodized. He taught. He was as close to the systematized man as football has produced, and his record has been stunning.

Among the people he has taught best are quarterbacks—either taught them himself or saw to it that they were taught. Greg Cooke was an unknown at Cincinnati. But he led the American Football Conference in passing his rookie year. He got hurt. Along came Ken Anderson, hardly the most renowned athlete in America when he quarterbacked at Augustana, Illinois. But who has been better in the AFC the past two years?

Nobody. Brown coached both Cooke and Anderson. And it was no fluke that two relative obscurities—referring only to their college careers—led the league in passing under Paul Brown.

So why doesn't everybody do it like Brown? For one thing, not many are that well organized, or so secure in the soundness of their coaching philosophy. It's no coincidence that Bud Grant and Don Shula played for Brown. Shula and Grant are opposites temperamentally but very much alike in their priorities and personnel judgments.

Am I saying that you can arrive at some kind of composite of the successful football coach?

Somewhat. You certainly can't ask a man with such a highly developed ego as a football coach to change his personality in accordance with what the computers define as a successful coach. But he can borrow and adopt some of the methods that a scientific profile would show are common to most, if not all, successful coaches.

If I were a coach, I would try to program myself, up to a point. I'd keep a lot of the present Francis Tarkenton, certainly, for better or for worse. But I know the game, and I think I can teach it. I understand player attitudes, where players are receptive, where they are antagonistic. I would study Grant, Shula, Brown, Landry, and Lombardi. What are the common denominators there, in terms of policies and attitudes? I would try to incorporate some of those within the framework of my own personality and philosophy.

As a general manager I would make more use of computerized data in making personnel decisions. As a part owner I'd like to move toward changing some parts of the football structure, although not radically, because the game's founders built well, and despite all its present court convulsions, pro football will survive. It's the most popular thing going on television, and there's no reason it won't remain that way for years to come.

But cut down the number of exhibition games, for one thing. They now schedule six. Two would be enough. And I wouldn't use the extra weekends to add games to the regular season, as some are recommending. We get into that "more is better" box. It doesn't always work that way. Take a factory that produces goods for five days a week and does it efficiently. Then somebody says, "Let's produce for six days a week." But for six days a week they end up producing no more than they did for five, because the workers don't work as hard. Instead of making more profits, the factory makes less profits, and the company has more problems. I know that by cutting the exhibitions and holding the regular season at fourteen games you will reduce revenues somewhat. But that can be made up by efficiencies in the organization and cutting some fat from the payroll, front office, and otherwise. The bonus would be for the fans: better football over the length of the season.

If the commissioner will excuse another heresy, I'd like to see the Super Bowl played in the stadium of one of the competing teams.

One of the reasons the Super Bowl has been so bland so often is the artificial environment in which the teams prepare for the game. There's the press saturation and all the other distractions. But the atmosphere in the arena itself is part of it. The game is watched primarily by people who don't have a high emotional stake in the outcome. It's played in a warm-weather city with a big stadium. Those are the criteria. What the Super Bowl needs is what any great athletic contest needs: real, red-eyed passion from the fans, not blimp-watching. The players respond to the crowd's emotion more than the average fan dreams. Yes, it would give the home team an advantage, although not an especially large advantage. The Greek might say a couple of points. But a championship game needs that kind of aura.

So the ballplayer, and certainly the commissioner, would rather not have the game played in subzero cold and Alaskan wind. You might get some of that, although even in Minnesota, January football is usually very bearable. And the historians will tell you that the truly memorable games have been played in adverse weather—the Packers and Cowboys in that title game at sixteen below, for example, and the whirlwind in Yankee Stadium in 1962 when the Packers played the Giants. You hear that foul weather does not provide ideal, laboratory conditions for a true championship test. But ballplayers are flesh and blood, not robots, and the game wasn't intended to be played in a laboratory vacuum. What's wrong with settling it in the wind and rain, if that's what the sky decrees?

My organization in pro football, if I have one, will want to know all it can about human behavior, so that in some way it might enrich the lives of its athletes and other employees. I admit I'm an evangelist on the subject. Should I apologize? My father was an evangelist. Maybe I can't help it. Daddy tried to save souls. I'm just trying to impart the good feelings I've had out of life to other people.

Yes, I'm happy. I think life is a real trip. I don't deny there are a few hundred things I'd like to try. I have energy. I'd like to invest some of it in the more worthy causes. Like most athletes I've been involved in several, but I see some that have a capacity to materially alter behavior for the good of society, and that's the kind of work I have some knowledge in. The Johnson Institute is one. It deals in treatment and prevention of chemical dependency. It has pioneered in the field and done tremendous work in humanizing the whole approach to salvaging the chemically-dependent person.

Every once in a while I ask myself, "What drives you?" Is it dollars? Sure, I like money. I like houses. But the money is just a measurement of how well you are doing, what you have that others want or need. You enjoy the things that money buys. I certainly don't mean flaunting wardrobes or partying lavishly. The house I bought a few years ago is large and expensive, but it has character, it permits us to have a lot of guests, and it gives me enjoyment in refurnishing. It also gives me privacy, which is important for a person who is before the public much of the time. I think that a person who has to nourish himself constantly with the attention of masses of people has a neurotic outlook on his importance and a twisted attitude on the true sources of fulfillment. I think that if there were no money in the world, I would still be doing the things I'm doing. It's really a dynamic world. I have appetites. I want to taste and experience as much of the world as I can. Some people with these urges explore and climb and look for sunken treasure. I explore with people and business and television and wherever I think my energies and opportunities might merge.

As a football executive, one of the things I'd like to explore is the dynamics of the fan's relationship to the game. There's a mystery and challenge in that. The football fan strikes me as an absorbing field for study. Every psychologist I know has examined his urges, and I've got a couple of theories of my own. Deep emotional involvement in a football game, I think, momentarily removes some of the confusion from the fan's life. There's disunity in his world. He's not sure whether he's making progress or not. In football, now, it's win or lose. It's the same in any game, sure, but pro football is mass-produced on television, so it's everybody's game. The fan doesn't really know what or who is ahead in much of his society. Most people in business do not know exactly where they're going from day to day. They see the bottom line or the balance sheet at the end of the month or quarter. That's about it. How many people can directly relate themselves to that? So they're lost about who's ahead, we or they.

There is no doubt about that when the fan goes to the ball park or turns on the television. When the game is over, he sees what's on the scoreboard. It's all very simple. If Dallas wins, Roger Staubach is a winner and Fran Tarkenton is a loser. Two years before it was just the opposite. Fans can be very intelligent and perceptive people, but when they escape to the stadium or the tube, they want it simple. Don't cloud the issue with gray areas like "We're doing okay but it could be better, although it could be worse." The fan is satisfied when he gets a decision, when the images he has about the players he follows are confirmed or repudiated. It must be hell to be a hockey fan and go home with the score 3–3. The game may have been exciting, but it didn't do much for his convictions about the players, and it didn't provide much escape from uncertainty, either.

I've been exposed to every kind of reaction from the fans, of course, from pretty wild acclaim to demands for my head. Thrown in with sixty thousand others, the fan may sound tremendously appreciative and loyal—or tremendously insane. I do remind myself all the time that away from the arena these people may be entirely different personalities. I think that many of them when they're in the stadium are privately gratified over the distress or defeat of a famous athlete. I think it pleases this kind of fan to know that even famous and moneyed athletic heroes have to bow to the humiliations of life. Maybe the fan isn't aware of it, but I've been to too many stadiums and heard too many crowds to question it.

Should that be cause for bitterness? Not at all. We all fill roles for each other in some fashion, don't we? The prominent athlete will fill one for the autograph seeker. I admit having trouble adjusting to that. I've given thousands of autographs. I find myself now not wanting to, under normal circumstances. I will not go to absurd lengths to avoid it, but I will go to medium-range lengths. I didn't always feel that way. The young athlete's ego needs the reinforcement of people standing outside the stadium gates with their autograph books and old footballs. But after a while it wears. And if you acknowledge that, people are likely to say, "That's a pretty arrogant attitude, isn't it? There was a time you craved the stuff. Remember, these are the people who pay your salary. You've got to have time for them."

There is some truth in all of that, of course, but some sophistry, too. The athlete cannot and should not try to seal himself off from his public. Yet he does have a private life. He must try to arrive at a balance there somewhere. If I have a chance to establish some kind of social relationship with a person, adult or youngster, so that we can talk or know each other in some fashion, then I don't have any objections at all to signing my name. I've also done it in crowds, and I will again. I'm simply giving my preference, and explaining why sometimes I just will not place myself in a position where I have to sign autographs because the crowd demands it. Somebody will thrust a slip of paper at you. You sign it. The autograph seeker will rush off to get somebody else. He has never really looked at you. The autograph, the trophy, was the thing, not the relationship.

I've been asked about this a lot of times, so I'm trying to explain my response to the fan without giving myself any elite attitude. I do value the respect of the person in the audience, but I think there is a middle ground between off-the-field seclusion and putting yourself in a showcase.

What a player does after a game, for example, varies in accordance with his emotional needs. You'll have guys who have to party, win or lose. That's their outlet. Other guys will do nothing more sensational than go home, have dinner with their families, and read a magazine. I'll concede that the majority of the players I know do not answer that description. Most of them need to wind down or seek a kind of solace.

Elaine and I usually try to keep our options open for game days. I just can't predict how I'm going to feel, or what I'm going to feel like doing. I might want to spend the night at home with friends, or with my family. Elaine and I may go out to dinner by ourselves or with a half-dozen friends. Except in unusual cases, I feel no great highs or great lows. The thing I try to avoid after a game is being with people I'm not well acquainted with. If we lose, the stranger will think he needs to talk about all the raw deals you got during the game, and try to salve your feelings. His intentions are good, but I don't need that. I find that losses affect people around me more than they affect me. I've never liked to call my mother and daddy after a loss, or my brothers. I know they are feeling badly for me, and there just isn't much a telephone conversation could do for any of us.

Elaine is no problem. She understands all of this the same as I do. After you win, though, you can talk to anybody, because the world is in tune.

It wasn't that way for me, even playing with a winning team, a month into the 1974 season. I can't remember a more anxious time in my career. It started on the flight home from Dallas after we had won, 23–21, on Freddie Cox's last-second field goal. My arm between the elbow and shoulder was throbbing. I told Fred Zamberletti about it the next day and started taking heat treatments. We practiced briefly that day. I couldn't throw the ball more than fifteen yards. I've thrown in pain many times, but I was always able to put the ball where I wanted. But all of a sudden my arm didn't have the strength to do what any ten-year-old could do.

I was plenty scared, mostly of the unknown. I couldn't imagine what the trouble was, and we never did figure that out until the off-season four months later. The soreness made it impossible for me, in practice at least, to throw those crossfield sideline patterns we call "out" balls. And I couldn't throw deep very well, either. The sort of stuff I was throwing in practice was so embarrassing I wanted to yell out in frustration. The players and coaches saw what was happening and didn't talk about it. Pretty passes in practice never mean much to them compared to what the scoreboard looks like on Sunday. I began taking butazolidin drugs to reduce the pain, but you have to be very careful with those.

The arm trouble never got much public attention that season because we were winning Sundays and I threw reasonably well. One or two of the Minnesota reporters with access to the dressing room saw the treatments I was taking and were aware of the seriousness, but they felt that what goes on in a football locker room the week of a game is privileged information, and I appreciated that. I don't think the opposing teams thought much about it, because it didn't really affect our strategy. You may not be able to throw the ball forty-five or fifty yards in practice, but when it's Sunday and the juices are running, you can do a lot of things that are beyond you on the practice field.

Grant curtailed the amount of throwing I did in practice, and we just went from week to week. It worked out. With my arm in that shape I threw for the second highest number of yards in the league, 2,598, and seventeen touchdown passes. I don't know whether this is a commentary on the quality of my receivers or the miracle powers of Sunday afternoon adrenalin. We won eleven games, hammered St. Louis in the first playoff game, and made it into the Super Bowl for the second straight year, by beating the Rams in a game people like Ron Yary and Ed White insist to this day was the most brutal football game they have played in. Most of it was legal, all right. The line play was savage, particularly the battle between Yary and Jack Youngblood of the Rams. They are two of the greatest in football, and on virtually every play they pounded each other as though this were the one play that would end the universe. It was just awesome. You rarely see that kind of game in the Super Bowl, because in addition to the high stakes and all the national impact and the quality of the teams, it had the grimness of a December day in Minnesota and a partisan crowd thundering from start to finish. So the emotionalism of it seemed to run deeper, and for me at least it had all the dimensions of a classic football game.

Maybe I can say that in retrospect, since we won. The Rams might not place that kind of reading on it at all.

We didn't have any illusions about the quality of the Pittsburgh defense we would face in the Super Bowl. Since that time, the Pittsburgh front four has been ranked among the most powerful of all time in pro football, and I'm prepared to go a little further. I just can't imagine any being greater. Here's Mean Joe Greene, 275 pounds and 6 feet 5; Ernie Holmes, 270. They are virtually as fast as Alan Page, who weighs 245. L. C. Greenwood weighs only 240 pounds, but he's 6 feet 6 and depressingly agile. When he's rushing the passer, he comes at you with arms so big and high they should call him for goal tending on every play. The other guy, Dwight White, is 255 pounds and meaner than Greene. White says he should be voted the most vicious player in football and every time I see him he looks like he's running for election. The linebackers, Andy Russell, Jack Lambert, and Jack Ham, are mobile, smart, and tough, and the defensive backs think they are more vicious than White. They also play a kind of coverage, the double zone, that I think is the most difficult in football to throw against.

Our team had no reason to be intimidated by all that, and it wasn't. We were big boys, after all, and had done an awful lot of winning the past two years. My arm immediately became the inspiration for a few million words in the pregame brainstorming. In accordance with league procedure, Grant had to advise the commissioner's office that I wasn't going to play in the Pro Bowl after the Super Bowl in New Orleans. We had to explain why. Grant told the reporters my arm had been sore most of the season but that neither he nor I expected it to affect my performance in the Super Bowl. I confirmed that. Yet I felt some uneasiness during the week because I was doing next to nothing with our passing game in the practices. We had the stuff in, all right, but I wasn't throwing much. There was no reason to risk complicating the arm condition. Bud and I knew from the experience of the season that I would be able to throw adequately in the game. And after all those years in pro football, a couple of days in practice weren't going to radically change my habits, style, or effectiveness in the game.

We had a rewarding week in New Orleans. But I can't say the same for my old friend Howard Cosell. He turned up the day before the game to tape an interview with me on the lawn of the Hilton Airport Inn, where we were quartered. Howard showed up in his canary-colored blazer and his adverbs and set up beneath the balcony that services the second-story rooms. Our session was moving briskly, Howard delivering his usual output of profundity and brilliance, when we were spotted from directly above by Wally Hilgenberg.

Now, Wally is an intelligent man, as any linebacker surely must be, but he does have the linebacker's typical suspicion of profundity and also a long-standing suspicion of Howard. Wally thought that an educational thing to do on the Saturday before the Super Bowl was to dump some water on Cosell's head. Wally went into his room, emerged with the wastepaper basket full of water, and was about to dump it on Howard's susceptible head when Bob Lurtsema intercepted him. Hilgenberg seemed annoyed and wanted to know if

Lurtsema had designated himself to be Cosell's bodyguard. Lurtsema said no, he wanted to pour some water himself. Hilgenberg told him to go get his own water. Lurtsema fetched a basketful of water from his room and was headed for the railing to join Hilgenberg when the two of them were intercepted by Alan Page.

"How come you guys get to pour water on Cosell's head?" Page demanded to know. "I thought this was an integrated football team."

They nodded and said, "Go get your own water." Which he did.

The director saw what was going on and tried to warn Howard. He ran his finger across his throat wildly, telling Cosell to stop. But Howard was in the midst of a profundity, and there was no way he was going to stop. The water splattered all over him. Cosell leaped up screaming and yelling words you never heard on Monday night. Lurtsema said this made him understandable for the first time in his life. What got Howard especially ticked off was not only that they interrupted his profundity, but they also unsettled his hairpiece. I said, "Howard, it's just a little water." He recovered beautifully, and in character. "A little water, hell," he said. "It was an absolutely unprecedented tidal wave they launched on me."

I had had a little of the same kind of treatment myself a few days before. From time to time a quarterback will want to let his offensive line know that no matter who makes the headlines and the bigger money, the quarterback has his head fixed squarely on reality as to who does the work. The best and most influential way to accomplish this is to spend some of that money. New Orleans being a city of such excellent cuisine, I thought that all the members of the offensive line —reserves and tight ends included—would enjoy a night at Antoine's, one of the world's finest restaurants.

We began the evening with a before-dinner drink in some storied old watering hole on Bourbon Street. Then we headed for Antoine's, where the waiter greeted us with all of his French-accented elegance and his tails and his boutonniere. We had the finest steak or seafood on the menu, with the full garnishments of wine, salads, cheeses, and breads. It was one of the unforgettable nights I have spent on the town. So was the check. When the tip was factored in, it came to more than eight hundred dollars. Rarely has a quarterback expressed his gratitude with so much feeling, and with so little left for cab fare back.

But I don't want to give the impression that all of the gratitude was one-way. When it was time to leave, my guests rose. In the full mellowness of the evening, amid all this welling comradeship, right there in one of the world's most elegant restaurants, they broke into song:

> Hooray for Francis, hooray at last,
> Hooray for Francis, he's a horse's ass.

Sentimentality like that somehow makes it all worthwhile.

We were ready physically and mentally for the Steelers, I thought. I was remarking on that the morning of the game to Stu Voigt, who was rooming with me, when the telephone rang. The operator said it was a call from Washington, D.C. In a moment I didn't have any doubt of it because the caller identified himself as Gerald Ford.

We had never met, but the President said he wanted to call because he was a Midwesterner himself, had gotten to know Bill Brown in a charity golf tournament in Minneapolis that summer, and just wanted to talk. It was a very pleasant interlude. He spoke of the enjoyable times the Vikings had given him on TV, and how he liked Minnesota and people up there. He also talked to Stu for a while, and the conversation left us with a very good feeling. It's one thing for a politician to make a phone call after a game, when he can harvest all the publicity. It's another for him to make a call before a game, when nobody else is aware of it. I think it says a good deal about the man and the sincerity of his interest.

It was a disagreeable, squally afternoon. The Pittsburgh defense played with the same character. There just wasn't much I could do to get us unhinged offensively. They swarmed us and muscled us. Our defense played a great game and deserved to win. We couldn't match that offensively, but I can't honestly blame the offense. I tried everything I had put together in fourteen years of professional football.

It didn't impress the Steelers very much. I couldn't believe

Greenwood. He knocked down three passes himself. The rest of the Pittsburgh front four knocked down three more. In all the time I played football I couldn't remember a defensive line blocking more than two in one game. We got down near the goal line in a critical point of the first half. I called a post pattern to John Gilliam, and he was breaking open. The ball was there. So was Glen Edwards, blasting Gilliam on the chin the moment the ball arrived. It was a legal tackle. The ball popped loose, and they intercepted. We came away with air.

Terry Bradshaw and Franco Harris generated the Steelers' offense in the second half, and we just never got into it. The final score was 16–6. Two straight Super Bowls down the tube. You can tell yourself before a game like that never to put yourself out on the cliff, and make it the most important thing in your life. But Lord, it hurts.

Howard might have had a word for it: demoralizing.

And yet Gary Larsen was right. About eight hundred million Chinamen can get up tomorrow and not give a good goddamn.

So why not quarterbacks?

There is some therapy in tomorrow for quarterbacks. But never that much.

All the Blue Ribbons

14

The price of durability in pro football can take novel forms. Nothing else will explain why in the winter of 1975, approaching his fifteenth season in the NFL, Francis Tarkenton found himself examining a dead man.

The encounter took place in East Lansing, Michigan, at the suggestion of a Michigan State University professor who certainly must be the most powerfully constructed professor in America. He is familiar to millions of baseball watchers as Mike Marshall, the relief pitcher with a tireless arm and incomprehensible theories about the athlete and physical condition. Few people can understand Marshall's technical language. The community of ignorance ranges from fellow athletes to reporters. But Marshall reacts to this befuddlement with huge indifference. He is a distant, strong-minded man who disdains the frivolities of the popular press. During the latter part of his remarkable career he has been not only unhittable but inaccessible. In the off-season he conducts a program on kinesiology at Michigan State, which means he is an expert on the performance of the muscle system.

Zamberletti arranged the meeting between Marshall and Tarkenton, a rarity because Marshall usually tries to avoid personal consultations with ailing athletes. As part of the program, Marshall took Tarkenton to the anatomy department at Michigan State. By letting the gulping quarterback view a cadaver, he displayed the muscles used in throwing a football.

"I had to hope," Tarkenton said, "that my own muscles were in better shape than the ones I was looking at."

At the time Tarkenton's own arm was semidead. Although he had rested it for more than a month, it still ached, and it seemed to have regained little of its normal strength.

The only journalist with enough valor to report Marshall's diagnosis of Tarkenton's arm trouble has recorded this description, which seems to subject credulity to far more stress than Tarkenton's arm had absorbed: "There was no doubt what muscle was giving him trouble," so Marshall had explained to Murray Olderman. "The muscle is the superspinatus and inserts at the apex of the greater tuberosity, and the pathway is under the acromeoclavicular joint. It's involved primarily with stopping the forward movement of the arm and is also primary, I believe, in initiating inward rotation of the humerus, the bone of the upper arm, as well as stopping the action."

Duly engulfed by this diagnosis, Tarkenton responded: "Well, I'll be damned. I just knew it had to be serious."

What it was, basically, was a sore arm caused by a weak muscle behind the shoulder, the muscle that is indeed involved in stopping the action of other muscles when the arm throws a football. The muscle apparently had never been strong enough, and it caused trouble when Tarkenton was in college and sometimes thereafter. But it never affected him as seriously as in 1974. Marshall told him it was wrong for a throwing athlete to let his arm lie dormant in the off-season. Without work, its muscles begin to atrophy and degenerate. Tarkenton began a program of weight-lifting and throwing in February and maintained it until the start of summer camp. He arrived with a revived arm and geysers of the old confidence.

He had never spent much time examining his unusual medical history in pro football, or speculating on the reasons for it. In Tarkenton's later years his durability gave him as much novelty among the veterans of the game as his scrambling style did earlier in his career. His coach capsuled this quality into a tidy maxim: "Of all the abilities in football," Grant said, "durability is probably the most important. It's one of the principal reasons Francis has become the greatest quarterback in pro football history. He's always there, always in condition to play. He's been that way every game for fifteen years, which means that when he runs out there you've got a knowledge and feeling for all parts of the game and all situations that is just about without equal in pro football."

In the second year of his pro career, Tarkenton was knocked dizzy by a sideline tackle in Baltimore and missed a quarter. A year later, Dave Whitsell of the Bears nailed him with a similar tackle and forced him to miss the last fifty minutes of the game with a possible concussion. It was half time before Tarkenton recognized that he was in Chicago, and it was 8 P.M. before it dawned on him that the game had ended in a tie. Aside from those two games, Tarkenton has never yielded more than a few playing minutes to injury or illness. Against the backdrop of the unrestrained scrambling of his early years, the fact that he holds the NFL record for most yards gained by rushing for a quarterback, and that as a passer he has faced the rush of carnivorous defensive linemen more times than any quarterback in history, his freedom from injury makes him a statistical freak.

His boyhood did not forecast such abnormal behavior. He had the usual kid illnesses and hurts, and as a ten-year-old he came close to death from double pneumonia. Arm injuries prevented what might have been a major-league baseball career and turned him into a nonpasser for portions of his high school football career.

As a pro, however, he has been touched by the good fairy or whoever has custody of roaming quarterbacks. The Viking team physician, Dr. Don Lannin, finds no special physical attribute in Tarkenton that accounts for it.

"What he's got," Lannin says, "are great reflexes and a sense of knowing what's happening all over the field. He knows enough to avoid situations that might be injurious. He's prudent, now, of course, about falling before a 280-pounder flattens him. All quarterbacks will do that. But Tarkenton doesn't do it all the time. The first down is more important to him than possible injury. If he's heading for it and it's close, he'll expose himself to the full impact of an open-field tackle. He chews out pass receivers all the time for making their cut a half-yard short of a first down. He certainly doesn't want to be one of the offenders himself."

Tarkenton's own theory lays some of the credit at his feet.

"I think some people have bones and bodies more brittle than others," he says. "I think I've got a strong body, although I weigh only 187 to 190 pounds. People look at me and say, 'God, you are small. You've got strong legs, but from the waist up you're not a big, muscular guy.' I don't have any brittleness, though. God gave me that, and it's probably the biggest asset I've got, a strong body. I've also got quick and big feet, which may seem a contradiction but isn't. I don't get caught in awkward situations because I'm adept on my feet, which contributes to good balance. I think I've also acquired good judgment over the years. I know where the danger points are, and I know how to protect myself when I fall."

The heavens may have been overrated in preserving Tarkenton as an able-bodied quarterback, but there is no question they had a hand in formulating the Vikings' 1975 schedule. It seemed precisely designed for a football team trying to restore its equilibrium after being shaken by two straight Super Bowl defeats and three in the past six years. The stabilizing agents included the New Orleans Saints, the San Diego Chargers, the Chicago Bears, the Green Bay Packers, the Cleveland Browns, the Atlanta Falcons, and the New York Jets.

To this comforting agenda, Tarkenton brought all his reawakened zests and optimism. His friends kept asking him about retirement. The thought was always worth some attention in January, when the lumps were still tender. It was also worth some public speculation when the general manager called about a new three-year contract. The general manager had to understand that retirement from football was a very serious option for a board chairman and television commentator. When he retired, Tarkenton told his friends, it probably would not be in weariness or in retaliation for an uninspired contract. "I will only play as long as I think my team has a legitimate chance to win a championship," he said. "When I see we don't have that chance, I think I will wake up some July morning and decide, 'Football doesn't excite me now.' And then I will quit."

He was thirty-five and approaching his fifteenth season. Although capable of playing another five seasons or so, he had no intention of shooting for George Blanda's Methuselah trophies. He would play three seasons after 1975, probably. From his quarter of a million from football in 1975 he expected to reach salary figures that would make him the commercial runner-up to Joe Namath and his five hundred thousand dollars. Some time before the 1975 season, the Philadelphia Bell of the young—and doomed—World Football League offered him half a million annually for three years plus one-third ownership. "How much," Tarkenton asked himself, "is one-third of nothing?" His arithmetic confirmed, he put in a call to Jerry Burns.

Largely at Tarkenton's request and sometimes at his insistence, the Viking passing offense became multidimensional. It took into account the peculiar skills of Foreman and Gilliam, and of Tarkenton himself. It also responded to the mounting complexity of the NFL defenses. The Vikings didn't move consistently on the ground despite Foreman's bravura and his one thousand yards. The left side of the offensive line was unsteady, and Tarkenton had no trouble curbing his enthusiasm for Ed Marinaro as a rusher, although Marinaro caught the ball with his usual productivity.

Statistically the Viking defense was still strong, but the aging of Marshall, Eller, Hilgenberg, Winston, and Krause, and an injury that removed Jeff Wright from strong safety, made it shaky against quality teams. One antidote for that was to keep the offense on the field, which pretty much laid it to Tarkenton's wisdom, Foreman's feet and hands, and the blocking punch of Yary, White, Tingelhoff, and Voigt. The quarterback's role had changed subtly over the past two years. Where before he had been a respected head and craftsman, he was now a playing consultant. Neither Grant nor Burns had any ego frictions there. Tarkenton deserved to be heard on matters concerning offensive personnel and strategy. All the parties accepted that it was much better in the interests of an open, positive atmosphere around the locker room to allow the quarterback to air his opinions directly. Behind the walls, lobbying and grousing belonged to another time.

Tarkenton campaigned throughout the early season for a backfield switch that would move Foreman from halfback to fullback. The distinction is largely technical, but under certain conditions it allowed the more versatile use of Foreman as a runner. In midseason, they made the switch successfully. Tarkenton also campaigned, with less success, for the greater use of McClanahan at halfback. "More tools," he would tell Burns. "He gives me more tools. He's just a helluva runner."

Marinaro did not earn such warm recognition from the quarterback, although the two had no problems personally. Tarkenton viewed Marinaro as an excellent pass receiver and a fine Italian figure on the dance floor. He viewed McClanahan as a first-rate halfback. Annoyed by his lack of running opportunities, Marinaro openly demanded more, and several times appealed to Grant to trade him despite his starting status on a championship contender. Most players will last two or three days on Grant teams with this kind of public outcry. Grant forgave Marinaro, who is a likable kid without guile, although probably optimistic about his chances to be a fearsome runner. He also had value as an outstanding receiver and fair blocker. Grant, the pragmatist, decided he could indulge Marinaro's boyish squallings. Marinaro was no troublemaker. Also, Grant recognized, the Vikings were thin in backs. "If you could run like Foreman," he would say paternally, "I'm sure Francis would give you the ball twenty-five times, like he does Foreman."

It took Tarkenton weeks to get accustomed to a locker room, a plane flight, and a huddle without Grady Alderman and Bill Brown. With Gary Larsen and Milt Sunde, they were removed from the roster in midsummer in an act that had the ritualistic quality of some valedictory of the aged warriors in a Wagnerian opera. It was accompanied by a rare effusion from Bud Grant, eulogizing them for their years of high performance, their character, and the professionalism with which they had represented Viking football and the NFL.

They responded in language of comparable grace and courtesy, but none of them believed Grant's verdict that they had extracted all they could out of their pro football careers. All of them sought new employers. Only Alderman and Sunde found other clubs receptive.

Sunde lasted only a couple of weeks with the New York Jets, Alderman somewhat longer with the Chicago Bears.

Tarkenton disagreed with Grant in his assessment of Alderman. In 1974 Alderman played as a reserve behind Charley Goodrum at left tackle, but played considerably and well. Grant's decision to release Tarkenton's best friend, Francis concluded, simply meant that Grant had fallibilities along with the rest of mankind.

Tarkenton and Burns retooled the passing game. They added motion series, more rollouts, more formations. Whenever their opponents were convinced that the Vikings had exhausted all possibilities in how to deploy Foreman, they offered him in new locations the next week. They had him at halfback, fullback, in the slot, on the flank. They ran him wide, up the middle, flaring on pass routes, and running deep. They also moved John Gilliam from one attacking position to another, constantly unsettling the defense, creating new responsibilities and a variety of confusion for the defensive backs.

It was the kind of offensive in which Tarkenton frolicked. It multiplied his options, and it offered the widest forum of his career for his tactical imagination and his dexterity. He passed more than he wanted, or than he should have. He attributed that to the absence of a second major running threat to complement Foreman, and unsettled conditions on the left side of the Viking offensive line, where Chuck Goodrum, Steve Riley, Andy Maurer, and John Ward were in and out of the starting lineup. The hoary doctrine of establishing a running game was largely sacked. With the Vikings in 1975, the run was a diversion. The pass set the tone of the offense and lit up the scoreboard.

The year became a statistician's feast. Unitas' record for career passing attempts, career completions, and touchdown passes began melting in the face of the bombardment. Eventually Francis overtook them all. They weren't the kind of records schoolboys write in charcoal on the backs of shovels. Pro football's mathematics has never been as important to the multitudes as baseball's. Tarkenton's 291st touchdown pass, to Foreman in the flying snowballs in Buffalo, was the counterpart of Henry Aaron's 715th home run in Atlanta. Yet it was interred in the seventh and eighth paragraphs of the dispatches that day, overplayed by O. J. Simpson's 23rd touchdown of the season and the hooligan behavior of the Buffalo crowd.

Tarkenton himself contributed indirectly to the general lack of frenzy that greeted his touchdown record, his 2,931 completions and his 5,225 attempts. They were more important to him privately than he was willing to acknowledge. But he had been denied the highest professional recognition for so many years, had been downgraded for so long by the sloganeers and mythologists, that when the records finally arrived it was almost as though he wanted to scorn his former detractors by refusing to accept the full flavor of his vindication.

So he made tepid public statements: "The records are nice, because they are a measurement of how you stand among the great quarterbacks who have played this game, but they aren't something I have spent hours dreaming about and craving."

He didn't spend hours, he spent years. It was not any sustained, egocentric trip. But he had known for years that he was within range of the records, and he decided somewhere in the late 1960s that he would get them. While he didn't dedicate his career to them, the possession of Unitas' old records to him meant simply what it said: that by achieving them, he had become the greatest passer in pro football history. It mattered, because the sloganeers always talked about Tarkenton the savvy quarterback or Tarkenton the scrambler or Tarkenton the charmed-life quarterback. Almost never about Tarkenton the great passer.

From the standpoint of physical strength, velocity, and artistry, he knew he wasn't. Yet you don't use those standards to scale greatness in a passer. You use figures, longevity. All right, add championships if you want. Do it softly, though, because Tarkenton wasn't overwhelmed by that argument in 1965, and he would be a transparent hypocrite to embrace it now in 1975, when he had been to the Super Bowl twice.

The statistics told Francis Tarkenton and the world that he was now the greatest passer. The quibblers could use whatever other criteria they chose to invent.

He savored that. Not vengefully. He didn't set the records in retaliation. He set them, he told himself with an excusable internal glow, as a kind of confirmation. Tarkenton had known it all the time. Isn't that the line? He grinned reflecting on it. He had known about it at least since his days in the attic arraying his bubble-gum cards.

Nobody beat the Vikings that year until they yielded to Billy Kilmer in the last minute of the eleventh week, in Washington. The games themselves became stage props for the statisticians. Tarkenton was there pursuing Unitas. Foreman was pursuing one thousand yards and scoring touchdowns and catching passes incessantly. When it was over, they hauled in the biggest Univac they could find and discovered that Tarkenton had all the records he wanted except John U.'s forty thousand yards for a career, which would wait another year. Foreman had caught seventy-three passes and scored twenty-two touchdowns. Marinaro and Gilliam had both caught fifty passes or better. Krause had intercepted tons of passes. To make the starting team you had to break a record, preferably your own.

The season was a continuing celebration like that. If the career counselor charting a livelihood for Tarkenton had said, "Someday all your aspirations and contentments will come together, the anxieties will be stilled, and you will be on terms with creation," his projections would all have merged in 1975.

Tarkenton could even absorb a bad day now and then, although not many in the crowds were aware when these occasions occurred. Years ago when he threw two or three interceptions in a game, he would torture himself inside and mutter, "What am I doing? What am I doing to the team?" He would pull in and refuse to throw risky passes the next week. But he had outgrown that. One thing a struggling football team didn't need was a gun-shy quarterback. Not so paradoxically, the older and wiser he got, the more daring he got. While the arbiters of quarterback conduct in pro football were saying, "Don't throw deep against the zone defense," Tarkenton was throwing deep against the zone defense any time he pleased. There were ways to unzone the zone, and he didn't wait for it to happen by accident. He made it happen.

The achiever syndrome that had driven him from boyhood propelled him even faster in 1975, when he was just one year removed from a twelve-month income that would yield him more than one million dollars from all his enterprises.

Yet he understood failure a little better in the very process of harvesting this abundance. Like all good athletes, he sought perfection on every play. But he was now prepared to accept that he wasn't going to get it, that sometimes he would fail. He had no trouble coping with that now, largely because the number of times he was failing in the 1970s tended to shrink each year. It also used to be crucially important to him that everybody liked him. He understood now that he couldn't please everybody, and he had given up trying. Here and there he would have to disappoint autograph seekers, or the fund chairman for a charity drive. He had tried to be a good guy and fund-raising front man for everybody years ago. It got chaotic. He wasn't sure that either he or the drive chairman wound up any closer to heaven for the effort.

It was impossible for a man of his optimism and verve ever to fall into the traps of cynicism, but Tarkenton long ago lost any reverence for the constancy or taste of sporting publics. He remembered giving his entire Super Bowl check to needy people in 1974 and then finding himself accused by some of doing it for publicity. He knew that adulation is conferred in brief if creamy sprays, and there is a preciously thin line for the athlete between this adulation and ignominy. Both may come to him (and had for Tarkenton) on the same afternoon. The knowledge of it had become an ingrained part of his psyche.

Because his public life tended to be tumultuous as a professional athlete, Tarkenton strove to make sure his three children did not have a lopsided idea of how he fit into the world. He would take Matthew to practice once a week as a means of showing him where and how his father worked and to introduce some of his friends. At home a few hours later he would explain to the boy that another youngster's father might work in a mill or an office, and his work was just as important as quarterbacking the Vikings. It filled him with love to see how quickly the boy grasped that and conveyed his understanding—and that the boy actually recognized what his father was saying a long time before he said it.

In their day-to-day lives with their children, Francis and Elaine

Tarkenton tried to achieve a blend of human sensitivity and self-reliance. They talked often about these qualities at dinner. Elaine understood his energies, his professional and emotional focus, and Francis' respect for her judgment deepened as he found his public life expanding. She had glamour, taste, beauty, and a gift for informality, but she also had much hard-shelled sense on what was best for Francis Tarkenton and his family. More than any other person's, her counsel was meaningful to him in the days of his frictions with Norm Van Brocklin. She saw, perhaps before he did, that he must leave for the comfort of his mind and the renewal of his zests. And in the end she helped guide him in the direction she knew he wanted to go.

Tarkenton's increasing depth as a person, quite apart from his professionalism, aroused the admiration of his coach as few players had.

Asked for his private evaluation of Tarkenton in the midst of the 1975 season, Grant said, "Come to a practice someday. Observe this fellow. I would be willing to bet a small stake that sooner or later Tarkenton has a word with everybody on the field, every player, coach, ballboy, water sprinkler. He's not being a politician. This fellow really fills out his life with something meaningful almost every moment. He involves himself. He cares what happens to his team-mates, in football and outside of it. He may walk by a rookie receiver and offer a suggestion about how the rookie can improve the last pattern he ran. He may walk by Carl Eller and razz him about his new hat. He may mimic Burnsie a little. Always interacting. He seems to be a man totally adjusted and excited about the way his life is going.

"As a ballplayer, he brings something to the stadium that is a lot deeper than all of his experience. He's got a gift. Maybe the word is instinct. Nobody ever figured out how he was able to survive all those years when he was charging around behind the line of scrimmage. The reason he could get away with it where others couldn't was that he had a sense for it. He knew when to turn or throw or run because he felt the pressure or sensed the open man. What a coach admires as much as his physical ability and his mental sharpness is his maturity. After all he's been through, he's more than willing to accept advice, from a coach or ballplayer. He's also learned how to accept the outcome of the game. Some guys after a big win will walk around starry-eyed for days, or like they've got bad news from the bank if they lose. Tarkenton has got it as well organized as I've seen. You know that when he goes out on a field on Sunday, nobody could possibly be more ready to direct a football team."

Tarkenton's sense for the game has reached a level where intuition, the "feel" of it, had become inseparable from his actual perception of what was in front of him. In a film session the day after a game with the Bears, Jerry Burns raised a professional question. "You got good yardage on that play," he said. "But how come you ran into the left side? The Bears weren't overshifted. Just looking at the Bear setup, you'd almost have to go right."

Tarkenton nodded. He had no way of knowing as he called the switch that the Bears had a play on to plug up the right side. "It just *felt* softer on the other side," he said. "I figured we better go there."

The season of 1975 was not only a kind of pluming out of his fifteen years in football, when the records and the recognition finally arrived, but also a proving hour for the codes by which he lived and played. All the little homilies his father had given him in his boyhood about working and being his own person and loving and fighting the good fight. No matter how much fame and worldliness and money he acquired, no matter how many great people he met, he kept his child's devotion to those homilies, although the language he used to define them had changed. And when this finest of all seasons ended for him, his team stood 12–2, he had completed 273 of 425 passes, and he had thrown 25 touchdown passes. Within a few weeks he would receive the Bert Bell Player of the Year award, the Associated Press Most Valuable Player award, the Washington Touchdown Club's highest honor, and the pro football writers' Most Valuable Player award. And his father would say he should be proud and thankful but he should not luxuriate too long in these because they were material ornaments. What mattered was how he gave of himself.

Cowboy Nelson was taping Tarkenton for the playoff game with

Dallas at the moment his father was delivering a farewell sermon to 1975 in his church in Savannah. He called it "Thank You, and Good-bye." The preacher's voice projected vigor and tenderness and the fire of the believing witness. For his text he had chosen a letter written by the Apostle Paul to Timothy from a Roman jail, forecasting his death. He had fought the good fight, finished the course, kept the faith. He had asked Timothy to bring Mark with him, Mark who had left Paul once and earned his enmity. The apostle was forgiving him and saying, "I need him." He was saying, "Thank you."

Too often, Dallas Tarkenton said, people are reluctant to give thanks for the times and gifts that do not bring them happiness. Man should give thanks for all, he said, the times of testing as well as the times of joy. They are what make him man.

The preacher said good-bye and thank you. He laughed and talked with the members of his congregation afterward. It was the kind of hour that was the summation of his own life and creed. Then he headed for his home with his wife Frances, his sons Dallas, Jr., and Wendell and their families, and in a few hours he would watch his other son play football.

Francis Tarkenton had never subjected himself to the kind of self-examination he fixed on his life on the flight to Georgia for his father's funeral. Perhaps he had never had the time. But he knew that was a deception. He had never taken the time. He was satisfied with his priorities. He was content with his life and had no guilt problems. But weren't there times when he was overwhelmed by all the excitement and the achievement, and lost touch with some of the fundamental truths of the good life? He was a man of heartiness and accomplishment. He knew he had insights that sometimes guided and inspired others. He was very much a citizen of his world and the keeper of his house. And yet what of love? He was capable of giving and receiving it. Did he express it as frankly and as often as those he loved, needed, and wanted?

The recognition of his own needs struck him the night of his father's death. The presence of his wife and family offered him solace. And he needed friends almost as much. No matter how self-sufficient the man, he saw now, he reached out desperately for the voices and hands of those he trusted. They gave him a comfort that was honest and therefore real.

Seeing and hearing his family again, he felt regret. If they could do so much for him without realizing it, how many times could he have done the same with a word or touch? "I love you" or "You're important to me." And "Thank you for being here" or "Thank you for being who you are."

He was not a callous man. He did try to be thoughtful. Not often enough, perhaps, nor to enough people. His father's death, extraordinarily, returned him to a truth his father had espoused his entire life: the basic goodness of people. In Minneapolis a truck driver walked into the Viking office and gave a clerk his Super Bowl ticket. He said he wanted to turn it in so that the money could be given to the memorial fund "for Fran's dad." A youngster sent a dollar bill with a note saying, "I asked my mother and father if I could use my weekly allowance for the memorial fund for your father."

Mrs. William Nelson of Brooklyn Park, Minnesota, wrote: "When I told my six-year-old that your father had died during the game, his face was very thoughtful and puzzled. 'Does Fran Tarkenton have a dad like mine?' he asked. 'Is Fran Tarkenton a son like me?' " Mrs. Nelson replied that he was, and that he loved his father very much. Her own son touched the No. 10 on his small purple jersey and wept.

People Francis hadn't seen since his high school days came to the house in Athens, Georgia, the day of the funeral. They brought food and their thanks for having known his father. Friends and relatives, yes, but also strangers who had heard of Dallas Tarkenton—or had heard of Francis Tarkenton, and knew that he grieved. And this, Francis realized, might have been the highest triumph of his father's conviction, that people will come when they know they are needed and it does not matter what their names are or where they come from. The Tarkenton brothers invited them in, and they talked. Among them was a man from Chattanooga, Tennessee. "I listened to the game," he said, "I heard about your father's death. There's no reason for you to know me, but I just wanted you to know I care."

Hundreds gathered in the Methodist church for the service, where three of Dallas Tarkenton's closest friends in the ministry shared the eulogy. They captured his spirit and his witness, Francis thought, and his buoyant humanity. And when the processional carried his father from the funeral home to the cemetery, it gained a hill from where he could look back down the road for more than a mile and a half and see cars with their headlights on, the motorcade for the little preacher who was born in the slums of Norfolk, Virginia.

He was an evangelist without blush, but friend more than minister. Because he lived so long without money, and raised a strong and affectionate family without it, he knew more than most the needs that transcended wealth. His pulpit appeals were always directed to the best in human nature, and on his very last day on earth he was asking the people in his congregation to look positively at everything they had done in 1975, the bad times included. St. Paul, he said, gave thanks for all, not just the good.

Strangely, at this very moment on his way to the burial of his father, Francis Tarkenton felt the deepest security of his life. He wanted to look into his father's eyes and tell him that he had spoken the truth, in his ministry and in his judgment of the people he tried to guide. Francis still felt grief, because the little man with all of the vitality and faith was gone forever. But he had never felt so proud, to see the hundreds in the motorcade, the kindnesses that had been offered by people both celebrated, such as John Glenn, and unknown to the world, such as a little boy with a purple jersey. They were a confirmation of what his father had preached and lived by.

Francis Tarkenton had never thought much about the allegories of the act of death, what it represented in terms of success and tragedy. He mourned a person who died, tried to remember all that was good in him, and wished him well in the hereafter. But John Glenn had seen something in Dallas Tarkenton's death, a hope, a kind of victory, and this he expressed in a card that touched the entire family. In celebrating Dallas Tarkenton's life, they were consecrating his teachings and his faith in people. Gerald Ford had joined that sentiment in a telephone call to the Tarkenton family. He said he had heard the news after the football game, that he remembered their conversation the morning of the Super Bowl. His wife and he wanted Francis Tarkenton to know they were thinking of his father and his family.

One of Dallas Tarkenton's friends delivered the prayer at the graveside and, before the final rite, his son Francis spoke. He thanked all who had come to comfort his family and express their respect for the good man they would now bury. So often, he said, we do not take the time to tell others how important they are and what they have meant to us.

As he spoke he noticed a familiar face, a face burned by the heat of a thousand football practices. He recognized Quinton Lumpkin, his freshman coach in college, the man who had driven to Stone Mountain to persuade him to come back to Georgia. The old coach's eyes were moist. "I love you, Coach Lumpkin," Francis Tarkenton said. The other's lips moved. "I love you."

The Quarterback Tells How to Quarterback

Psychologists tell me that millions of people in America imagine themselves quarterbacking a professional football team. This mass fantasy is said to cut across all social and economic levels, from six-year-olds holding their plastic minifootballs to their grandfathers holding their beer steins. I don't doubt it, because I did the same kind of fantasizing as a boy.

Quarterbacking has acquired a slick façade in the minds of the football watchers and also a fair amount of money and notoriety. I'm not going to challenge or defend the reasons here. But I would like to conduct an informal lecture on how I look at quarterbacking, on the chance that youngsters might be guided by it and that their elders might find it useful in reinforcing what I'm sure is their high level of wisdom on the game of football.

There is no such creature as a quarterback type. The people who have become successful quarterbacks occupy the full range of the personality spectrum. You have extroverts and tough guys like Bobby Layne, folksy characters like Sammy Baugh, and quieter people like John Unitas. All of them have had mechanical skills, of course, but the one critical quality they all have in common is a sense of command. It doesn't really matter how they exercise it, as long as the team understands that the quarterback knows what he's doing and that he can reap the full potential of his offense. If he achieves that position, his team will respond. The young quarterback should recognize that he does not simply walk into a huddle and say, "I'm the boss." If he's a boss, his team does not have to be told. It will accept his leadership because he has demonstrated his right to it, not because he has announced it. And he earns it by learning and mastering the techniques of quarterbacking and the tactics of the game.

The young man who quarterbacks the East Cumberland Junior Lions should do it just as earnestly as the man who quarterbacks the Detroit Lions. But the young quarterback should realize above all else that he has just begun to play the game, and he cannot do it on the same physical or mental level as the professional quarterback. So the first rule in Fran Tarkenton's classroom is "Listen to your coach." He may not have played professional football, but he has played more football than the young quarterback, and he has access to more expertise.

If the young quarterback learns nothing else here he should learn this: The quarterback can beat his own team in more ways than any other player. He handles the ball on every offensive play. He can beat his own team by carelessness in the way he takes the center snap, in handing off to a running back, in throwing the ball too soon or to the wrong man, or in throwing the ball at all. He must discipline himself to avoid making critical mistakes in the routine mechanical parts of his job. So you can call that part of his assignment "prevention." That is not negative thinking; it is fundamental in the making of a good quarterback. Don't beat yourself or your own team. Once you have established that discipline you can go about the business of learning how to beat the other team, and you can do that by executing the handoffs right, by throwing the ball right, and with sound play selection.

What does the quarterback mean by execution? He means carrying out the fundamental parts of the game—how he positions himself, how he handles the ball.

You can't get anywhere without the ball. All right, how does the quarterback handle the exchange from center? First, his position under the center. The basic rule is make yourself comfortable in the stance. For some this might mean a flat-footed stance; others like to stand on the balls of their feet, or the heels. I don't think it's smart

Figure 1   Figure 2

to have your feet any wider or any narrower apart than the width of your shoulders. I think you can make yourself comfortable from there. Crouching under the center, I like to get up snug. *(Figs. 1 and 2)* Do whatever is comfortable, but everything else being equal, it's better to be up close; the more you increase the distance between your body and the football, the more likely you are to get yourself in an awkward position on the snap. The smoother you handle the snap from center, the faster you can move.

The handoff of the ball from the quarterback to the running back is a routine part of the game, but it's very important, because an error there often means losing the ball, which often means losing the game. It happens more than the fan realizes. The responsibility for the smoothness of the exchange is the quarterback's because his job is the easier of the two. The runner has it tougher. He's got to receive the ball, find the right hole, think about his blocking, and also worry about the defense. And while doing all that, he's got to hang onto the ball.

I believe in lifting the ball immediately into the target area of the

Figure 3

Figure 4

exchange, which should be slightly above the belt buckle. *(Fig. 3)* That's where the ball should be placed. The quarterback should raise the ball to that level as he pivots. He should bend at the knees, and his eyes should be very close to the level where the ball is. The idea is literally to "watch the ball into the belt buckle." As you're sliding the ball into the runner's arms, your eyes should follow it in. *(Fig. 4)* If they don't, and your eyes are someplace else, you're very likely to miss the target area with the ball, and you're inviting a fumble. How many times have you seen a quarterback pivot, hand off, and the ball pop into the air or go flopping around among all the bodies on the line of scrimmage? The quarterback may have been a few inches off line in his handoff. The back was surprised, and he never had control of the ball. A nice, gentle touch on the handoff is much better than slapping it into the carrier's midsection. He may come up high with his knees. Or he may not be ready for all that velocity, and the impact actually takes his breath away. I've seen it happen.

Once the ball is handed off, the quarterback should let his hand ride the ball for a split second to be sure the exchange is stabilized and the back actually has possession. You hold the ball with both hands until you make the exchange. You then use the hand closer to the line of scrimmage to slide the ball into the runner's midsection. In that way you're not making a backhanded exchange. In pro football, quarterbacks do not do much faking, because most defensive backs will not be looking into the backfield once the play is under way. In school football, it is extremely important to carry out the fakes because younger defensive players do have a tendency to try to follow the ball in the backfield. So you will want to make your moves very decisive. Convince your opponent that you are actually handing off when you are simply faking. Or after you have handed off, convince him you still have the ball. Do you like to act? That's what faking is all about.

The problem with many young quarterbacks is that they want to hurry everything—the snap from center, the handoff, the fake. What you are seeking is precision. This means crispness in how you make your moves. Haste and sloppiness mean broken plays and fumbles.

If the quarterback is pitching out instead of handing off, there are two basic tosses. One is the two-handed throw, usually end over end. It's the surest and the easiest way to deliver the ball four or five yards. The spiraling underarmed pitchout, thrown one-handed, is used when the ball has to travel much farther. *(Figs. 5, 6, 7 and 8)* You can get it out there faster that way, but greater precision is required, and it is more dangerous for young quarterbacks than the two-handed toss.

There is a third kind of pitch, used on the option play when the quarterback is running down the line of scrimmage and can either pitch out or keep the ball, depending on the reaction of the defensive team. As he is coming down the line, the quarterback should look immediately for the nearest aggressor, the defensive end or a linebacker usually, who has not been blocked. The ball should be in front of the chest. As soon as a defensive player commits himself to making the tackle, the quarterback should pitch the ball one-handed from the chest, leading the running back slightly so that he will catch the ball at full momentum without breaking stride. To get the ball out quickly and smoothly, the quarterback should toss it left-handed

Figure 5   Figure 6

when the play is going left, right-handed when the play goes right. The other hand is used to fend off the man-eaters who are trying to break up the play.

How about some forward passing?

The distance the quarterback drops back varies with the kind of pass he expects to throw. If he's figuring on something short—five yards or so downfield—he will want to drop back three yards. If he plans to throw ten yards downfield, he should set up five yards back. For deeper throws he needs a drop of seven to ten yards. The play may not be there, of course, and he will have to throw something else. But we're talking about probabilities. It's important that the quarterback be precise about these drops because his offensive line usually gears its blocking to the kind of pass he plans to throw. If it's a short one requiring a short drop, his offensive line will try to block straight ahead near the line of scrimmage. On deeper patterns it will use the drop-back type of blocking.

In executing the drop, I pull my right leg back from the center and head toward the designated drop area, crossing over with my left

gure 7   Figure 8

foot as I begin the drop back in order to see what's happening downfield. I would advise the younger quarterback simply to get back into his drop as quickly as he can. The defense scanning can come later in his career, when he has more experience. The quarterback who does have that kind of experience will want to read the defense as he is setting up. What does that mean? It means he will want to work with his coach to pick out one or two men in the defensive secondary whose movements will determine where he can throw effectively.

You've heard a lot about peripheral vision. Forget it. I don't know any quarterback who can read the entire field at a glance. Yet most young quarterbacks try to see too much. What they see is a maze of jerseys, their own and their opponents', running in different directions. The quarterback is likely to get confused, and he is very likely to throw for an interception. So wipe all of the peripheral-vision business out of your head.

The first thing you want to do in reading a defense is to eliminate half the field.

Key on the free safetyman or a linebacker, or whatever defensive player is most likely to tell you what kind of pass is open by his reactions after the ball has been snapped. The message is instantaneous to most pro quarterbacks. They have studied these defenses and the keys for years. Younger quarterbacks will want to work with their coaches to get the same kind of information.

We'll take something basic. Say I'm dropping back and I see the opposing middle linebacker going to my left. My knowledge of their defenses and tendencies tells me I better go to my right with this pass. What I've done is to eliminate the left side, or half the field. So now as I'm dropping back I can concentrate on the right side. I know there is nothing but trouble the other way. I want to avoid a situation where we've got two receivers out there and they have four defenders. What I'm looking for is a part of the field where we have two and they have two. I can't ask for any better odds. That's one-on-one. If I know anything about this game, I should be able to get the ball to one of the friendlies better than 50 per cent of the time. And when I'm doing that, I'm in business. Yes, the defense sometimes tries to disguise what it's doing. But it's not as easy as it sounds, and that is a lesson left for another class.

How do you throw the football?

Again, the watchword here is to be comfortable. Start with the grip. People have different physical characteristics, which pretty much determine how they will grip a football. Don't copy somebody else's grip because that somebody else is famous or related to you. Use what works for you. A fundamental part of any grip, however, is to use the fingers on the strings in a way that permits you to spiral the ball. Your thumb will wrap naturally on the narrower part of the ball, the exact place depending on how big your hand is. The control of the ball, the sensitivity, is all in your fingers, not in the palm of your hand. You can use the fingers on the strings in any position, just so you use them. *(Figs. 9 and 10)*

In delivering the ball, you want to throw overarm. There have been good quarterbacks who have thrown the ball sidearm, but they will tell you they could have completed more passes if they had learned to throw overarm. You'll have more passes blocked throwing sidearm.

Figure 9

Figure 10

Figure 11

Figure 12

Figure 13

As you are setting up, you want to position the ball somewhere from the shoulder up to a point behind your ear, holding it in your throwing hand, stabilizing and protecting it with your other hand. *(Figs. 11, 12 and 13)* When you release the ball from this position, the two parts of the hand that should be most sensitive to you are the forefinger and the thumb. You actually release the ball with these two fingers and impart the spin with them. Right now, picture a baseball pitcher throwing a curve ball. If he's a right-hander, he will snap his wrist to the right. In releasing the football, it's just the opposite. The passer will snap his wrist to the left. You don't want to exaggerate that movement, but that is the action your wrist should have to give you the spiral and the greatest distance and velocity. *(Figs. 14 and 15)*

After the ball is released and your arm is following through, the little finger of your throwing hand should be pointing straight up in the air, and the thumb should be pointing straight down. *(Figs. 16 and 17)* If you have exerted the correct wrist action, you will get that position. Try it. The wrist twists left if you are a right-hander; it

Figure 14

Figure 15

twists right if you are left-handed. That is a constant. It never varies. If you have released the ball any other way, you have not released it properly, and until you do, you can't throw the football. It's that simple.

Why the spin? A spiraling ball will encounter less wind resistance and follow a truer course, giving you more velocity and distance than you would have with any other kind of delivery. Again, the forefinger and thumb control the spin. The exact amount of pressure you apply will vary with the individual. You don't have to squeeze the ball with the thumb. All you have to do is apply whatever pressure is necessary to control and launch it.

In setting up to throw, your feet should be at about shoulder width, but whatever is most comfortable. Don't be spread out so you can't get the power you want. If you're right-handed, step out with your left foot. Not too long a stride. You'll be spread out that way and sacrifice a lot of strength, because the body will not be completely behind the throw.

Imagine yourself as a whip. That's exactly what you are when

Figure 16   Figure 17

you throw a football. You are in your stance about to throw the ball, which you have in the two-handed position high. You draw the ball back in your right hand, cocking. Stride forward with your left foot, no more than six inches. Your free arm is important here, which you may not have realized. As you are striding forward and bringing your arm overhead for the delivery, draw your free arm into the body. This gives you a whiplike action as you propel the ball with your right hand.

As you release the ball, allow your throwing arm and hand to move forward at maximum extension, pointing in the direction of the target. The follow-through is important for maximum velocity, distance, and accuracy. What is not important—as a matter of fact, what is wrong—is to let your body fall forward the way the baseball pitcher does. This used to be taught, but incorrectly. What you should do after you finish the delivery is pull your body back sharply, creating the last stage of the whiplash effect.

Those are the basics in forward passing. You use adaptations of those basics in any kind of pass, whether you're throwing from the stationary position or throwing on the run. Naturally, you don't have time for all of the ideal footwork if you throw on the run, but the actions of your upper body will be about the same whether you're running or standing. You definitely want to create this whiplash effect in all forward passes. There will be times, however, when that's impossible because you're throwing under great pressure, or your vision is obscured or you have to lob the ball out beanbag fashion.

One note of caution there.

I've just described three conditions where you probably should not be throwing the ball in the first place. And that is *very* important to remember. There are times when you can rescue a play. There are other times when it is just stupid to try, when the odds are all bad. I have salvaged many in my career. Because of the amount of football I've played, I think I've made the right calculations a lot more than the wrong. One thing I'm sure of: There is absolutely *no* excuse for an interception. There might have been a fine play by the defense. But in every case when you throw for an interception, either you have been guilty of bad execution, of faulty judgment, such as trying to force the ball into a crowded defense, or just plain failure to anticipate a defensive move you should have anticipated.

Are you ready for some strategy?

People smile a little now when the coaches and quarterbacks in pro football talk about the importance of establishing the running game. It is one of those proverbs of football. But it still has a solid ring, and I still try to achieve it in every game I quarterback. With a running threat, you can pass almost when you please—and not when the defense forces you to pass. If you can't run, they start teeing off on your passing game, and almost everything you throw is under duress. Can you win without establishing the ground game? Sure. You can win a game, but you can't win many championships. At that level of competition, the defenses are so good you just can't get by with 50 or 75 per cent of an offense.

You can now ask how to get a ground game going so the defense will respect it if you don't have strong running personnel or the kind of line blocking you need.

It's not easy. But it's not impossible. There are not many defenses in football without weaknesses. You can try to discover those weaknesses, and if you know what they are, you can devise a list of plays —some people call it a game plan—that will give you a chance to exploit them. At the schoolboy level, the best way to do that is to be sure who your strongest runners are, and not be bashful about letting them run with the ball. You have to be certain what plays your team runs best, and what the most reliable ones are in certain situations.

Then study the opponents' defense, with film if it's available, with scouting reports otherwise. Go over it with your coach. What is available to you from that defense? Does their defense play the inside game harder than the outside game? During the game those tendencies might change, and you have to be aware of that. But no matter how much information you have on your opponents' defense, the crucial information available to you is this: What does our team do best on offense? Learn that and never forget it. You will try to go with that first, in all probability. And make them stop your strength before they do anything else. If they can't, you have the blueprint.

If they can, then go to your alternative plays. Maybe they are stopping your strength because they are overplaying it, and they are vulnerable to the other stuff. Often that is exactly the case.

How about the quarterback and play selection?

What do you do on first down, for example? The computers will tell you that most teams run on first down. If you pass on first down and come up empty, you've forced yourself into a probable passing situation on second down and ten, and the defense will demonstrate no surprise when you do pass in that situation. That is the rationale behind running on first down most of the time. But you certainly don't want to ignore a first-down pass, up to and including a first-down pass when you're on your own goal line. I throw from down there quite often—relatively safe passes, of course. My experience tells me that the risk of a running-play fumble and an almost certain touchdown by the opposing team is greater than the risk of an interception. I'm talking about my preference and my outlook. Another quarterback, in different situations, may look at the percentages differently.

Under normal conditions if you're going to throw on first down, you'll want to throw a high-percentage kind of pass. In my arithmetic that means a pass you're confident will be completed 85 per cent of the time. If you don't have that kind of confidence in the play, you shouldn't call it. The pass best calculated to give you that kind of percentage on first down is one where you will fake a running play —since they are expecting a run. We call that a play-action pass. It doesn't always have to be a short pass, either. A sizable percentage of my deep passes are thrown on first down. If you're going to throw deep, that's often the best down to do it. The defense has to respect the run. Further, if you're going to pass, they are inclined to look for the short stuff.

When you get into a must-pass situation, you don't have to wring your hands. So the defense knows you're going to pass. It doesn't know where, and to whom. Read your coverages. If the pass is there, throw it. But don't be reckless. These are the downs when the interception risk is the greatest. There are three things you can do if you're not sure you can get the ball to the receiver. The first is to hunker up and take the loss or throw the ball safely away, which is easy to say but not always easy to accomplish and could also cost you fifteen yards. The second is to throw and hope nobody intercepts and runs for a touchdown. The third is to run away from the rush and try to rescue the play, either on your own or by throwing to some available target. This is scramble football. I do it less now than I once did, but I don't hesitate if it's a choice between that and throwing wildly and accepting defeat, meaning taking the loss. Sometimes eating the football is the only choice open to you. But I've never liked it, and my statistics will tell you I've gone to some pains to avoid it.

There's no standard way to run a football game other than trying to keep the defense off balance while at the same time running the plays with the highest success ratio. In other words, do what you do best. But don't let yourself get typed. The defense has to understand you are capable of unorthodox calls, a departure from the script. You've got to be aggressive about that. Maintain pressure. Sometimes I'll do this with a first-down pass. I've thrown on four or five straight first downs early in the game. With the right kind of personnel and a sound grasp of the good-percentage passes, you can make those tactics work.

The quarterback should also be the leader of the offense. And a word here about style and protocol in the huddle. The way the game is played today, the huddle is strictly for the quarterback's announcement of the play. There isn't time for anything else. If another player wants to give him information or make a suggestion, the time for that is while the team is walking back to form the huddle. The quarterback sometimes will ask one of the players a specific question in the huddle. Maybe he hasn't had time to talk to him beforehand. He might ask the center, for example, "Can you block the guy over your head?" He expects a straight answer. No wishful thinking. If a man can't make a play, there might be all kinds of reasons. The player doesn't have to regard a negative answer as a confession of anything. He helps his team very specifically by being honest. As a rule I don't ask questions in the huddle. I should be able to get the information I need before I get there. The best approach to play calling is simply to step in there, call the play right away, and break the huddle.

You better know exactly the play you're going to call when the huddle forms. If you are indecisive, the team will recognize that immediately and lose confidence in that play. And that is usually fatal. If you stammer and meditate, your team is going to say, "He really doesn't believe in this play," or worse, "He really doesn't know what he's doing." You have to be positive, firm, and quick. Now, you can be all those things and still have doubt about the play. But you're not going to get away with those contradictions very often. The team will read you pretty fast when you come over with a phony ring. The answer to that is to know what you're doing, and the way you achieve that is by working and studying. Good quarterbacks are born that way only in fiction.

When you get to the line of scrimmage, you'll want to look over the defense to see whether the opponent is in a formation that will completely wreck the play you've called. If he is, you will want to change the play by making an audible call on the line. A few years ago the football fans were hypnotized by all the mumbo jumbo and masterminding that were supposed to go into audibilizing. It's been romanticized and talked to death. In pro football there have been games when I called everything at the line. We had decided to run our offense that way because our opponents—typically the Chicago Bears—had a habit of confronting us with constantly changing defenses; so we could save ourselves a lot of time just by making the play selection at the line.

The experienced quarterback should be able to do that without any great stress. But usually, I won't call more than a handful of audibles. Unless you are suddenly faced with a big-gain opportunity, or a potential disaster, you are better off going with what you called in the huddle. Your team has had a chance to prepare itself mentally for its assignments. Also, calling a new play at the line exposes you to the danger of somebody blowing the call or just not hearing it in the noise of the crowd, or the wind, or because of his distance from the quarterback.

Naturally, the audible plays available to the quarterback should be laid out in advance. You can't expect the team to dig into the whole playbook on the spur of the moment and carry out all assignments flawlessly. So the coach will prepare certain plays to be used as audibles, based on anticipated defenses. And they will be practiced during the week and become a part of the standard ready list.

The quarterback, then, should know exactly the audible to call when he's facing a situation that requires one. I think most fans understand now, and certainly players at all levels must, how important it is to keep this ready list of plays small and workable. Against any given team you only want to use the stuff with maximum potential for success, based on the matchup of the teams, what you do well, what your opponent does well, where you are weak, and where your opponent is weak. If some changes have to be made during the game, they can usually be made without calling a constitutional convention.

I'm not underestimating the value of audibles. Our teams have won many games on an audible play called in a critical situation. I'm just saying that the quarterback should be realistic in how he approaches audibles. The audible, incidentally, doesn't necessarily involve changing a running play to a pass play or vice versa. Let's say that in the huddle you've called an off-tackle play to the right. But when you set up at the line you discover your opponents overshifted to your right. This means you overman them on the left side. Call an audible to exploit that situation.

Some principles of tactics might be offered here. When to call a reverse, for example. This is a play you will usually see once or twice a game, intended to take advantage of the opposing team's pursuit and aggressiveness. Usually it means that your flanker will come crossfield and take a handoff or lateral well behind the line of scrimmage. If it's executed right and the surprise factor is operating, most if not all of the defense will be going the other way. The time to call that play is when you're across the fifty-yard line and beginning to threaten the opponents' goal line. A good zone would be between the twenty and forty. The defense has to react quickly down there to protect against a touchdown. That makes it vulnerable to a finesse.

Let's say the defense reacts quickly to a play that looks like a sweep to the right. The pursuit starts galloping from the other side of the field, because nobody over there has been blocked. So now the halfback hands off to the flanker, who has delayed a few counts. Here comes the flanker back the other way. When it happens against his team, the fan might accuse the defensive end of stupid play for letting himself get suckered. When the good guys do it, the fan says it's a brilliant piece of strategy. It all depends on where you are sitting. The defensive end isn't stupid at all. He's simply reacting the way he's trained himself to react for years. It's very difficult to tell himself, "Stop. They may be coming back this way." If he does that every play, he's just not going to pursue very much, so the flanker reverse is a sort of occupational hazard for him. The other reason you call the reverse in your opponents' territory is one of caution. If the play breaks down, you're in midfield and haven't killed yourself.

The draw play, or delayed line buck, is a good call on any play in which a pass is a logical call. Last season the Vikings frequently passed on first down, and the opponents knew it. So a draw play would have been a reasonable call on first down every now and then, because as the play begins it has the appearance of a pass. In most cases, of course, the draw will be used on third down, which is the obvious passing situation. Like the draw play, the screen pass is called when you're getting a lot of pressure from the defensive line. You will want to call trap plays when you are faced with especially aggressive linemen. What you do there is to take advantage of their charge by letting them come across the line and then sending the running back into the hole thus created. If you've played any football at all, you know that's a lot tougher in practice than in theory, because the defensive linemen—especially the more experienced ones —know all about the dangers of getting trapped.

But still they can be trapped.

The kind of passing game you use will vary with the kind of personnel available to you as much as with the kind of defense you are facing. You've seen a major trend in pro football toward using the great running backs as the team's primary receivers. That tactic is largely a response to the sophisticated defenses of today, and the realization that often the best way to get your good running backs into the open is to throw to them. You don't see many teams tearing up the opposition with end sweeps today. They take too long to

develop against quick defenses. In many cases a better way to get
your back out there fast is to swing him out and throw to him. We
did that all the time in 1975 with Chuck Foreman. I don't know if
there have been one or two more spectacular individual performances than Foreman delivered that year, when he gained more than
one thousand yards on the ground and caught seventy-three passes.
The quarterback will want to throw to a man like that five to ten
times a game or he should face a sanity hearing. The quarterback can
throw that pass either off a rollout or from a dropback. Because the
play develops quickly, he doesn't need maximum protection back
there.

If the linebackers happen to be covering your backs hard and
close, you'll have to go downfield and throw to your ends, breaking
either in or out, depending on the pattern you've called. Usually
you've got an option to throw deep or short when you're going
downfield. Don't get hung up on throwing to the so-called primary
receiver. In my first year in the league, I often decided in advance
who I was going to throw to, and I never took my eyes off him. Now
I tell the reporters practically every Sunday, "There's no such thing
as a primary receiver," as though it's a private anthem I have to sing
after every game. I don't mean that I look at everybody on a given
pass pattern. I'm just saying that I have to be alert to throw to the
open man, and it can't be predicted who's going to be open.

About the blitz, or the rushing linebackers. The good quarterback will usually welcome that situation. It means if he keeps his wits
about him and he gets a minimum throwing time, he'll find somebody open. The blitz creates one-on-one situations downfield, and
quite often one-on-none. The desirable thing there is to spot the open
man before some linebacker removes your head. The best strategy
against the blitz, when you see it coming, is to keep your backs in
for protection and throw a quick slanting pattern or quick sideline
pattern to the outside receivers. With the defense thin downfield,
there's a fair chance that a play like that can go for a touchdown.

If you have gotten the impression that I believe the quarterback
can help his team win more with his head than with his arm, you're
right. Many quarterbacks have the physical qualifications and, given

time or ideal situations, can lacerate a pass defense. But on Sunday afternoons in the heat or wind or rain and the pressure, it doesn't often look the way it does on the blackboard. So you can't have enough knowledge. Ask questions, read, play. Remember, the position doesn't confer any genius on you. Listing you as the quarterback doesn't make you smart. You've got to be smart to deserve to be quarterback, and being smart involves work.

The quarterback has to be in command, all right, but that doesn't mean he's some kind of lofty general, above the battle. He has to involve himself emotionally. I've done it all my career. Sometimes the fans and the officials believe I overstep. If I do, I regret that, but you have to care. You have to be in the middle of it. I'm not advocating retaliation, but sometimes there's no option. A big Washington lineman came in once when I was playing with the Giants, threw me down on a pass play, and walked away laughing. I stood up, got his attention, and drilled him with the football between the eyes.

All I'm saying is that the quarterback sometimes has to take care of himself. He can have no objection, though, if he has a few 270-pound friends.

If the quarterback has done his work and acquired a position of leadership, he should be careful how he exercises it. I didn't say timid, I said careful. Years ago the tough quarterbacks could get away with calling their people names in the huddle, chewing them out publicly. It won't go now, and it shouldn't. If a guy is loafing, the coach will know about it and pull him. You don't see much loafing in pro ball, by the way. The money is pretty big. Nobody's going to jeopardize it with that kind of behavior. If a young football player loafs, he really shouldn't be playing, should he? Because if he doesn't enjoy and doesn't want to involve himself, he has no excuse for taking up space where another boy would give of himself.

So if the quarterback sees a player making a mistake, yes, he will want to talk about it. What went wrong? Is the play understood? If one of my teammates makes a bad mechanical mistake, such as missing an easy catch, I might say something like, "Come on, we've got to get this thing together." I'm asking him to concentrate. Once should be enough. I'm not going to call him names or degrade him in front of his teammates, his opponents, or the crowd. That's not the kind of involvement I want, and it isn't the kind the young quarterback should want, or be allowed.

And now you know all my secrets.

Let me add this. Whether the quarterback gets a quarter of a million dollars or just a couple of raps on the head, whether he's in the National Football League or some playground behind the school, the biggest reward for him is the recognition of his teammates: that he was not only a leader but also one of the team, that all their contributions were important, and that each is dependent on the other. If you can have that feeling at the end of the game or the end of the season, you will have achieved something very special and honorable.

FRANCIS TARKENTON YEAR BY YEAR

	Team	Passes Att.	Comp.	Pct.	Yds.	TD	Int.	Yds. Rushing	Avg. Per Carry	TD
1961	Vikings	280	157	.56	1,997	18	17	308	5.5	5
1962	Vikings	329	163	.49	2,595	22	25	361	8.8	2
1963	Vikings	297	170	.57	2,311	15	15	162	5.8	1
1964	Vikings	306	171	.56	2,506	22	11	330	6.6	2
1965	Vikings	329	171	.52	2,609	19	11	356	6.4	1
1966	Vikings	358	192	.54	2,561	17	16	376	6.1	2
1967	Giants	377	204	.54	3,088	29	19	306	7.0	2
1968	Giants	337	182	.54	2,555	21	12	301	5.3	3
1969	Giants	409	220	.54	2,918	23	8	172	4.6	0
1970	Giants	389	219	.56	2,777	19	12	236	5.5	2
1971	Giants	386	226	.59	2,567	11	21	111	3.7	3
1972	Vikings	378	215	.57	2,651	18	13	180	6.7	0
1973	Vikings	274	169	.62	2,113	15	7	202	4.9	1
1974	Vikings	351	199	.57	2,598	17	12	120	5.7	2
1975	Vikings	425	273	.64	2,994	25	13	108	6.8	2
	Totals	5,225*	2,931*	.56	38,840	291*	212	3,629†	6.0	28

*all-time NFL record
†all-time NFL record for quarterback

Index

269